The Westminster Story

The Westminster Story

1852 - 2002

GLORIOUS, GRAND AND TRUE

BY W. PAUL GAMBLE

with editorial assistance by

RICHARD H. GAMBLE

Westminster College, New Wilmington, PA 16172-0001
© 2002 by Westminster College. All rights reserved.
Design: Valenta Platt Design Group Inc. ♦ www.vpdg.com
Printed in the United States of America.

ISBN 0-9715652-0-1

Dedication

Dedicated to my great-grandfather, William Dickey, one of the founders of Westminster College, and to my grandmother, Ellen Dickey Gamble, a graduate of 1857 in the first full class to include women, and to my father, William Dickey Gamble, a graduate of 1896 and a member of the Board of Trustees from 1924 to 1944. ❖

James Patterson, D.D.
1853-1866

Robert Audley Browne, D.D.
1867-1870

E. Tupper Jeffers, D.D.
1872-1883

Robert Gracey Ferguson,
D.D., LL.D.
1884-1906

Robert McWatty Russell,
D.D., LL.D.
1906-1915

W. Charles Wallace, D.D.
1916-1931

Robert F. Galbreath,
D.D., LL.D.
1932-1946

H. Lloyd Cleland, Ped.D.
1946-1947

Will W. Orr,
D.D., Litt.D., LL.D.
1949-1967

Earland I. Carlson, Ph.D.
1967-1981

Allen P. Splete, Ph.D.
1982-1985

Oscar E. Remick, Ph.D.
1987-1997

R. Thomas Williamson, J.D.
1997-

Table of Contents

About The Author
W. Paul Gamble

The *Westminster Story, 1852-2002* was developed as a father-son collaboration between W. Paul Gamble, College historian, and his son, Richard H. Gamble, freelance journalist, who provided significant editorial assistance. (See Preface for details.)

W. Paul Gamble is the author of *Westminster's First Century* (1952), *The History of Westminster College, 1852-1977*, and *The History of Westminster College, 1852-1992*. He has served on the Westminster faculty or staff for the past 55 years, including administrative posts as alumni secretary and executive assistant to the president, and faculty positions in the speech and English departments.

Richard H. Gamble taught English at Coe College (1969-74) and has been a financial journalist since 1977. He has written book-length histories of two banks and now lives in Colorado. ❖

Richard H. Gamble
and his father,
W. Paul Gamble

Preface

The origin of this history might be traced back a long way. As a small child trying to come to terms with the adult world around me, I became aware of an invisible presence in our family of something called Westminster College. Later, when I could understand that my Grandmother Gamble was in the first regular graduating class at the College, that her father was one of its founders, and that my father and his brother and sister were also graduates, I realized why I had been hearing fond and frequent references to Westminster. When I was a little older, references to the College assumed a current flavor as my father began serving what would be a 20-year stint on the Board of Trustees. By the time I was in high school, my sister and brother were students at Westminster, and one of my favorite weekend activities was to visit my brother and learn what it meant to be "collegiate." After he graduated, I became a student myself, then an alumnus and then a part-time member of the College faculty.

In 1949, with Westminster's centennial anniversary approaching, I was recruited by President Will Orr to serve as alumni secretary. My duties included editing the College magazine, the *Blue and White*. Because of centennial preparations and family ties, I decided to write a series of articles for the *Blue and White* about the College's history. As part of the 1952 centennial celebration, these articles, with minor additions and editing, became the first published history of the College, *Westminster's First Century*. That collection, as the original preface stated, made "no pretense of being a formal or analytical history of the College. It is rather an informal year-by-year summary of the things that have happened at Westminster."

As 1977 grew near, the committee planning Westminster's 125th birthday observance requested a revised and updated history. This second edition of the College history, published as *History of Westminster College, 1852-1977*, added 25 years to the account and strengthened coverage of academic development and certain pivotal controversies, but it followed the same year-by-year format as the original. As the preface stated, "It is packed with detailed information which may tend to clutter the story for the continuous reader while at the same time increasing the value of the history for reference purposes." When we ran out of copies of the 1977 history in 1992, we turned out a hurried third edition — essentially a reprint of the second edition with 15 additional years summarized briefly in outline form.

One hundred copies of this 1992 edition were thicker than the others because they included "A Personal Perspective on the History of Westminster College." After I retired from the faculty, while I was still serving part-time as curator of the College archives, my conscience began to nag me because a lot of what I knew about the College's history had not been included in the published editions, largely to avoid offending anyone by discussing controversial topics. For the benefit of future historians, I put down what I knew about these episodes and placed a copy of this "Personal Perspective" in the College archives. When we were preparing the 1992 history, President Oscar Remick, who had read the "Personal Perspective," wanted to include it in copies that would be distributed to the Board of Trustees, so this material was added to about 100 bound copies of the 1992 history. Much of this material has become less sensitive with the passage of time and now can be included in this sesquicentennial edition of the College history.

For many years I have wanted to rewrite the history and break away from the limitations imposed by the year-in-review format. I wanted to cover major story lines coherently rather than in annual fragments. I also wanted to accommodate more analytical discussion of major events, problems, and trends. With the approach of 2002, thanks to good health, plenty of time and some help from my family, I finally got that opportunity. This history takes a more thematic, less chronological approach. The earlier histories, while out of print, are available in libraries to those who need to look up key facts in a chronological reference book. This text is written for the reader who wants a readable account of how the College grew. The voluminous records of annual faculty additions and retirements and the won-lost records of the various sports teams that made up a large part of the earlier histories are here relegated to appendices. Those who want to consult them may do so, but the general reader will not find them cluttering the text.

I knew that preparing such a substantially different history would be an ambitious undertaking for a man approaching 90, so I collaborated with my son, Richard Gamble '63, who brought to the project a computer and experience gleaned from 20 years of magazine editing and two book-length bank histories, as well as the relative youth of a man approaching 60. He agreed to help rearrange already written material from the earlier histories, "Personal

Perspective" and several speeches and magazine articles of mine, and to supply necessary transitions as well as a more journalistic writing style. This history would not have been possible without his skilled contributions. Needless to say, collaborating with my son on this project has meant a lot to me. The other indispensable family tie is to my wife, Anna Mary Shaffer Gamble, whose support has made possible almost everything I have done since we were married in 1938.

In preparing this and all earlier editions of the College history, my principal sources have been the minutes of the Board of Trustees and faculty meetings, College catalogs and other College publications: *Holcad, Argo, Blue and White*, and *Westminster Magazine*.

I am indebted to Robert Gracey Ferguson, Westminster's president from 1884 to 1906, for insights contained in his *The Early History of Westminster College*, first published as magazine articles and later reprinted as a 20-page booklet. Some additional sources for particular sections will be identified in the text.

I want to express my gratitude to Oscar Remick, Art Rathjen, and Amy Rose Wissinger for their support in getting this history off to a good start, and to Tom Williamson, Gloria Cagigas, Mark Meighen, and Pat Broadwater for bringing it to a successful conclusion. A special thank you goes to Dewey DeWitt, my successor as curator of the archives, for helping to round up information for this history, and for preparing the appendix on faculty and staff additions and retirements. My thanks also to Joe Onderko for compiling the appendix of year-by-year sports summaries.

In covering his subject, any historian needs to find the right balance between reporting events and interpreting them. Understanding the past usually requires not just collecting and ordering the facts but also explaining why events happened and how they are interrelated. Finding that balance is an art, not a science — certainly influenced in this case by my close association with the subject and the sheer accumulation of decades of memories. During the 50 years I have worked on the College history, I have had access to a mountain of relevant documents and conversations with participants, many of them now dead, whose clear memories of events and personalities went back even further than my own 1921 memories of meeting President Ferguson and seeing the previous "Old Main." I have known personally all of Westminster's presidents and interim presidents since W. Charles Wallace (1916-1931). I worked for 16 years in administration, 15 years in the classroom, and 20 more years as archivist and historian. Because of this background — and because few authorities now are likely to rise to contradict me — I run the risk of indulging in too much interpretation. When clear personal memories supplement the written record, I have used them freely, shifting from third person to first person when doing so would improve this account. Even when I follow the conventions of an objective, third-person historical account, the reader should know that I am telling the story from my own perspective. Clearly, I am fond of "Mother Fair." I have tried to deal candidly with her controversies and fairly with those who fall within the bounds of this history, but if readers suspect a bias and a tendency to present the College in a favorable light, they probably are right. Age has its privileges, and familiarity brings insights as well as blind spots. Hopefully, my collaborator has brought added objectivity to the project.

As we prepare this sesquicentennial history for the printers, it is our hope that it will bring to its readers a better appreciation for the host of people — teachers, presidents, trustees, students, and alumni — who have made their contributions, large and small, to Westminster's rich heritage. ❖

— Paul Gamble

THE WESTMINSTER STORY
SECTION ONE
1852 — 1902

George C. Vincent

CHAPTER 1

Conflict and Tranquility:
Westminster's Three Cycles

The entire sweep of 150 years of Westminster history can be divided logically and rather naturally into three periods of approximately a half-century each. The formative first period, from the College's founding in 1852 until the turn of the century, was a time of trial and development, indeed a struggle for survival. Many colleges were founded during the middle years of the nineteenth century; most of them did not live to see the twentieth. What enabled Westminster to grow into a firmly established institution in its first 50 years? Was the College's bold experiment with coeducation critical to its survival? How important were the forward-looking changes it made to its curriculum? Its ties – both spiritual and financial – to the church? Its early financial strategy of selling scholarships? Its early leadership? Support provided by the town of New Wilmington?

From the beginning, like-minded men (and very soon women) united behind a common vision and worked hard to bring Westminster College into existence and drive it forward. But it also is true that, from the very beginning, Westminster attracted forceful, ambitious personalities who contributed to controversy as well as progress. The sentimental picture of Westminster as an idyllic site filled with gentle scholars who patiently learned and proudly taught is both profoundly true and seriously limited. In fact, Westminster, particularly at the highest levels, has been no stranger to tension, conflict and struggle. Sometimes the tensions between different visions of what the College should be and the different temperaments and ambitions of its leaders have been creative and productive; at other times, they have boiled over into power struggles that have been difficult and painful to resolve.

The first 20 years, from the time Westminster opened its doors in 1852 until the arrival of President E.T.

First main building. Occupied in 1855, it burned in 1861.

Jeffers in 1872, was clearly a period of struggle. Westminster coalesced quickly into a community to work together to survive a fire and stave off insolvency. From the very beginning, almost miraculously, Westminster worked as an educational institution. The students came; the faculty taught; the graduating classes swelled. But behind its strong success in the classroom were both nagging financial problems and friction that led to a certain instability of leadership that dragged on until 1872.

Clearly, the young institution did not survive because it led a charmed life and was able to avoid crises and serious problems that threatened its existence. The physical College was essentially wiped out in 1861 when a fire destroyed its only building. Fiscally, the College had to struggle through dark days when it could meet its small payroll only by asking its faculty to accept significant salary cuts until revenue recovered. The wrenching Civil War turned students and professors into temporary soldiers. Social changes challenged the College's original classical curriculum and led to Westminster's active participation in the curriculum revolution that took place in the last half of the nineteenth century. The first of three major conflicts forced the resignation of Westminster's first president, James Patterson, in 1866, and continued through the troubled administration of Robert Audley Browne (1867-70), and the following two years when the College was without a president. It took dedication and resilience to overcome such challenges. This period of instability more or less ended with the arrival of E.T. Jeffers in 1872.

The second period, from the turn of the century until 1952, saw a number of important developments. Public relations and fund raising became significant programs, pulling college presidents away from their traditional role of academic leadership. Separate faculty and administrative staffs developed and sometimes found themselves at odds. Tenure protection introduced tensions between the faculty and Board of Trustees, sometimes catching the College president in the middle of disputes. These tensions led to a second major period of conflict that became apparent when President Robert Galbreath submitted his resignation in 1945. It continued through the one-year administration of Lloyd Cleland and the following two years when the College was once again without a president. The tensions carried over into the early years of the Will Orr administration, but were essentially over by 1955. The curriculum continued to change as majors and minors were introduced, and the Great Depression encouraged a trend toward vocational training. Intercollegiate athletics grew from casual recreational activity into well-publicized contests between select groups of skilled, highly trained stu-

Second main building. Occupied in 1862, burned 1927. Known after 1900 as 'Old Main.'

dent-athletes. At Westminster, at least, they remained bona fide students.

The third period, from 1952 to 2002, saw the modern college evolve in response to the social, economic and technological influences that were reshaping American culture. The G.I. Bill that followed World War II helped popularize the idea that college training belonged to the masses of able, ambitious young people, certainly including those returning from the war who wanted to pursue commercial careers. Colleges like Westminster struggled to outgrow their traditional roots as elite cultural centers for the academically gifted (and financially independent) – those who intended to become educators, clergymen or professionals with a liberal arts education. The dramatic post-war expansion in student enrollment required a comparable expansion of the physical plant. The number of major buildings on Westminster's campus more than doubled during the last half-century. Financing this expansion meant one major fund-raising campaign after another, reinforcing the emerging role of the president as the College's leading fund-raiser. Finally, the computer age made significant changes not only in the curriculum, but in the physical and communications infrastructure of the College. It pointed toward even more drastic changes as Westminster moved into the twenty-first century.

Student unrest that swept the nation's college and university campuses in the 1960s and early 1970s never became violent or destructive at Westminster, but there were confrontations. Student activism led to a new code of students' rights and responsibilities. Growing friction between the

Old Main Memorial. Occupied 1929 to present.

faculty and Board erupted in the third major crisis – Who should lead the College and in what direction? The major conflict that marked the third half-century started in 1978 with the death of Board president John Miller and the election of Robert Lauterbach as his successor. It continued through the later years of President Earland Carlson, the interim College presidency of Lauterbach (1981-82), the short administration of Allen Splete (1982-85), and the interim term of Jerry Boone (1985-1987). It wasn't fully over until the arrival of Oscar Remick in 1987.

Westminster College has proved to be a remarkably resilient survivor, but also a sensitive organism whose peak performance depends on several delicate balances. The inevitable internal tensions can constructively maintain those balances when the different factions regard each other with mutual respect and work to reach common goals. But the tensions also can feed surprisingly destructive conflicts when they are not handled with the greatest care.

Tensions within the Westminster family have existed since the College was founded but have, of course, changed over time as the nature of the College has changed. The early College was a comparatively close-knit and homogeneous organization. The president was a teaching member of the faculty; there was no separate administrative staff. Institutional polarization between faculty and administration developed gradually after the turn of the century. Also, in the early years a high percentage of the faculty and the leaders of the Board of Trustees were ordained ministers who shared some common perspectives about Christian higher education. Clearly the College, in its early years, was not immune to differences of opinion and personality clashes. Doctrinal differences sometimes led to disagreements, typically between the more conservative clergymen on the Board and the more academically minded clergymen on the faculty.

The first Board of Trustees was evenly divided between six ministers and six laymen. When the Board was enlarged to 24 in 1858, the even division continued. The number and percentage of ministers, however, increased over the years until, in 1900, the Board comprised 21 ministers, eight lawyers, and two others.

Throughout the twentieth century, both the faculty and the Board became more diversified and less dominated by clergymen, but cooperation became more difficult as the faculty became more scholarly and the Board grew less academically oriented. Clergymen on the Board gave way to a growing number of laymen, first lawyers and then business executives. The pattern of having a clergyman preside over the Board lasted until 1957, when leadership passed to two attorneys, Clyde Armstrong (1957-1964) and Judge Miller (1964-1978). Since 1978 the Board has been headed by a corporate executive.

During this period, the number of ministers serving on the Board dwindled until there was just one clergyman in 1985 (but two by 2001). The exodus of clergymen was offset by an influx of corporate executives, partly due to a shift in the College's financial support from church to corporate contributions, charitable foundations and philanthropic businessmen. As the Board came to be dominated by people who live in a world of commerce that is quite different from the academic community, the College president has had to serve increasingly as a conduit between the faculty and Board, working to see that each group understood the priorities and concerns of the other. The mediator, however necessary and constructive his role, was in the line of fire and sometimes was shot.

In reviewing the sometimes hostile historic relations between the Board and the faculty, we should keep in mind that members of the Board are capable people who give generously of their time to advance what they believe to be the best interests of the College. Many of them are Westminster graduates whose ties to the College go back many years. And the faculty members, while they are paid employees of the College, often look beyond their paychecks and fringe benefits and work earnestly to improve the quality of education at Westminster, foregoing opportunities to make more money elsewhere because of a loyalty they feel for the College and its students.

The three extended periods of disruption will be discussed in detail in their respective time periods, but all three involve some common factors. In all three cases, the Board saw fit to put a leading member of the Board in the front office at the College to take control of a situation when fundamental change was deemed necessary. In all three cases the action was followed by a number of years of uncertain leadership, including short, troubled presidential terms and periods when the College was without a regular president.

Another way to view the turmoil that disrupted Westminster's stability on three occasions is to recognize an internal tension between two opposing philosophies of college governance. One view favors a strong central authority and could be called an authoritarian or, as a Middle States Association of Colleges and Schools evaluating team more diplomatically put it, a "paternalistic" approach to governance. The other extreme, which favors broad sharing of power among a college's many constituencies – board, administration, faculty, students, alumni, even parents – can be called a participatory approach to governance.

Both models have their advantages. Advocates of paternalism see it as a more decisive and efficient way for a college to make necessary, sometimes difficult decisions. Advocates of participatory governance argue that sacrificing consensus to efficiency undermines the cooperative effort that is needed to make any decision work. We must be careful not to pin oversimplified labels on specific presidents. Most of them pragmatically advocated various mixtures of paternalistic and participatory governance. The record doesn't tell us whether opposing views of governance were involved in the Patterson-Browne period of disruption. We do know, however, that they played an important role in the other two major upheavals. Galbreath was caught between faculty support for participatory governance and the Board's preference for paternalism. Will Orr and the Board seemed to agree in a preference for paternalism. Then, under the leadership of Judge John Miller, the Board and President Earland Carlson worked together in a period (1967-78) that was basically participatory. But the change in Board leadership from Miller to Lauterbach caused the pendulum to swing back toward paternalistic governance and brought on the third upheaval. When the selection of Remick put an end to this last unsettled period, he put in place a new mix of paternalism and participation. How this has worked out in practice is something to be examined later. ❖

CHAPTER 2

The Founders and the Cause:
Affordable Instruction in the Arts and Sciences, and Pure Principles of Protestant Christianity

Westminster College was born at a time when the winds of change were sweeping across America. The middle of the nineteenth century was marked by westward expansion, industrial development, educational progress, and religious revival. Industrialization was producing a moneyed middle class that was demanding and paying for higher education.

As Westminster was getting started in 1852, people were reading Harriet Beecher Stowe's *Uncle Tom's Cabin*, published that year in book form, and slavery was the dominant issue of the day. Congress was between the Compromise of 1850 and The Kansas-Nebraska Act of 1854 in its efforts to avert a civil war. Franklin Pierce was elected president that year. The Know-Nothing Party was flourishing in Pennsylvania. It would be another two years before the Republican Party was formed. Abraham Lincoln was an obscure lawyer in Springfield, Ill. Railroads were uniting the country. You could travel as far west as Chicago by rail, but it would be another four years (1856) before trains could cross the Mississippi, another 17 before tracks spanned the continent. The world had yet to hear of Pullman sleepers (introduced in 1859) or dining cars (1863). A letter mailed from St. Louis could reach San Francisco by stagecoach in just 25 days. It would be another eight years before the Pony Express was organized and cut the time to a speedy 10 days. Melville recently had finished *Moby Dick* (1851), Hawthorne *The Scarlet Letter* (1850). Thoreau had moved back to Concord from his sojourn at Walden Pond, but had yet to publish his account of the experience (1854). Immigrants, especially from Ireland and Germany, were flooding into Ellis Island.

And the country was in the midst of an explosion in higher education. In 1820 there were only 38 colleges in the United States, but the next 40 years

George C. Vincent

The Rev. George C. Vincent, leader of the founders, and first principal (presiding officer) of the College.

saw the appearance not only of Westminster, but of 193 other new colleges. Almost all of them were founded by religious groups, partly to train future ministers and partly to provide to the rising middle class the cultural, religious, social and vocational advantages of a college education.

Christopher Jencks and David Riesman cover the effect of these movements on American higher education thoroughly in *The Academic Revolution*. What they refer to as pre-Jacksonian education had been dominated by the European classical tradition. But, by mid-century, American education was being drawn into the accelerating currents of change. Progressive educators noted that the traditional classical college curriculum, dominated by the ancient languages, was not meeting the needs of a changing American society, and they advocated more utilitarian courses and more choice for students.

The Rev. D.H.A. McLean, a leading founder, and half of the original faculty.

Currents of change were also stimulating a growing interest in intellectual development for women. A rising feminist movement was encouraging women to seek higher education, but so were economic forces. Expanding public schools demanded more teachers at all levels, and school boards were discovering that women could teach as well as men for salaries from one-quarter to one-half those demanded by male teachers. These factors combined to encourage experiments in both coeducation and women's colleges.

Religious revivals, immigration, and western expansion were feeding a melting pot of religious and ethnic communities, many of which wanted to sponsor their own colleges. The result was a proliferation of colleges beyond what the country needed and could support. As Jencks and Riesman report, "Almost all of these groups felt impelled to set up their own colleges, both to perpetuate their distinctive subculture and to give it legitimacy in the larger society." Of all the colleges founded before the Civil War, only a relatively small percentage survived into the twentieth century. Most of those that survived emphasized collegiate rather than sectarian issues.

Westminster's sectarian foundation in the Associate Presbyterian Church was a result of an eighteenth century split in the National Church of Scotland. A group that insisted on the democratic election of ministers by congregations seceded from the main church in 1733 to form the Associate Presbyterian Church, then emigrated in large numbers to America, many of them to western Pennsylvania. They brought with them the Calvinist traditions of respect for learning and demand for an educated clergy. Through the years, this hardy, independent group must have nourished a dream of a college of their own, but no concrete plans moved forward until the mid-nineteenth century.

The place where the seed first took root and started to grow was Shenango Presbytery on the western border of Pennsylvania, midway between the north and south boundaries. The first suggestion to receive any official action seems to have come in a letter from Duncan Forbes of Rock Spring, addressed to the presbytery. In the presbyterial minutes under the date Dec. 25, 1849, there is this entry: "Mr. Wolfe and Dr. Cowden were appointed to consider and report upon a suggestion made by Duncan Forbes, respecting the establishment of a Presbyterial school for the education of young men for the ministry."

No tangible progress seems to have been made for almost two years. Then at a meeting of Shenango Presbytery in Mercer on Dec. 2, 1851, according to the minutes, "A preamble and resolution were presented setting forth the duty of taking into consideration the establishment of a literary institution. A committee was appointed ... to take the subject into consideration and to request the cooperation of the brethren of the Ohio Presbytery." The organizing committee included three pastors of neighboring Associate churches – George C. Vincent from Mercer, J.D. Wolfe from Wolf Creek (now Slippery Rock), and D.R. Imbrie from New Wilmington – and two elders, William Dickey from Salem (Greenville) and Edward McElree from Harmony (Harrisville).

The committee proceeded with plans for a joint meeting of representatives of both the Ohio and Shenango Presbyteries, to be held in New Wilmington on Jan. 21, 1852. The stated objective of the meeting was "to take into consideration the establishment of a seminary of learning for the material benefit of said Presbyteries." Subcommittees were appointed to study and report on certain phases of the undertaking.

When the joint commission convened, Ohio Presbytery was represented by the Reverends J. P. Ramsey (New Bedford), David H. Goodwillie (Poland), J. R. Sleatz, and Jon Anderson McGill, and by elders Isaac P. Cowden, David Houston, and R. Davidson. Shenango Presbytery, in addition to Vincent, Wolfe, Imbrie, Dickey and McElree, was represented by the Reverends D.H.A. McLean (Greenville) and G. Small, and by elders H. White, Livingston Carman, G. Allen, W. Maxwell, and D. Bower. Ramsey was chosen as chairman, Vincent as secretary.

The Rev. David R. Imbrie, a member of the exploratory committee, founding commission, original Board of Trustees, treasurer of the Board, and pastor of the New Wilmington Associate Presbyterian congregation.

McLean House, built by McLean in 1852 or 1853, it stood on the present site of Galbreath Hall. The oldest building owned by the College, it is now located on Prospect Street, and has been converted to apartments for faculty housing.

Deciding just what they should establish was part of their mission. Preliminary suggestions, as we have seen, included a "school for the education of young men for the ministry," a "literary institution," and a "seminary of learning." As a practical matter, the group responsible for organizing such an endeavor focused at the outset on the establishment of a presbyterial "academy." Starting a "college" instead was first perceived to be a very ambitious undertaking. McLean, participating as pastor of the Greenville church, describes how plans changed. "After nearly a day in conference over the matter, Edward McElree, an elder from Harmony congregation, moved that a college be established under the care of the two presbyteries. This caused a hearty laugh, but before the conference closed it was unanimously agreed to establish a college. This changed the whole aspect of the affair, and the members felt they had ventured upon a large undertaking." At that time, the only Pennsylvania educational institution of higher rank than academy between the Ohio River and Lake Erie was Allegheny College, which had been founded in Meadville in 1815.

The meeting at which Westminster was born established a number of important goals and policies for the new college. In a critical decision with far-reaching consequences, the founders defined the mission of the College broadly. Rather than simply preparing young men for the ministry, they would seek to provide "the mental and moral training of youth of both sexes." As a result of this decision, Westminster became the first integrated and unrestricted coeducational college in the country. The name "Westminster Collegiate Institute" was chosen in honor of the Westminster Confession of Faith. Curricular goals were established for "affording instruction in the arts and sciences" and "the promotion of the pure principles of Protestant Christianity."

Vincent was chosen to be principal of the College, at an annual salary of $500, and April, only three months away, was picked as the target date when the school would open its doors for a spring term. Vincent and McLean were directed to secure a charter. A fund-raising plan was adopted under which perpetual scholarships would be sold for $100, family scholarships for $80, and individual scholarships for $60. A perpetual scholarship entitled the bearer to free tuition (and such scholarships evidently could be transferred at will and never expired). Family and individual scholarships were somewhat more restricted, as the names imply. As we will see in Chapter 8, this policy soon proved to be controversial because it all but eliminated income from tuition. However, the strategy was being used by other colleges at that time, and the founders considered it to be the quickest and most effective way of securing immediate funds and insuring a steady flow of students to the new college.

McLean's handwritten account of how he and Vincent were chosen is illuminating. Referring to the original proposal to establish an academy, he recorded, "I was not friendly to it, but did not openly oppose it. I was then in charge of the Greenville Academy, which the trustees had placed under my absolute control for five years, and our prospects for a full school were then very bright." The decision to found a college put the matter in a new light. McLean's account says Vincent was elected "president," although the Board minutes more accurately record him as being named "principal" of the proposed college. By his account, McLean was offered a professorship and, when he turned it down, he was offered the presidency. He declined this offer as well and reported, "If I consented at all to go, it would be in this condition, that all the teachers should be placed on an equality, and each made responsible for his share of the work, until the college was past an experiment." (Since McLean did consent, he evidently was satisfied that he and Vincent would teach with equality, or else he changed his mind.)

The destinies of Westminster, the founders decided, should be vested in a 12-member Board of Trustees, six members to be elected by each presbytery. Wolfe was appointed to canvas for funds in Shenango Presbytery, and the Rev. J.W. Logue to do the same in Ohio Presbytery.

State Senator William M. Francis offered a free building site if the College would locate to New Wilmington.

One of the first problems to resolve was the selection of a site. The claims of New Bedford, New Wilmington, and Wolf Creek (Slippery Rock) were all considered, but when New Wilmington citizens pledged $10,000 toward the endowment of the new college, and both A.P. Moore and William Francis offered free building sites, it was decided to locate in New Wilmington, which, at that time, was a village of about 200 people, without paved streets or sidewalks. Its only connection to the outside world was by stagecoach. But it was beautifully situated in the Pennsylvania hills and, as the first College catalog expressed it, "free from those causes that might attract an idle or vicious class of people."

The newly elected Board of Trustees met in New Wilmington on March 3, 1852, but did not elect permanent officers since the charter had not yet been received. The six original Board members from Ohio Presbytery included the Reverends Goodwillie, Ramsey, and S.T. Heron, and elders Houston, Cowden, and Thomas Dungan. Shenango Presbytery had elected the Reverends Wolfe, Vincent and Imbrie, and elders Dickey, McElree and Andrew Jackson Burgess. At this March meeting, with the opening of the first term just a month away, the Board tapped McLean to serve as professor along with Vincent.

The initial term had been scheduled to start the first Monday of April, but the opening had to be moved back to the third Monday because McLean was not available until then. News of the postponement failed to reach everyone, however, and several students showed up on April 5. Vincent took care of these early arrivals by hav-

First classroom
building. Used from
1853 to 1855.

ing them recite in his home. By the third Monday, April 19, classes started in the Associate Presbyterian Church, located in the northeast corner of the village on what is now Church Street. McLean writes of those first days, "Dr. Vincent and the writer took charge of the school, having for classrooms the old Seceder Church, he at one end of it and I at the other." About 20 students, including both young men and women, attended the first session.

On June 22 and 23 the Board of Trustees met in New Wilmington. The new charter, which had been granted by the state legislature on April 27, was read and approved, and the Board proceeded to elect permanent officers on June 22: Goodwillie as president, Wolfe as vice president, Burgess as secretary, and Imbrie as treasurer.

The Board then recessed in order to consider a possible site for the College. The Board minutes give no reason why the offers of free land made by Moore and Francis were declined, but circumstances suggest a possible explanation. Free land offers for attracting a new college were not unusual because surrounding land still in the possession of the donor usually increased in value. Professors McLean and Vincent must have become interested in a possible profit from the purchase of land that would surround the College campus. They made arrangements to purchase a farm of approximately 158 acres just south of New Wilmington from Thomas Porter. The professors worked out a deal whereby the College Board would lend them funds to purchase the farm, with the professors paying 6 percent interest on the loan. The Board would retain 20 acres, more or less, on the north for the College campus, and another 30 acres on the south end of the farm. The professors would retain the remaining 108 acres in the middle at the rate of $37 an acre, meaning they would owe the Board approximately $4,000. If the Board paid the same rate for their 50 acres, the total purchase would amount to about $5,850.

After agreeing to the land deal with the professors, the Board appointed a committee of trustees and New Wilmington citizens to take care of the property, reserving four or more acres in the northwest corner for College buildings, using their discretion about the sale of lots, and taking necessary steps toward buildings to house the College. This original buildings and grounds committee consisted of McLean, Burgess, Francis, Moore, Carman, Thomas Pomeroy, and J.A. McLaughry.

Dickey and the two professors were appointed agents to work with Wolfe and Logue in selling scholarships. As a result of their efforts during the summer, students arrived in such numbers for the fall term that the little village was hard-pressed to provide room and board. Classes overflowed the old Associate Church into the Associate Reformed Church and the public school building. David Goodwillie, son of the Board president, and the Rev. John Harshaw were added to the faculty on a temporary basis, and the latter subsequently was elected to a permanent position.

When the Board met Sept. 8, 1852, agents reported that more than $25,000 worth of scholarships had been sold. The sale had not raised that substantial sum, however, because most of the scholarships were financed; the buyer would make a down payment and pay the rest in installments, along with 6 percent interest.

The Board decided to erect a temporary College building that could later be sold as a dwelling. A motion to provide a separate classroom for female students was defeated. R. Rambo was employed by the buildings and grounds committee to construct this building. The same committee had lots laid out on three sides of the campus area, and on Nov. 4, 1852, these lots were sold at public sale for prices ranging from $52.50 to $117, the total receipts being about $1,400. (The expanding College eventually would buy back most of this property at a much higher price.)

Westminster Families: The McLaughrys

James A. McLaughry, a member of the original buildings and grounds committee and subsequently on the Board of Trustees, started a connection with the College that went on for generations. Livingston Carman, his father-in-law and fellow committee member, was also a member of the founding commission. His son, James A. II '84, was a prominent Mercer County judge who served on the College Board from 1916 to 1943. His daughter, Margaret '74, was professor of English on the College faculty from 1887 to 1903. Another daughter, Elizabeth '87, was a pioneer woman doctor and founder of the Overlook Sanitarium. Three other sons and four other daughters of James A. II also attended Westminster.

In the next generation, James A. III '19 served on the College Board from 1942 to 1954. His wife, Margaret Miller McLaughry '17, taught modern languages at the College from 1927 to 1930. His brother, DeOrmond "Tuss" McLaughry '15, coached sports at the College the year after his graduation before going on to a distinguished coaching career at several Ivy League colleges. Three other grandchildren of James A. I attended Westminster.

Among his great-grandchildren, Mary Beth McLaughry '42 served as director of annual giving and parents' relations from 1970 to 1978. Her sister and two brothers all attended Westminster. Her brother Bill, at age 69, received his degree from Westminster in 1999, 80 years after his father. Bill's wife, Katherine, also a Westminster graduate, was a member of the College computer staff in 2001.◆

From Family Fireside to Weatherbeaten Building: A Young Man's Journey to Westminster

J.B. McMichael, president of Monmouth College (Ill.), speaking at the funeral of George C. Vincent in October 1889, recalled his introduction to Westminster as a young prep student at the beginning of the College's first regular term in the fall of 1852:

"The fame of the founding of Westminster Collegiate Institute went into all the country round about, and so did the financial agents who 'talked the night away' at family firesides where the subject of a college education had never been thought of as a possibility. It was thus in a family well known to the writer, and when the head of the household invested in a one hundred dollar scholarship, entitling a student to perpetual tuition in the new College, it began to be a practical question which of the family should get the benefit of the scholarship.

"Among the early friends and active agents of the college involved in this case was a fast and lifelong friend of Dr. Vincent, Jackson Burgess, an uncle of the boy to whom I refer, and whose name is the only correct and authorized interpretation of the boy's initials. With these influences around him ... the boy set out on foot for the seat of the college twenty-five miles distant, and reached it without any inconvenience before day was done. ...

"The structure was neither beautiful, imposing, nor convenient, but every feature of the old weatherbeaten building is well remembered. It was the old Seceder church which stood in the twilight of Porter's woods (at the east end of Church Street in the northeast corner of town), near a copious spring of purest water which even at this distance of time is as 'good news from a far country.' Professors Vincent

At a Board meeting on Jan. 4 and 5, 1853, bylaws outlining the duties of Board officers, professors and students were discussed and approved. The bylaws provided that at the close of each of the three terms, "it shall be the duty of the Professors to present their respective classes for examination in the presence of the Trustees." The bylaws also specified that "all the pupils shall be required to preserve the utmost propriety of deportment, not only while in session, but in going to and from the College and in their boarding rooms." Dickey, at the Board's request, "read the By-laws, accompanied with some pertinent remarks, to the teachers and pupils."

At the same Board meeting, plans were approved to erect a permanent building large enough to accommodate three or four hundred students. The building committee was authorized to contract for a half million bricks as soon as $1,000 was raised toward the building. In March, the Board authorized erection of a main building not to exceed $6,000 in cost. It was specified that the building be three stories high, and 60 by 80 feet or larger if the price would permit.

By the spring of 1853, the temporary building had been completed at a cost of $1,134, and occupied by faculty and students. It was a two-story brick structure located immediately south of the Associate Reformed Presbyterian Church (where the south wing of the New Wilmington Presbyterian Church now stands). The first floor was one large room for assembly purposes, and the second floor, reached by an outside staircase, was divided into two classrooms. The Board took action in March 1853 to expand the faculty for the following year by electing the Rev. Andrew M. Black of Franklin College as professor of Hebrew and Greek, and Miss Janet Lowrie of Washington, Pa., as "female professor" to take charge of the young ladies and teach in the English and scientific department. In June 1853 three new members joined the Board, Shenango Presbytery having elected the Rev. Joseph McClintock and Carman to replace Vincent and McElree, and Ohio Presbytery having elected Logue to replace Heron.

With the completion of the first full year of instruction, Westminster Collegiate Institute was more firmly established than the most optimistic among the founders might have anticipated. The finances of the infant institution were precarious, for the sale of scholarships brought in very little cash and effectively eliminated most tuition income. But thanks to those scholarships, the enrollment had exceeded all expectations, and this demand for the services of the College was a key factor in its survival.

In addition to their liberal use of scholarships, the founding fathers made a number of other bold decisions that greatly increased the odds for its survival. Quite progressively, they adopted a policy of non-discrimination; as the first catalog succinctly stated, "No person will be refused admission on account of Color, Caste, or Sex. ... We will sacredly respect the rights of conscience, and whilst we will honestly endeavor to inculcate the pure principles of Christianity, every student of different religious sentiments shall enjoy full liberty of conscience as to place and mode of public worship." This policy, liberal for church-related colleges of the day, broadened the appeal of the College in its region – especially among young women – and contributed to its survival.

and McLean were in charge. The latter I had known as pastor of the home congregation and principal of Greenville Academy, but the former I saw for the first time. He was tall, well-formed, straight as an arrow, prominent features, dark hair, heavy eyebrows, keen, kindly blue eyes, and high and receding forehead. He spoke kindly to me, said he knew my father and my uncle, and hoped I would make as good a man as they. I thought I would. He made me feel bigger than I ever felt before."

(Jackson Burgess McMichael was a cousin of John McMichael and his sister Sarah; all three of whom were among the earliest students at the College. According to a story handed down in the family, the two McMichael men were called Black Jack and Red Jack by their college friends in reference to their hair color. Jackson became president of Monmouth College; John was president judge of Lawrence County, and Sarah was among the first women in the country to earn an A.B. degree and become a college professor.) ◆

A progressive approach to the curriculum also increased the College's appeal and broadened its market. Westminster was born at a time of vigorous controversy over college curricula. Critics of the traditional classical curriculum, which was centered in ancient languages, advocated an alternative for students who preferred more utilitarian courses taught in the English language. The founders established such a program. In addition to the traditional "Classical Course," there was also an "English and Scientific Course" designed for students preparing to teach in public schools and others preparing for professions that did not require classical learning. The College also included, from the very beginning, a preparatory department that offered secondary instruction to prepare students to meet the qualifications for college entrance. This turned out to be a valuable asset in building enrollment.

Who were these founders who were, by turns, traditional and progressive, devoutly conservative and liberally tolerant? True to Presbyterian tradition, laymen had equal representation with ministers on the founding commission and the first Board of Trustees, as reported above. (Three ministers and two laymen had served on the earlier exploratory committee.) Responsibility for the operation and instruction of the College was delegated primarily to Presbyterian clergymen who were also educators. In some cases, we know little more about these individuals than the names that are noted in the records.

But several stand out, even from the limited information that now is available to a historian. There is the Rev. George C. Vincent, the man who never would be Westminster's president. He was the first to arrive, a founder as well as the original "principal" when a faculty of two shared a common classroom. And he was the last to leave, in 1871, a persistent presence during this first period of leadership instability. Whether that presence was disruptive or supportive remains somewhat unclear.

There was the Rev. James Patterson, the outside leader recruited in 1854 to take charge of what was already a burgeoning institution. He won respect and endured resentment until he was ousted in a controversial maneuver in 1866 and replaced by an ambitious and influential Board member and local (New Castle) pastor, Robert Audley Browne. Browne may well have been instrumental in forcing Patterson's resignation, and he reaped continuing dissension among the Board and staff until, after several threatened resignations, he finally departed in 1870. While the available records of this period raise far more questions than they answer, Vincent, Patterson and Browne appear to have been central figures in a sometimes bitter power struggle.

Then there was the Rev. D.H.A. McLean, a founder and original faculty member who resigned twice in protest, first from the faculty and then from his position as president of the Board of Trustees. He was an influential, if not prevailing, member of the inner circle. And there was William Dickey, the founding layman charged with the heavy burden of keeping the College solvent. He became controversial (and was burned in effigy) when he was chosen to deliver an unpopular message to students. Another name to watch is that of Sarah McMichael, who, first as a student and then as a faculty member, played sometimes conspicuous roles in this 20-year period.

Vincent is credited by McLean, his original faculty colleague (and his real estate investment partner), with being the originator and moving force behind plans for the College. Vincent was born of Irish ancestry on April 4, 1813, near Harrisville, Pa., the youngest of ten children. He was graduated from Franklin College, New Athens, Ohio, in 1836 and from the Associate Seminary in Canonsburg, Pa., three years later. He served a pastorate in Washington, Iowa, before coming to Mercer, Pa., in 1848, where he was pastor of the Associate church and principal of the local academy. He was elected at age 39 to serve as principal at Westminster, a post he held for two years until the College called Patterson as its first president. Vincent continued on the faculty for almost 20 years, part of the time as vice president of the College, and he was a member of the original Board of Trustees from 1852 to 1853.

McLean was himself a leader among the founders. He was pastor of the Greenville church and head of the academy there when he was elected to serve as half of Westminster's original faculty. After resigning from the faculty in 1855, he was elected to the College Board in 1858 and served as president of the Board from 1859 until he resigned from that body in 1866.

Early fiscal leadership fell largely to Dickey, an elder in McLean's church. Dickey was a member of the original committee, the founding commission, and the first Board of Trustees. He served the College for a number of years as financial agent, which combined fund raising and business management. Burgess, another member of the original Board, also served briefly as financial agent and for many years was secretary of the Board.

That is what the record shows. We get a more personal glimpse of the early leaders through the eyes of Dickey's daughter, Mrs. Margaret Dickey McKee. Her reminiscence is quoted by subsequent President Robert G. Ferguson (1884-1906), in his *The Early History of Westminster College*: "The three men, mutual friends of each other, who were most deeply interested in the welfare of the college at the start were Dr. Vincent, Dr. D.H.A. McLean and William Dickey; and in helping in securing financial aid and fighting the battles for the institution, we will add the name of Jackson Burgess. I still remember their talks together; especially do I recollect the earnest prayers of these four men, and their future hopes for what seemed to me then to be the very idol of their hearts." ❖

CHAPTER 3

Tough Vines:
Opening Doors to Women in Higher Education

The claim that Westminster was the first integrated and unrestricted coeducational college in the nation does not minimize the significant contributions made by other colleges in breaking down the barriers and opening the doors of higher education to women. Extensive research indicates, however, that educational history was being made on the morning of April 19, 1852, when some 20 young ladies and gentlemen met with two professors in the old Associate Presbyterian Church in New Wilmington to open Westminster College. Never before in our country, it seems, had male and female students been received on such an equal basis into the pursuit of a college education. (Did some of the many colleges that did not survive attempt coeducation? Perhaps, but answering that question is beyond the scope of this history.)

The young women in that church building that morning faced a double challenge.

Many educational leaders of the day believed that women had neither the mental capacity nor the physical stamina to keep up with men in academic work at the college level. And these experts had additional reservations about coeducation, believing that it would be unsafe to educate young men and young women together at this highly combustible age. Westminster's early coeds helped to demonstrate how wrong the experts were.

Drawing of female and male students from first 1904 *Argo*.

While Westminster's embrace of coeducation was bold and progressive, it also was part of a broader movement that affected other colleges as well. The main barrier to women receiving college degrees already had been broken at Oberlin College in Oberlin, Ohio. Chartered in 1834, Oberlin started with an all-male "Collegiate Department" and a separate "Female Department" that offered a special course much like the ladies seminaries or "finishing schools." The female department had its own curriculum, its own female principal and board of managers, and its own commencement exercises. Oberlin obviously was not founded as a coeducational college.

In 1837, however, four ambitious young women from the ladies department sought permission to take courses in the male college that would lead to the A.B. degree. The female principal and some of the faculty opposed the idea at first, but the young women prevailed, broke through the barrier, and thus made educational history. In 1841, three of them – Mary Hosford, Elizabeth Smith Prall, and Caroline Mary Rudd – received from Oberlin College probably the first authentic bachelor of arts degrees awarded to women in this country. However, coeducation continued to be controversial at Oberlin, as we shall see, and barriers of segregation and discrimination remained.

Westminster College started with a different premise – an integration and a freedom from discrimination that were remarkable for the time. However, Westminster also discovered that coeducation did not come without complications. Westminster had started, largely by necessity, with "coed housing." With no dormitories, students made their own arrangements for room and board with the village householders. As a result men and women students sometimes roomed and boarded in the same house. After two years of this freedom the Board, perhaps responding to parental concerns, passed a resolution prohibiting male and female students of different families from rooming and boarding in the same house. That action, taken in March 1854, was to become effective with the beginning of the fall term, and William Dickey, a founding trustee and College financial agent, was directed to announce this ban on coed housing to the students and faculty.

This action may have been the cause of a student demonstration the following September, during which Dickey was burned in effigy. According to the Board minutes, these "disgraceful and riotous proceedings" resulted in faculty actions, Board hearings and other repercussions over the following six months. Before the matter was closed, freedom of student expression became an issue. Meeting March 28, 1855, the Board directed the faculty to find out who had written the article relating to the burning of Dickey in effigy that had been read by Sarah McMichael as editress of a student paper titled *Gathered Leaves*, and, if written by one of the students, "deal with him or her accordingly." By resolution the Board "disapproved of the freedom used in the paper read by Miss McMichael in offering such remarks as recall those scenes of wickedness and seem to justify such proceedings against an honorable and worthy member of this board."

Students of both sexes were subject to rather strict rules of conduct. They were not allowed to "frequent taverns, groceries, and places of idle amuse-

A group of Westminster coeds in the 1880s.

ments or vice," to leave their rooms after 9 p.m., or to leave town during the term without the permission of the president. In the early years, these rules applied equally to men and women. Later, women would be "protected" by stricter regulations than those imposed on men.

Both the English and scientific course and the traditional classical course were, from the very beginning, open on an equal basis to both men and women at Westminster. In the early years most men took the classical course while most women took the scientific course. (At that time "science" referred not specifically to the natural sciences but to any body of practical knowledge, much as we use the term today in "political science.") Originally graduates in the scientific course received diplomas instead of degrees, but when Westminster leaders learned within a few years that other colleges were conferring bachelor of science degrees for a similar course, Westminster followed suit and awarded the degree retroactively to the earlier graduates in this course.

Westminster granted its first bachelor of arts degree in 1854 to William P. Shaw, obviously a transfer student, who became a United Presbyterian minister. The first commencement exercises took place in 1856, when President James Patterson addressed five graduating men; three of whom had started their college careers elsewhere and completed their last two years at Westminster. The class of 1857 might be called the College's first full graduating class. It included 11 men and 10 women, almost all of whom had taken their entire college work at Westminster. And one of the women, Sarah McMichael (having survived the controversy over her written remarks about the Dickey effigy burning), received a bachelor of arts degree for completing the classical course. She was listed in the commencement program as delivering the "Latin Valedictory." She became the first woman in Pennsylvania and one of the first in the nation to earn an A.B. degree.

Another pioneer in coeducation, Antioch College, was conceived at the same time as Westminster when a committee from the Christian Church decided to found a coeducational college in Yellow Springs, Ohio, on the same day – Jan. 21, 1852 – that the committee from the Associate Presbyterian Church simultaneously was agreeing to found Westminster College for the education of both sexes. Westminster was "born" less than three months later under the modest circumstances recounted in the previous chapter. The founders of Antioch, however, had more ambitious, more expensive plans and took longer to prepare their college for opening. They enlisted as their first president Horace Mann, a prominent Massachusetts educator who was advocating, against strong opposition, coeducation for high schools and normal schools. He aspired to make Antioch a model coeducational college and waited until funds could be raised to construct a main building and two dormitories, one for women and one for men. As a result Antioch was not "born" until the fall of 1853, about a year and a half after Westminster.

Thanks to the fame of Horace Mann, the Antioch experiment attracted national attention and made Antioch's early years the subject of many published accounts. With two dormitories, Antioch could provide segregated residential life. But there was no segregation or discrimination in the classroom. The first graduating class in 1857 included 12 men and three women who received A.B. degrees. Two of the women and six of the men had transferred from Oberlin, allegedly to get away from continuing segregation and discrimination there. A specific complaint was that women who earned degrees at Oberlin were required to write commencement essays, but their essays were read by men at the graduation exercises.

Robert S. Fletcher's two-volume *History of Oberlin*

Ladies' Hall and Conservatory of Music. Occupied in January 1885, it is the oldest major building on the Westminster campus.

College From its Foundation Through the Civil War presents a clear picture of the role of women in the early years at Oberlin, including the restriction on women's participation in commencement exercises. Various female A.B. candidates petitioned the faculty and the ladies board for the privilege of reading their own essays, but the petitions were denied "on the grounds that it was improper for women to participate in public exercises with men." The essays continued to be read by men up through the 1856 commencement. There were no women candidates for the A.B. degree in 1857, probably because the women who had been in the Oberlin class of 1857 were reading their essays and receiving their degrees at Antioch. The following year Oberlin lifted the ban on women reading their own commencement essays.

The parallel courses of Westminster and Antioch, conceived with such similar purposes, contain interesting ironies. In seeking an auspicious beginning, Antioch incurred a heavy burden of debt. By 1855 both Antioch and Westminster were having difficulty meeting their faculty payrolls, but Antioch had the more expensive operation to finance. In April 1859, Antioch was declared bankrupt and auctioned off to the highest bidder. Many supporters of the college suffered heavy financial losses. President Mann became ill and died before the end of the summer. The college was reorganized and reopened, but the struggle for solvency extended for another 60 years. On two more occasions Antioch was closed by its trustees for lack of funds, first in 1864 and again in 1881. On both occasions sufficient funds were gathered to reopen the college after a one-year hiatus.

Enrollment was also a problem. In the 50 years between 1860 and 1910, there were 34 years when Antioch graduated five or fewer, and in five of those years there were no graduates. By 1919 Antioch faced another financial crisis, and it appeared that nothing short of drastic action could prevent the college from failing. Trustee Arthur E. Morgan proposed such drastic action and thus launched the Antioch experiment in cooperative work-study education. Morgan was made president, and under his direction Antioch enjoyed a rebirth and went on to win widespread recognition not only for its work-study program but also for other academic innovations.

In contrast with Antioch's dramatic ups and downs, Westminster had a modest beginning with meager financial resources, but, thanks to a steady enrollment, managed to keep going and keep growing. By the turn of the century Westminster's graduating classes were averaging more than 45 students per year.

Waynesburg College also has a place in the beginnings of coeducation.

According to *The Waynesburg Story* by William H. Dusenberry, the college was an outgrowth of a male academy started in 1849 and a female seminary started in 1850, both by the Cumberland Presbyterian Church. The male academy was chartered as Waynesburg College in 1850, but the female seminary was not included, and operated with a separate administration and separate commencement exercises. When Jonathan Weethee became the second president of Waynesburg in 1855, he wanted to unite the two schools into a coeducational college. He met with strong opposition but effected a compromise whereby the seminary became a female department of the college but still retained its own principal and separate commencement. In 1857, Waynesburg conferred its first degrees on women, three of them receiving bachelor of science degrees for completing a scientific course that omitted classical languages. When Weethee resigned in 1858, one of his reasons was continued opposition to making Waynesburg a truly integrated coeducational college.

The year 1857, when Sarah McMichael received her A.B. degree from Westminster, saw Otterbein College in Westerville, Ohio, grant its first mistress of arts degrees to two women who completed a special ladies' curriculum. The following year two more women received that degree, while three men received Otterbein's first bachelor of arts degrees. Founded in 1847 as a preparatory school, Otterbein expanded to the college level in 1853. Thus Westminster, Antioch, Waynesburg, and Otterbein all conferred their first degrees on women in 1857, but only Westminster and Antioch awarded A.B. degrees to women who had taken the same courses as men.

Hillsdale College in Hillsdale, Mich., could also be considered a pioneer in coeducation. It traces its roots to an earlier school, Michigan Central College, founded in Spring Arbor by the Free Will Baptist Church. Starting as a coeducational preparatory school in 1844, it was chartered as a college in 1850, but closed in 1853. Between 1850 and 1853, it awarded B.S. degrees to seven women and two men, and A.B. degrees to one woman and three men. According to V.L. Moore's *The First Hundred Years of Hillsdale College*, when Michigan Central was chartered, "the conferring of an A.B. degree to a woman was not anticipated." However, an able and ambitious Livonia Benedict managed to transfer from the female department to the college department and in 1852 earned an A.B. degree.

It appears then that Michigan Central was second only to Oberlin in awarding an A.B. to a woman. The closing of Michigan Central was followed by a "distressing period of controversy and litigation," but its successor was opened in 1855 in Hillsdale as coeducational Hillsdale College. The first degrees were conferred at Hillsdale in 1860, when five men received A.B. degrees and eight women received diplomas for completing the "ladies course." Hillsdale awarded its first A.B. degrees to women in 1863.

Two coeducational secondary schools started in the mid-1840s grew into colleges. The frontier village of Olivet, Mich., started a school in December 1844 and applied for a college charter in 1845. Instead, it was chartered as an academy, known as Olivet Institute, with its enrollment divided almost equally between male and female students. It was chartered as a coeducational college in 1859. A select school, open to both sexes and all races, was founded in Alliance, Ohio, in October 1846. By 1849, it was known as Mount Union Seminary. A normal department (for training teachers) was added in 1853, and the venture was chartered as Mount Union College in 1858.

Eureka College, Eureka, Ill., was chartered in 1855 as the first college in that state to receive men and women on an equal basis, and the University of Iowa, Iowa City, also chartered in 1855, is the only state university started before the Civil War to have a continuous record of coeducation. Any college that was involved in coeducation before the Civil War can credibly claim to be a pioneer in higher education for women.

Faculty Women

Westminster's significant role in opening up the teaching profession to women was not limited to preparing her female students for elementary and secondary classrooms but soon extended to her own faculty. There were openings for "female professors" as early as 1853, and, before long, this included openings for some of its own graduates. We have already noted the roles of Janet Lowrie, Westminster's first female professor, and Sarah McMichael, the first woman to earn an A.B. degree. Women also played a role in the expansion of curriculum at Westminster. In 1866 when the Board created chairs of modern language and music, Mrs. M.H. Wilson was added to the faculty to teach French, German and Italian, while Ella Mehard was named professor of instrumental music. When Sarah McMichael joined the faculty in 1867, the Board minutes record that "an effort was made to rent a boarding house for her and as many of the young ladies as could be accommodated." We do not know what the result was, but we do know that when the Ladies' Hall and Conservatory of Music was completed in 1885, Mary Samson was named "Governess" of the young women. Linnie Hodgens came in 1887 to teach art, and Grace Acheson arrived in 1897 to teach elocution.

As the faculty expanded, the number of women professors also increased. In 1902, at the end of the first half-century, there were six women on a faculty of 14. We don't know much about the early faculty, but surviving comments have identified several women as noteworthy. Oella J. Patterson, who served as professor of English from 1877 to 1887, was considered an outstanding teacher. When she retired to travel for her health in 1887, she was replaced by Margaret McLaughry, a Westminster graduate of 1874 and a member of a family with many Westminster associations. She taught until 1903. Many of the "old grads" seemed to have fond memories of Hodgens, who taught from 1887 to 1908.

Oella Patterson, outstanding professor of English, 1877-1887.

The Civil War, for all its tragic consequences, was a watershed event that produced fundamental changes, including a change in attitude toward women's capabilities. With so many men in the military, women stepped in and performed ably all kinds of jobs that previously had been considered beyond their range. Other battles for women's rights lay ahead (women would not get the right to vote until 1919), but the fight for admission to higher education had been won, thanks, in part, to those far-sighted and fair-minded college presidents and trustees who insisted, in spite of determined opposition, that women should not be denied access to higher education. But coeducation prevailed not only because women were given a chance, but because they capitalized on it. The real heroines are the coeds of Oberlin, Westminster, Antioch and the other coeducational colleges who proved that women not only could keep up with men in higher education but, in many cases, would set the pace. ❖

McMichael vs. Dickey

Sarah McMichael, who so angered the Board by recounting the Dickey effigy burning, was the first woman to receive a bachelor of arts degree from Westminster in 1857. She returned to serve on the College faculty from 1867 to 1869. *Gathered Leaves* was an early student publication, one copy of which survives in the College archives (but not the offending issue). As "editress" of this magazine, she evidently found herself, at least in the eyes of the Board, as an antagonist to William Dickey, a College founder and fiscal savior. This "confrontation" between Westminster pioneers was resolved at the altar by future generations. Sarah McMichael was a cousin of Jacob McMichael, my grandfather, and William Dickey was my great-grandfather. They would no doubt have been surprised to learn that the McMichaels and Dickeys would be united when my mother, Mabel McMichael, married my father, William Dickey Gamble. ◆

CHAPTER 4

Trials by Finances, Fire and War

Westminster's most critical fight for survival probably occurred during its first 14 years, and the person most responsible for that survival probably was the Rev. James Patterson, the first president of the College. Following a successful first full year of operation in 1852-53, with student enrollment growing robustly, the Board, meeting Oct. 18-20, 1853, proceeded to bring in Patterson to take the helm of an expanding endeavor. By choosing Patterson, the Board passed over its two founding faculty members, George C. Vincent, who had been serving as principal, and D.H.A. McLean. At that time Patterson was serving as pastor of the Scroggsfield and Yellow Creek churches in Ohio. Born in Pittsburgh July 15, 1812, he had been graduated from Jefferson College in 1830. He was described by a former student, the Rev. J. R. Johnston, in an account published in 1873, as tall and somewhat angular with "a high forehead, a piercing eye, and a very pleasant countenance."

The Board minutes record only that "after mature deliberation Rev. J. Patterson was declared unanimously elected." However, McLean's handwritten account of the process reveals more controversy than the minutes admit. "Two members of the board made a motion, and it was adopted without suspicion, that no one should be declared elected unless he had the twelve votes of the board," he wrote. "On the first ballot I had ten votes, then Dr. Cooper, Dr. Peter Bullion, Dr. Easton, were tried with like result, these two voting 'no.' When Dr. Patterson was tried, these two voting for him, but two others, who now saw the trick, voting against him, and thus the balloting went on for the whole day, no one receiving more than ten votes. On the second day near noon the two who had voted against Dr. Patterson withheld their votes, and Dr. Patterson was declared elected. I never knew how many votes Dr. Vincent received."

When the announcement was made, resistance from outside the Board became evident. Before the Board meeting adjourned, petitions were presented from students and townspeople asking the Board to delay the selection of Patterson so that other possibilities might be considered. These petitions might well have been prompted by local support for Vincent or McLean. The Board declined the requests, however, and proceeded to hire Patterson, who managed to

The Rev. James Patterson, Westminster's first president (1853-1866). He nurtured the College through the difficult early years.

disarm many of the skeptics when he proved to be a fine scholar, an able teacher, and a man of lofty character. He took up his duties as Westminster's first president in March 1854 at the age of 41, and he was formally inaugurated the following Sept. 6.

Recognizing the need for expanded academic offerings, the Board already, in November 1853, had approved a course of study prepared by the faculty and assigned courses to each professor. The preparatory program would offer two years of English, Latin, Greek, and mathematics; the English and scientific program would offer a three-year course featuring English, Bible, mathematics, history, and philosophy; and the four-year classical program, in addition to the above, included courses in Latin, Greek, and Hebrew. The Board approved the curriculum "with the understanding that the expurgated editions of the heathen Classicks be read."

The first College catalog, which came out early in 1854, outlined this course of study in detail, along with the faculty assignments. It listed 251 students, 154 men and 97 women. However, not all students were in attendance at the same time. There were three terms each year, and enrollment for individual terms varied in the early years, ranging from slightly over 100 to almost 200. The tuition charge was $8.33 per term, and the average price for room and board was $1.50 per week. A report to the Board by President Patterson in December 1855 highlighted both the strength and the weakness of the College. He reported 165 students in attendance, 100 males and 65 females. A total of 32 classes were being taught, five each by Patterson, Vincent, the Rev. Andrew M. Black (a fall 1853 addition), and McLean, and six each by John Harshaw, who started in the fall of 1852, and Janet Lowrie, another fall 1853 addition.

But along with the good news came a serious cash-flow problem: There was no income from tuition because 105 of the students had entered on borrowed or rented perpetual scholarships, and the other 60 had used family scholarships. The scholarship certificates, whether perpetual, family, or individual, were identical in text, stating only that they were valid "according to the provisions of a resolution of the board of trustees." The minutes of the early meeting when this resolution was passed have been lost, but the terms of the perpetual scholarships evidently indicated that tuition would be waived for anyone who presented the certificate. (Scholarships and the College's financial struggles will be discussed in more detail in Chapter 8.)

The minutes for Sept. 7, 1854, report that Patterson, Vincent, Black, and Lowrie (but not McLean and Harshaw) had "released the board from $100 of their salaries." The following December the Board petitioned the state legislature, evidently without success, for an appropriation to ease the financial bind.

In December 1855 the Board cut all salaries by $100, reducing the president's annual salary to $600 and the other professors' to $400. McLean, Harshaw, and Lowrie promptly resigned, and the Board encountered some difficulty in replacing them, sometimes enlisting student tutors to teach classes. The Board authorized hiring a mathematics teacher to replace McLean at a salary not to exceed $300. Evidently a replacement could not be found at this figure, for the vacancy continued for several years. The minutes for March 24, 1857, discuss the need for filling the vacancy, and question whether the "present state of funds would permit." The Board resolved that Dickey should be "instructed to make every exertion… to raise the necessary funds." The vacancy caused by McLean's resignation finally was filled in September 1858 when the Rev. William Mehard became professor of mathematics at a salary of $500 per year.

William Dickey already has been identified as the founder most directly involved in financing the infant institution. From the very first he was active "as an agent in selling scholarships." Then in July of 1855 he was elected general agent to devote full time to the financial affairs of the College. This included, in addition to selling scholarships, soliciting gifts for the College, collecting interest on outstanding notes, paying bills, etc. In his travels for the College he rode around western Pennsylvania on horseback. While he was raising money to pay faculty salaries and fund essential operations, he evidently was foregoing his own salary. By 1859, he seems to have brought the fiscal crisis under control.

A vivid account of the arduous nature of Dickey's fund raising is provided by his daughter, Mrs. Ellen Dickey Gamble, in a letter published in the New Wilmington *Globe* and cited by Ferguson in *The Early History of Westminster College* pamphlet:

"In the spring of 1854 my father removed his family to New Wilmington so he could give all his time to his work as financial agent. It is needless to say that there were difficulties to meet and overcome continually, for it was a different thing to collect money in the early 50's to what it is at the

---

'A Credit to His Race'

Although, from the very beginning, Westminster's doors were open to all students, regardless of race, there is little evidence of African-American enrollment either before or after the Civil War. But we do know that there was at least one – John F. Quarles. In a story recorded in the *Holcad* of April 15, 1885, the Rev. David Strang '61, recounts: "Though never personally acquainted with Mr. Quarles, I felt a personal interest in him as one of the few colored students of Westminster College. He studied there when the Rev. R.A. Browne, D.D., of New Castle, was president of the institution. Dr. Browne described him as a 'bright mulatto,' and on that point turned the story he told me of the young man's ready repartee. In his turn he gave a speech in the 'morning hall' [chapel assembly]. It was a good one and well delivered, and the Doctor in remarking on it before all said, 'That was an excellent speech, Mr. Quarles – a credit to your race.' 'Which one?' he responded instantly." Quarles was graduated from Westminster in 1870 and pursued a career as a lawyer. ◆

present time, for there were few men of wealth in the church at that time, and the school had yet to be established. Early in the crisis, he associated with himself Mr. A.J. Burgess, of Greenfield, as his assistant – a man of faith and energy, who was for many years secretary of the board of trustees.

"Those years were of unceasing toil before them. They would meet and make their plans and then start out on a collection tour in different directions, to be gone for several weeks at a time. My father rode on horseback with his saddle-bag thrown across the saddle, being out in all kinds of weather and enduring much exposure, and no doubt, it was the same with Mr. Burgess, each one bearing their own expenses the greater part of the time."

In March 1859, Dickey resigned, possibly for reasons of health, three years before his death. In accepting his resignation, the Board expressed appreciation for "the fidelity, energy, and diligence with which he prosecuted his labors on its behalf, the value of which is seen in the present prosperity of the institution." They also resolved "that Mr. Dickey, having refused to receive the salary allowed by the board for his services as General Agent during the first two years of his connection with the college, the board now on accepting his resignation, appropriate to Mr. Dickey the sum of $500 as a testimonial of their appreciation of his services and an acknowledgment in part of the obligation to Mr. Dickey under which the college rests for his laborious and self-sacrificing zeal on its behalf." The Board also accepted Dickey's offer to continue to aid them "in closing any business that may need his attention." This last action evidently kept Dickey somewhat involved in College financial matters until he was incapacitated by a stroke in 1862.

William Dickey, a member of the exploratory committee, founding commission, and original Board of Trustees. Financial agent who brought College through a financial crisis, 1855-1859.

The Board minutes are missing from July 1859 to June 1863, but during this interval the financial affairs of the College evidently continued to improve. By June 1864 the president's salary had been raised to $900 and each professor's to $700 per year. In January 1865 the Board voted to discontinue the sale of scholarships, but at a Board meeting the following June, the Rev. G.K. Ormond, a financial agent for the College, reported that he had raised $20,000, much of it contingent upon the availability of scholarships. Upon his recommendation a new plan was adopted that made perpetual scholarships available for $500, family scholarships for $250, and individual scholarships for $125. The new plan also provided for endowed professorships for $10,000. In June 1866, Patterson's salary was raised to $1,200, and J.B. Cummings, a professor who joined the scientific department in the fall of 1856, was singled out for a raise to $1,000. Given raises to $800 were Vincent, Mehard, and the Rev. William Findley, a Latin professor hired in December 1856.

The financial position of the College had been strengthened in 1858 by the union of the Associate and Associate Reformed Presbyterian denominations to form the United Presbyterian Church of North America. Control of the College was transferred to the First Synod of the West in the new denomination. An amendment to the College charter granting university powers and providing for a Board of Trustees of 24 members was approved by the state legislature and governor in March 1859. Doubling the number of trustees brought new men into the Westminster picture, but the expanded Board expressed confidence in the former leaders by electing McLean president of the Board, the Rev. Robert Audley Browne vice president, A.J. Burgess secretary, and the Rev. J.P. Ramsey treasurer.

On Feb. 27, 1861, while the nation hung on the brink of the Civil War, disaster struck Westminster in the form of a fire that burned the College's main building to the ground. It was a serious threat to the survival of the College and reopened questions about whether Westminster should be moved to another location. Tempting offers to relocate the College came from New Castle, Poland, Mercer and Beaver. Xenia Seminary offered a plan to combine the two schools under the name of Westminster University if Westminster would move to Xenia, Ohio. But the citizens of New Wilmington raised $8,000 for rebuilding on the same site, providing a strong incentive to remain. After much discussion and several ballots, the Board decided on April 10 that the College would remain in New Wilmington.

Classes resumed quickly. The original small building was reoccupied and used along with the Associate and Associate Reformed churches for classes. The Board, meeting March 26, approved plans for a new building and contracted with J. and G. Frazier to erect it for $9,000. The new building was finished in time for the opening of the fall term in 1862. It was a three-story structure 100 feet long and 60 feet wide. The first floor included six recitation rooms, and one room for a geological cabinet. The second floor included the chapel, a reading room, and two society rooms. The third floor included two more society rooms, a gymnasium, and a literary room. Originally there was no central hall on the first floor; each room was entered from the outside. This building, later known as "Old Main," was to serve the College as a main building for 65 years until it too was destroyed by fire in 1927.

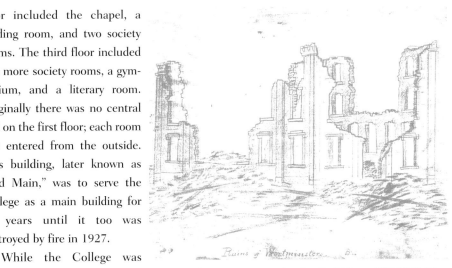

Ruins of Westminster

Ruins of first main building after 1861 fire, drawn by student John Bower.

While the College was rebuilding its main building, the nation was being torn apart by the Civil War. The College had inherited from its parent church a strong antislavery sentiment, and New Wilmington was an active stop on the "Underground Railroad," which sheltered runaway slaves and helped them on their way to freedom in Canada. It was natural that the College should strongly support the northern cause and that many of her sons would join the Union Army. However, the war did not cause a large-scale exodus of male students. Many of Westminster's young men entered the army upon graduation. A reserve company of students, organized in September 1862 as the Westminster Guards, was called to active duty on just two occasions. The first activation occurred immediately, in response to Robert E. Lee's Army of the Potomac crossing into Maryland and threatening Pennsylvania.

With Vincent as captain and Mehard as chaplain, the company left New Wilmington Sept. 15 and traveled successively by farm wagons, canal boats, river boats, railroad box cars and on foot to a camp within several miles of the spot where the bloody battle of Antietam was raging. Although not involved in front-line fighting, the Westminster men had plenty of excitement, with night alarms, hurried marches, tentless bivouacs, and the capture of several Confederate soldiers. They returned to New Wilmington on Sept. 28 to resume their studies. The company was mobilized again in the summer of 1863 and served during July and August near Parkersburg, W. Va., guarding a railroad against Morgan's Confederate raiders.

Most of Westminster's soldiers in the regular army served either with the famous Roundheads or with the 134th regiment. Browne, the vice president

'Soldiering Is Very Hard'

Sam Taggart and Joe Montgomery were friends and classmates at Central High School in Pittsburgh before they both came to Westminster, where they were roommates as they prepared together to become ministers. But when they graduated together in 1862, they deferred their plans for seminary and they went in the Union Army together, serving in the same company. Then their paths diverged when Montgomery got sick and spent the rest of his service as a patient and then as a staff worker in a hospital near Washington, D.C. The two friends corresponded and Montgomery kept a diary.

The healthy Taggart went to the front lines. His letters to Montgomery tell of the rigors of those campaigns. In a February 1963 letter, written right after the battle of Fredericksburg, he advised his friend not to rejoin the regiment. "I would be delighted if you were here but I fear the consequences. I tell you plainly, soldiering is hard, <u>very hard betimes</u>." (Taggart's underlining) In his last letter of May 17, 1864, Capt. Taggart wrote, "We have had a most terrible experience during the past two weeks, but it's impossible to give you an account of it now. Our regiment has suffered heavy losses in the late battles. I brought 28 men from camp in my company and now have 17. I had my canteen perforated by buckshot when our corps charged on the enemy works on the

of the Board who was later to serve as College president, left a pastorate in New Castle to serve as chaplain of the Roundheads, the popular name for the 100th Pennsylvania Volunteers. Among the Westminster graduates killed in the war were Hugh L. Sawhill '61, who was killed June 27, 1862, at the Battle of Gaines Mill; John Walker Vincent '60, killed Dec. 13, 1862, at Fredericksburg; Samuel Taggart '62, killed Aug. 7, 1863, at Reams Station; David P. McCallister '63, who died in 1864; and Benjamin Waddle '61, and John Carson '63, both of whom died in 1865.

As the war was ending, the College picked up additional support from its growing number of alumni. In June 1865, a committee of alumni asked the Board of Trustees for permission to schedule alumni exercises the evening before commencement. This is the first recorded instance of

Joseph Montgomery (left) and Samuel Taggart (above), both 1862 graduates who entered the Union Army. Taggart was killed in action in 1863. Montgomery survived to become a minister. His wartime diary and letters he received from Taggart are in the College archives.

organized alumni activity. The annual College catalog now published a tally of graduates by classes. That tally indicated that, by 1866, about 150 men had been graduated with A.B. degrees; almost 100 of them had gone into the ministry. Twelve women had earned A.B. degrees and 63 others had been graduated from the English and scientific course.

The end of the Civil War ushered in an era of prosperity, one that also lifted Westminster's fortunes, as we can see from the generous raises approved by the Board in June 1866. But another crisis was building that would shake the College more deeply than any yet in its short history. What happened is the subject of the next chapter. ❖

morning of the 12th.... We will have some terrible work soon."

On Aug. 7, 1864, while leading a charge at Reams Station near Petersburg, Va., Taggart was shot through the heart. Heavy casualties suffered earlier had made him the commanding officer of his regiment by that time. Montgomery returned from the war and, carrying out the plan two friends had made together, attended seminary and became a minister. (The letters cited above were donated to the Westminster archives by Montgomery's granddaughter.) ◆

CHAPTER 5

Intrigues and Departures:
How Westminster Got and Lost its First Two Presidents

Years of research have failed to shed much light on the dramatic turn of events that took place in the autumn of 1866. The preceding June the Board, in an apparent show of confidence, had approved generous raises for the president and faculty. The next Board meeting was scheduled for Sept. 25 in New Brighton, where many members were attending a church synod meeting. In the absence of Board president D.H.A. McLean, vice president Robert Audley Browne presided. According to the minutes, "The Board agreed to go into the Committee of the Whole to have a free conversation on the condition of the College." Some time later the Board emerged from this off-the-record session with a resolution declaring the presidency vacant and requesting the resignations of the president and the faculty.

The Rev. Robert Audley Browne, Westminster's second president (1867-1870). He was directly involved in the College's first period of controversy.

The Board met again the following day with Browne still presiding. The old penciled minutes, with certain parts crossed out, are confusing; it's not clear whether a motion to reconsider the action of the previous day passed or failed, but a committee was appointed, headed by Browne, to "act in an emergency." The following day, Sept. 27, the Board reconvened with Browne again presiding. On recommendation of the synod, the Board voted to amend its resolution of Sept. 25 so that it did not declare the presidency vacant but still called on the faculty to resign. Since the president was considered part of the faculty, his resignation still was requested. The change probably meant that the president was to continue in his executive capacity pending his resignation and the Board's acceptance of it. The resignations were to be presented at a Board meeting on Oct. 23 and to take effect Jan. 1, 1867.

McLean was back in his chair as the presiding officer when the Board met in October in New Castle and the requested resignations were duly presented. As one of the founders of the College, a member of the faculty from 1852 to 1855, and as Board president since 1859, McLean was intimately familiar with all the players in the controversy, and he, more than the others, might have realized how deeply the action contemplated by the Board would shock the College community. To forestall the damage, McLean moved that the whole matter be tabled until the spring meeting of the Board and that the faculty be asked to continue. After some discussion he was persuaded to withdraw his motion. Then Patterson's resignation was accepted, but a motion to accept the faculty resignations was defeated. Browne then moved to reconsider this last motion, and the faculty resignations were accepted. Then professors Vincent, Mehard and Cummings were re-elected to their former positions. Findley was to continue teaching until the end of the academic year, at which time he was to become general agent for the College.

With all other faculty members restored to their positions, the result of all this maneuvering was the removal of Patterson. The minutes give no hint as to the reason for his firing, and this question remains shrouded in mystery. But, in a process that would recur in the early 1980s, a high-ranking officer of the Board had presided over maneuvers to oust the president of the College and replace him with that same high-ranking officer of the Board.

The meeting continued with the unanimous election of Browne as president of the College at an annual salary of $1,500, followed by the election of Vincent as vice president. At this point, McLean resigned both the Board presidency and his membership on the Board, apparently to protest the actions taken by the Board. At a subsequent meeting the Board denied Patterson's request for $1,500 as compensation for past services.

The circumstances surrounding the ousting of Patterson cannot dim the significance of his contribution to Westminster. He assumed the presidency of the College in its infancy and, for almost 13 years he labored with patience and persistence in the face of a devastating fire, fiscal belt-tightening that reduced his own salary, and evidently some political infighting. His efforts brought growth, prestige and financial stability to the College. Clearly, he left Westminster better off than he found it. He was highly regarded by his students, who petitioned without avail for his reinstatement. Of the man himself, we know little, but we do have the testimony of one of his former students, the Rev. J.R. Johnston, class of 1859. In a sketch published in the *Evangelical Repository* in 1873 and quoted by Ferguson in *The Early History of Westminster College*, Johnston said of Patterson, "Nobody ever looked on him and thought him trifling. No more did anyone blame him with being insincere. It was as a teacher that Dr. Patterson excelled.... If among those he taught there be any who possess his scholarship, his fidelity, his devotion to the truth and to the church, learning shall not be without an advocate and the Master's cause without a champion."

Having forced his resignation, the Board then issued a statement recognizing Patterson's "earnestness, marked ability as a scholar and instructor, and their high sense of his private worth." He returned to the pulpit, serving as pastor of the Living Lake United Presbyterian Church near Washington, Iowa. Three years later, when Patterson attended the United Presbyterian General Assembly, meeting in Monmouth, Ill., some of his former students arranged a testimonial supper for him at the home of his friend, Andrew M. Black, the former Westminster professor who by then had moved to the faculty of Monmouth College. After the meal they presented Patterson with a gold-headed ebony cane. According to a hand-written account in the College archives by Johnston, "The good doctor sank down, overcome with emotion and leaning his head on his hands, wept – wept tears of honest gratitude." (That cane is a cherished memento still kept by Patterson's descendants.)

The actions at those September and October Board meetings precipitated a five-year period of unrest that included the three-year term of President Browne and two years when the College was without a president. When the Board met June 27, 1867, Browne had not yet accepted the College presidency, but he did so when the salary was increased from $1,500 to $2,000. Browne came to Westminster's presidency at age 46 with a varied background. A graduate of Western University and Allegheny Seminary, he had served Associate Reformed pastorates in Pittsburgh, Eastbrook, Shenango, and New Castle. When the Civil War broke out, he joined the famed Roundhead regiment as chaplain and experienced the hardships and dangers of military life. After the war, he ran successfully for a term in the Pennsylvania State Senate, where he became a leader in reform movements. He assumed the presidency of a college still plagued by factions and resentments following the forced resignation of Patterson and, perhaps, by the decision, once again, to pass over Vincent, the College founder and vice president, in favor of someone from outside the faculty and staff. It may not have helped morale that the salary gap between the president ($2,000) and the male faculty ($1,000) was much greater than it had been one year earlier, when the president was paid $1,200 and the other faculty members earned either $1,000 or $800.

While the higher pay scale reflected an easing of the crisis of 1854-58, chronic financial problems continued. Income from the $50,000 endowment was not sufficient to support operations, and tuition income was meager, as we have seen, due to the widespread use of scholarships. Salaries, the College's primary expense, totaled $6,600 when Browne took office, including his own $2,000, $1,000 for each of the four male professors, and $600 for the female professor, Sarah McMichael, Westminster's historic first female A.B., who was hired in June 1867. Dissension within the faculty seems to have led to Browne's first letter of resignation in November of 1868.

The Board called a special meeting for Nov. 30 to consider three resignations – Browne's and those of professors W.H. Jeffers, who had succeeded Findley as professor of Latin, and McMichael. According to the minutes, Browne cited as his reason the lack of unity in the faculty. The Board also heard statements from other members of the faculty. Then the faculty withdrew, and the Board passed a resolution requesting Browne to withdraw his resignation. When Browne agreed, the other two professors also withdrew their resignations. But the issue was not really settled, and Browne was again presenting certain requests dealing with faculty dissension when the Board met in June 1869.

While the Board minutes offer little insight into the problems he was struggling with, Browne wrote a revealing letter to his wife from Pittsburgh on May 1, 1869, in which he candidly and emotionally described the conflict as he perceived it. Excerpts from the letter follow: "The problem is thus forced upon me – can the institution (Westminster College) ever be lifted up? And I am only left to answer it one way. It can and must. If not with the favor of some men, then without it. The problem is also forced upon me – must I carry on my back the impracticable, old fogy incompetency that has made and makes all this trouble? I answer, I will not without a protest effectual enough to bring relief sometime. When the Board next meets they must understand the difficulties. I shall ask an adjourned meeting to consider them, at which I shall suggest reforms in certain departments and distinctly tell them I ought to be removed or sustained. It requires an immense amount of determination in me to persevere. Happily I think I am nerved to it, and also to make firmer demands of the board to grant the conditions of success."

Clearly Browne was using the threat of his resignation as leverage to get the Board to grant his "firmer demands" and give him "the conditions of success." It was intended to be "a protest effectual enough to bring relief," rather than a final resignation. And the relief he was seeking was from "the impracticable, old fogy incompetency that has made and makes all this trouble." While Browne did not explicitly identify the "old fogy incompetency" he was battling, suspicions that he meant Vincent would seem to be confirmed by the June meeting, when the Board heard separately from Browne and Vincent. At this meeting, Browne only withdrew his second letter of resignation after

A Suitable Memorial: Long-Delayed Recognition for Westminster's First President

As Westminster's physical plant expanded, buildings immortalized the names of six of Westminster's first seven presidents, as well as several generous donors. The forgotten man was James Patterson. When Oscar Remick arrived as the College's 12th president in 1987 and took a keen interest in the history of the College, I had found the ally I needed to bring tangible recognition to Patterson's contributions. Within two years, Remick was able to report success: "I carried your banner into battle and we emerged the victors. The Board of Trustees, at its meeting on Feb. 24 [1989], voted unanimous approval of the recommendation that the Arts and Science complex be named after the first president, Dr. Patterson. Knowing how long you have crusaded for this, I hasten to congratulate you on the victory." I attended a brief but effective program on May 20, 1989, when the Arts and Science Building was officially renamed James Patterson Hall. A long-standing debt of honor had been repaid. ◆

Vincent had submitted his unconditional resignation as vice president of the College, but not as a member of its faculty. At this point, the Board formally commended Vincent for his generous spirit in resigning the vice presidency.

In the handwritten letter to his wife, Browne apparently added the words "has made" to the phrase "has made and makes all this trouble," indicating that he considered the "old fogy" to have a history of trouble-making, perhaps one that stretched back to the ouster of President Patterson. Since we have no record of Vincent's point of view, speculation is risky. However, Patterson's departure paved the way for Browne, not Vincent, to assume the presidency of the College (at a salary that was increased quickly from $1,200 to $1,500 to $2,000), and McLean, not Browne, resigned in protest when Patterson was forced out, so it is hard to conclude that the actions taken at that time went against Browne's wishes. However, the same Board meeting that forced out Patterson and elevated Browne also promoted Vincent to vice president of the College. Browne and Vincent may or may not have been allied at that time.

In any case, even Vincent's generous resignation from the vice presidency at the June 1869 Board meeting did not finally resolve the conflict. Professors Jeffers and McMichael, who had earlier linked their resignations with Browne's, did leave the College that summer, but their reasons are not known. Matrimony probably played a role in McMichael's decision; she became Mrs. M.M. Brown within months after her resignation. By the following June (1870), financial pressures put Browne and the Board on a collision course. That month the Board resolved to operate on a balanced budget even if it meant curtailing salaries. The following September, at a synod meeting, the Board reported that the president's salary had been reduced to $1,500 and that any additional deficit would be deducted on a pro rata basis from the salaries of the president and the professors. The synod responded by passing a resolution that recognized the right of Browne to receive his full salary of $2,000 and directed the College to pay this amount until the close of the current year. Following that meeting Browne once again resigned the presidency of the College, and this time his resignation was accepted with formal regret at a Board meeting on Oct. 18, 1870.

Browne returned in 1873 to the pulpit of the First United Presbyterian Church of New Castle, where he had been the pastor from 1850 until he assumed the Westminster presidency in 1867, having been granted leaves of absence for his service in the Union Army and in the state senate. He continued to serve this congregation until his death on May 15, 1902, at the age of 80. Browne was active in community affairs and was highly regarded by the citizens of New Castle, who later raised funds for construction of Robert Audley Browne Hall in 1928, a dormitory which stands today on the Westminster campus as a reminder of her second president.

Westminster operated without a president for almost two years following Browne's departure. During this period the Board labored persistently to find a scholar and administrator who would give up a successful ministry to undertake the difficult assignment. For the first year after Browne left, leadership of the College once again fell upon Vincent, the enduring leader among the founders who had held his post for almost 20 years. But in 1871 Vincent resigned to accept the pastorate of a church in Brookville, Pa., perhaps when it became apparent that he would once again be passed over for the Westminster presidency. But Vincent did get his chance to be a college president – at his alma mater, Franklin College. He served that college with distinction until his death Oct. 16, 1889, at the age of 76. With the departure of Vincent, temporary leadership of Westminster passed to the Rev. William Findley, who was named professor of Greek and mental science in addition to his duties as general agent.

During this period of unrest, the College's base of church support continued to expand. In September 1871 the First Synod of the West invited the Synod of Pittsburgh to share in the sponsorship and control of Westminster College, and the following month the Pittsburgh Synod accepted the offer. An amendment to the College charter, approved Feb. 17, 1872, provided for 12 trustees to be elected by each synod. When the new Board met to organize, the old leadership was continued. J.H. Pressly of Erie was reelected as president of the Board, Findley was reelected as treasurer and general agent of the College, and the Rev. J.M. Donaldson of New Wilmington was elected secretary. At the same meeting the Board passed a resolution requesting the alumni of Westminster "to use their influence to the utmost in raising funds for the endowment of the institution."

The search for a new president ended in June 1872 when the Rev. E.T. Jeffers accepted the Board's offer. He entered upon his duties immediately and was inaugurated as Westminster's third president in the fall. Eliakim Tupper Jeffers (his friends called him E.T.) had been born April 6, 1841, in Upper Stewiacke, Nova Scotia. He had been graduated from Jefferson College in Washington, Pa., in 1862 and had just been honored in 1872 by his alma mater (by this time Washington and Jefferson College) with a doctor of divinity degree. He had attended Princeton and Allegheny Seminaries and was pastor of the United Presbyterian Church in Oxford, Pa., when he accepted the call to Westminster. He was only 31, the youngest man ever to hold the office.

Described as a polished gentleman, a brilliant scholar, and a man of excellent character and winning personality, Jeffers proved to be the rare combination of scholar, teacher, diplomat, and administrator that was needed to put the College back on an even keel. His primary interest was scholarship, and his administration concentrated on improving the curriculum, strengthening the faculty, and developing among the students a more profound respect for scholarship and a deeper desire for learning. We shall follow his efforts in the next chapter and see how he led Westminster through the revolution in curricula that took place during the last half of the nineteenth century. ❖

CHAPTER 6

E.T. Jeffers and Practical Education

Westminster College was an active participant in the curriculum revolution that swept through higher education in the United States during the last half of the nineteenth century. Particularly in democratic America, the idea that higher education was reserved for the intellectually elite came under heavy fire. It was hard to argue that doctors, lawyers, engineers, school teachers, businessmen and journalists needed to be steeped in Latin, Greek and Hebrew, those mainstays of the traditional classical curriculum. And increasingly, students enrolling in American colleges were bound for the "useful" professions instead of the "learned" professions.

Western expansion and Jacksonian democracy fed a popular contempt for traditional European culture in general and for the standards of classical education in particular. Benjamin Franklin's pragmatic curiosity and disciplined self-improvement provided a more appealing model for the rising middle class, which by the mid-nineteenth century had the ambition and the cash to send its children to college. After the Civil War, both feminism and increased demand for school teachers sent growing numbers of women to American colleges, most of them seeking something other than the classical curriculum.

The Rev. E.T. Jeffers, Westminster's third president.

Finally, the ethnic and religious groups that emigrated to America in such quantities in the nineteenth century frequently organized colleges to preserve their values and traditions while they educated their youth. Their sectarian views encouraged diversity rather than classical standards in academic curricula.

All these factors had some influence on the founders of Westminster and the kind of institution they shaped. While the single largest group for which Westminster was intended probably was young men preparing to be Presbyterian ministers – a learned profession that required knowledge of Hebrew, Greek and Latin – the founders consciously rejected organizing a college for any one constituency. They chose instead to provide a classical education as part of a broader menu. In this regard, Westminster's early leaders, notably E.T. Jeffers, developed a curriculum that was often progressive but rarely unique. Westminster's first pragmatic alternative, for example, the three-year English and scientific course – started in 1852 – was much like the one introduced by Francis Wayland at Brown University in 1848-49.

From the first, Westminster divided its academic year into three terms: fall, winter, and spring. The classical course, which required four years of study to earn a bachelor of arts degree, comprised 61 course units, 22 of them in Greek (equally divided between the New Testament and the expurgated versions of the "heathen Classicks"). It also included eight units of Latin, six of Hebrew, six of mathematics, seven of natural science, five of Bible, and seven in social sciences and philosophy. Non-ministerial students were permitted to substitute various mathematics and social science courses for the six Hebrew courses.

The English and scientific course, which initially covered three years or nine terms, included nine units of grammar and composition, ten units of mathematics, five in natural sciences, nine in social sciences and philosophy, and three in Bible. (In 1850s academic circles, "English" meant that the courses were taught in English, not that the subject was literature. In fact, literature was studied largely in the classical languages at that time, not in the English program.)

Both the classical and English courses were open to men and women alike, but women usually enrolled in the English course, which was considered good preparation for teaching in the public schools. Thus, the women who came to Westminster brought more demand for the practical English and scientific program and encouraged development of this part of the curriculum. Men at first bypassed the English course, but after 1865 men appeared with increasing frequency among the English graduates. A cumulative listing of graduates through the class of 1889 indicates that Westminster had conferred the A.B. degree on 31 women and the B.S. on 178, while 515 men had earned the A.B. degree and 39 the B.S.

The first catalog also outlined a two-year preparatory course that included in the first year, English grammar and composition, Latin grammar and Caesar's commentaries, geography, arithmetic, and algebra. The second year covered Cicero's orations, Virgil, algebra, geometry, and Greek grammar and readings. The first catalog did not classify students beyond listing 154 males and 97 females. But the next catalog (1854-55) listed 30 students in the classical department (nine juniors, eight sophomores, and 13 freshmen); 26 students in the English and scientific department (11 juniors and 15 in the primary class); and 78 students in the preparatory department (27 in the second year and 51 in the first year). Another 53 students were listed but not classified. A

The Westminster faculty of 1873-74 (from left to right): James W. Stewart, E.T. Jeffers, William Mehard, James B. Cummings, John Edgar, and John Knox McClurkin.

third year was added to the preparatory department in 1877. The preparatory department continued to be larger than the college-level departments in the early years, but College enrollment increased every year, shifting the balance. The 1901-02 catalog listed 194 college students and 39 prep students.

The importance of Westminster's preparatory department has not been generally recognized. In the mid-1800s public high schools were just beginning to appear in the larger cities. In other areas students got their secondary education at private or church-sponsored academies for boys and, more rarely, at seminaries or finishing schools for girls. Since the Westminster scholarships being sold presumably covered tuition for the preparatory department, it might have been economical for prospective college students to receive their preparatory work at Westminster. This department then became an important feeder for the College and a significant factor in its survival.

At the other end of the academic spectrum, Westminster expanded to include graduate degrees during its first half-century. The master of arts had been conferred as an honorary degree as early as 1858. The 1866-67 catalog made this degree available to any graduate of the College who for three years pursued "professional or other studies" and who paid a $5.00 diploma fee. In 1887, the writing of a thesis was added to the requirements. By the time the M.A. program was phased out in 1911, the College had granted 128 degrees. Starting in 1887 the College also offered a doctor of philosophy degree for graduate work done at an approved university. A total of 16 Ph.D. degrees were granted during the 12 years this program was in effect.

Jeffers' Legacy

Various professors and college presidents played important roles in shaping Westminster's academic development, and E.T. Jeffers, Westminster's third and youngest president (31 when he assumed the office in 1872), certainly was one of them. (See Chapter 5 for his biographical information.) An excellent scholar, he was aware of the sweeping changes in college curricula that were taking place around the country and moved quickly to bring Westminster into the mainstream, and sometimes the vanguard. By 1875, nine courses in English, Anglo-Saxon and German had been added, including Westminster's first courses in English literature, Shakespeare, and Milton. The faculty roster for 1874-75 included for the first time a professor of English language and literature.

But in 1883, one of those unspecified points of difference developed between Jeffers and the Board, and he submitted his resignation, bringing to a close an 11-year administration. He returned to Oxford, Pa., but not to the United Presbyterian Church he had been serving when he was called to Westminster. Instead, he became professor of theology at Lincoln University, a school for African-American students. He later served for many years as president of the Collegiate Institute of York, Pa.

The curriculum revolution continued into the administration of his friend, classmate and successor, the Rev. Robert Gracey Ferguson. Ferguson, like Jeffers, had graduated from Jefferson College in 1862. He had served as a lieutenant in the 21st Pennsylvania cavalry in 1863 and 1864. Following his graduation from the Allegheny Theological Seminary in 1866, he served pastorates in Mercersburg-Cove and Butler, Pa., until his call to the Westminster presidency in 1884. He was officially inaugurated as Westminster's fourth president Sept. 6, 1884, at the age of 42.

Rise of Music, Art, Literature

From the early years, training in instrumental and vocal music and modern languages was offered as extracurricular study. These classes were considered so extracurricular that they were not mentioned in the early College catalogs. We know they were offered because they are mentioned in student publications. But in 1866 the Board approved chairs of modern languages and music, and subsequent catalogs did include the names of teachers in these fields in the faculty listings. However, no courses in music or modern languages were included in the prescribed curricula of either the classical or English programs. Once Ladies' Hall (Hillside) opened in 1885, containing a music conservatory, a five-year music course was introduced leading to a certificate.

T.M. Austin was hired to develop a five-year program of instruction in piano, organ, voice, harmony, theory and notation for students preparing to be performance artists or music teachers. The first "music major" graduated with a certificate in 1887. Later, a bachelor of music degree was conferred – and extended retroactively to earlier music graduates.

Instruction in art, previously an extracurricular activity, moved into the catalog in 1885; one instructor and 24 students were listed.

Natural Sciences Arrive

The natural sciences became the most dynamic part of the growing curriculum during the 1880-1900 period. Chemistry, botany, physiology, astronomy, and geology all had been taught from the earliest years, but mainly as textbook courses. A move toward hands-on laboratory training began in 1878 with the purchase of $1,000 worth of chemistry equipment and continued the following year, when $600 worth of physics apparatus was ordered from Germany. It remained, however, for a particular "man of the hour" to arrive and light the Bunsen burners, so to speak. That man was Samuel R. Thompson, a Westminster graduate of 1863, who returned to his alma mater in 1884 to teach physics and botany. He was a staunch advocate of laboratory experiments and moved aggressively to secure laboratory equipment, sometimes at his own expense. (Thompson did his first teaching at Westminster back in 1855, when, as a precocious student, he stepped forward to tutor the classes of D.H.A. McLean when McLean and two other faculty members resigned rather than have their salaries cut during a bout of fiscal belt-tightening.)

Professor S.R. Thompson, an 1863 Westminster graduate, and leader of the College's move into the natural sciences.

Thompson set out to establish a scientific course, completely separate from the old English and scientific course, that would emphasize the natural sciences and include enough classical content to make the bachelor of science degree as highly respected as the bachelor of arts. The 1889-90 catalog announced this new four-year scientific course. The old three-year English and scientific course was renamed the literary course, and the first bachelor of literature (B.L.) degrees were awarded in 1891.

The science department Thompson envisioned required space for labs and equipment. He wanted a building so badly that he sank his personal fortune into it. In 1893 he offered the Board $20,000, a large sum in those days, to build and equip a building for physics and botany if the Board would pay interest on the sum to him and his wife as long as either lived. The building, completed and occupied in January 1894, was named the Mary Thompson Science Hall in memory of Thompson's daughter, who had died as a Westminster student in 1886. Thompson continued his campaign for the sciences by persuading W.A. Clark, a prominent New Wilmington citizen, to make an annuity gift for a chemistry wing in the new science building. In his efforts to develop the natural sciences, Thompson was aided by Charles C. Freeman, professor of chemistry, who joined the faculty in 1894. Freeman was a master teacher, and his work in the classroom, together with Thompson's campaign to attract resources, combined to bring new respect for the natural sciences and the B.S. degree at Westminster.

One minor academic development surfaced in June 1886 when the Board adopted a Three Study Plan that cut back the daily student class load from four to three and foreshadowed the "Three-Three Plan" (three courses per term; three terms per year) that became popular in the 1980s. It was an idea whose time had not yet come in 1886, however. The faculty reportedly felt that three classes a day left students with too much free time, and subsequent catalogs continued to list four courses as the normal load.

Thompson-Clark
Science Hall.
Gift of S.R.
Thompson (1893)
and W. A. Clark
(1895).

By expanding the curriculum and adding instruction in modern languages and literature, as well as music and art, and by taking a rigorous, laboratory-based approach to the study of the natural sciences, Westminster was in step with the trends in higher education in America in the second half of the nineteenth century. The classical curriculum steadily lost ground. Westminster's courses in Hebrew gradually were reduced, then finally eliminated in 1894. The 22 units of Greek originally required for the A.B. degree had dropped to seven by 1900. ❖

CHAPTER 7

Pranks, Frats and Sports:
Student Life at Nineteenth Century Westminster

Westminster's football team of 1895. It posted a 4-1 record, outscoring opponents 108-4.

The record does not show that the founders of Westminster College ever said, "Build it and they will come," but such faith would have been vindicated. The early College may have struggled to survive fire, leadership clashes and cash flow crises, but from the very beginning there was no shortage of students. In fact, as we have seen, the first students arrived two weeks before classes officially began, and Principal Vincent had to put them through their paces at his home. The early influx of students strained the capacity of New Wilmington to provide room and board for these temporary residents, the College being organized to provide instruction but not dormitories and dining halls.

From the very beginning, student life thrived, and by the 1880s, extracurricular activities flourished. Although most of the early students grew up on farms in pre-industrial America and many of them were young men preparing to become Presbyterian ministers, their attitudes, activities and enthusiasms will seem familiar to students of any generation. Both the euphoria and melancholy that students have experienced with "going off to college" were displayed from the beginning.

One of the first students waxed enthusiastic about the camaraderie that

Old Sharpie and the Grand Old Man — A Personal Recollection

Traveling to Westminster probably had not changed all that much between 1881 and 1921, when I made my first visit to the College and had my first ride on Old Sharpie. I was ten years old that year. My father was going back for his 25-year class reunion and had decided it was high time for me to get personally acquainted with the family school. In 1921, going from Sharon to New Wilmington still meant riding Old Sharpie, and I had grown up on Sharpie jokes and was looking forward to a memorable train ride. I was disillusioned when the Sharpie turned out to be much like other trains. Our coach was a bit shabbier, but there were no stops to get cows off the track, and no old ladies got off to walk on ahead because they were in a hurry.

At the time, the outing was a pleasant boy's holiday, but in retrospect, it was an important and well-timed visit for a future college historian to have made. I saw Old Main, the one built in 1862 after fire had destroyed the original main building, and I saw the old gym east of Old Main and north of the old Science Hall, which was about to disappear because the new gym (Old 77) was being dedicated that day. Best of all, my father introduced me to Westminster's "Grand Old Man," Robert Gracey Ferguson, then professor *emeritus*, the longest serving of any Westminster president and the College's first historian. I still remember how Ferguson greeted me with a twinkle in his eye and asked me several questions about my studies.

Seven years later, when I arrived at Westminster as a student, I traveled by automobile. Old Main was gone, and so was Ferguson. My class was the first to occupy Browne Hall and to move into Old Main Memorial the following spring. ◆

resulted from the early scramble for housing: "The upper story was all in one and we all slept there and we sometimes had a gay old time." But a classmate encountered New Wilmington as "a ragged old town – as ragged as despair, no side walks and endless mud." Both these reflections were recorded by Ferguson in *The Early History of Westminster College*.

Student life at Westminster, even in the nineteenth century, was marked by fraternities and hazing; sex and dating; sports; horseplay; defying authority; and an avid appetite for extracurricular activities. Early students shaped the culture and influenced the history of the College as surely as the Board and faculty did.

The smallness of the town, which had grown from 200 in 1852 to 500 by 1873, and the lack of convenient transportation threw early students on their own resources to create a social and cultural life to supplement their classroom experiences. In the early years, the nearest railroad connection was at Pulaski, five miles to the west. Daily stagecoaches connected New Wilmington with New Castle and points south, and with Mercer and points north. By around 1870 a railroad line from New Castle to Franklin opened a Wilmington Junction station about a mile and a half south of town. Passengers for New Wilmington either walked into town or rode in on a horse-drawn "hack" that sometimes met the trains. Students would talk about "coming up from the Junction on the hack." In 1881, the Sharpsville railroad opened a short line from Sharpsville to Wilmington Junction with a stop in New Wilmington. Jokes about the slowness of the "Old Sharpie" became a campus tradition, but the railroad in its day greatly improved the options for moving both passengers and freight.

Complaints of "no sidewalks and endless mud" could have continued until 1875, when stone sidewalks finally were laid in town. A *Holcad* campaign against the practice of allowing pigs and cows to roam the village streets – and the unsightly fences that this practice necessitated – finally bore fruit in 1886 when the New Wilmington Council passed an ordinance banning such in-town grazing. A short time later the campus fence mysteriously disappeared, reportedly torn down and carried away under cover of darkness by the boys in the class of '87. In March 1891 another *Holcad* complaint was put to rest when two new gas lamps were installed on campus. In 1892 New Wilmington finally got street lights, electricity and running water.

The *Holcad* itself had been launched in June 1884, published semi-monthly by a student staff until September 1887 and monthly thereafter. The familiar *Argo* yearbook did not appear until the spring of 1904.

Extracurricular Activities

Social life revolved around the eating clubs and literary societies. Eating clubs were organized as a practical solution so that students could feed themselves efficiently in the pre-dining hall years. During the Jeffers administration, for example, average board costs ran $4.50 a week for students not affiliated with an eating club, compared to $2.75 for eating club members. (Tuition at that time was $9 for the fall term and $8 each for the winter and spring terms.) The emphasis soon shifted from "eating" to "clubs" as members of these cooperative feeding troughs bonded and formed fraternities that, as we will see, were secret and forbidden until well into the twentieth century.

The Kelly eating club, a sub-rosa fraternity. They became Sigma Phi Epsilon when the ban on Westminster fraternities was lifted in 1920.

By the 1880s, if not sooner, drama had arrived at Westminster. The *Holcad* reports that the Adelphic literary society presented Shakespeare's *Julius Ceasar* in May 8, 1887, and the rival Philomath society responded by staging *Othello* the following month. Adelphic and Philomath were male clubs; women belonged to the Leagorean and Alethean (later Chrestomath) societies. There is no reason to assume that a pioneering coeducational college emulated the original productions and used all-male casts.

In April 1885, the library progressed from disorganized piles of books in a room that was open only on Friday afternoons to an arranged collection that was available every afternoon, under the care of professor John Mitchell. In 1889 the Reading Room Association, a dues-supported, members-only private library of sorts, dissolved and donated its collection of magazines and newspapers to the College library, where they became available to all students free of charge. The library's book collection got a big boost in 1891 when the literary societies turned over almost 3,000 volumes from their reading rooms.

Jim-Billy Quartet:
James Robertson,
William Barr, James
Barr, and William
Robertson.

Musical performances included the "Jim-Billy" quartet, organized during the 1887-88 school year, which toured western Pennsylvania with Miss Lela Boardman, an elocutionist who entertained with readings. The quartet got its nickname because it was made up of two sets of brothers: James and William Barr and James and William Robertson. Will Robertson '88 also played cornet solos during the performances. The introduction of a piano in chapel services in 1898 was a "breezy innovation" that greatly improved the singing, the *Holcad* reported. A glee club directed by professor M.L. Peterson sang the Westminster Hymn ("Hail, Hail to Thee") for the first time at a concert in March 1901. The words were written by Morgan Barnes, professor of Greek, (his 'heresy trial' still a year away) and set to music from Meyerbeer's opera "Les Huguenots."

Many future academic departments like art, music, speech and drama, physical education and journalism started as extracurricular activities largely led by students; classroom instruction was added after the programs already had demonstrated their value.

Healthy bodies go with healthy minds. Early Westminster advocates of this classical ideal generally took their exercise outdoors. The first gymnasium, a crude, cross-shaped structure built just east of the main building in 1878, was a project of the students in the class of '80, who contributed or solicited approximately $900. Three wings had sawdust floors and weatherboard walls, but one wing was floored and equipped with ladders, trapezes, bars and other equipment. That building, remodeled and improved several times, remained in service for 43 years.

Athletics

Organized athletics surfaced at Westminster in 1884 when the College organized a baseball association, 13 years after the National Association of Professional Baseball Players, precursor of the National League, was organized in New York. Most early baseball games were intramural contests between classes or school club teams, although a varsity team did play local community and high school teams and an occasional intercollegiate contest with Grove City or Geneva College. Resplendent in new gray and maroon uniforms in the spring of 1890, the team played up to its appearance by beating Washington and Jefferson and Western University (later Pitt). The following year, the team took two of three from Grove City and beat Allegheny once, but lost games to New Castle, Kiski and W&J.

By 1896, the baseball team was playing a full 20-game schedule and winning 12 behind the pitching of Harry Wilhelm and Don McKim. In the spring of 1898, Westminster's intercollegiate championship team defeated Indiana, Kiski, Volant, Grove City, University of West Virginia, and Waynesburg. Strong pitching carried the 1900 squad to another championship; John Cameron '01 pitched a 23-0 shutout against Bethany and a 34-4 victory over Geneva.

A Lawn Tennis Association was organized in the spring of 1888, four years after the baseball association, and sports backers already were pushing that year for an athletic association to sponsor a full program of sports. Individual athletes from Westminster won medals at intercollegiate track and field events, including three at an intercollegiate meet in May 1891. The first collegiate track meet had occurred in 1864, when Oxford challenged Cambridge. The revival of the modern Olympics in 1896 produced a surge of interest in track and field activities. R.G. Deevers '02, representing Westminster at the 1901 Pan-American Field Meet in Buffalo, took first in the broad jump and second in the 100-yard dash, putting Westminster in fifth place, ahead of Yale, Princeton and many other large universities. In the spring of 1902, Westminster's one-mile relay team took first at the National Intercollegiate Field Meet in Philadelphia. News of the victory was telephoned back to New Wilmington, where students celebrated with a parade and bonfire.

Westminster's proud tradition of intercollegiate football got off to a somewhat shaky start in the fall of 1891, 22 years after Rutgers and Princeton played the first intercollegiate game, although that 1869 game resembled soccer more than today's football. Football took on a more modern look in 1882, when the field was lined (in five-yard intervals) and teams were given three "downs" to advance the ball or lose possession. The present system of having four downs to gain 10 yards or lose possession wasn't adopted until

The 1895 Westminster baseball team.

1912. Kicking prowess dominated the early game. A drop-kicked field goal scored five points, a touchdown only four.

Westminster lost a lone game to Geneva, 42-0, in 1891, then went 3-1 in its first real season in 1892, beating Grove City twice and Butler once while losing to Geneva. But football was thrown for a loss off the field. The young *Holcad* editorialized against it as a rough and ungentlemanly sport and predicted it would be banished. Indeed, Harvard officials had banned the sport briefly in 1884 as "brutal, demoralizing to teams and spectators, and extremely dangerous," but its popularity in the 1890s proved irresistible. At Westminster, the ladies at the Hall burlesqued the male football program at their Halloween social in the fall of 1892. The following year the team beat Youngstown twice, but lost twice to Grove City.

By 1895, the Westminster team was flexing its football muscles – winning four games by a combined score of 108 to 0. But that season also provided ammunition to critics who considered it a brawl among roughnecks. A disputed game with Youngstown ended after dark when an opposing player claimed to have scored the winning touchdown. Westminster partisans argued that the player had run out of bounds, but they had to accept the touchdown and the loss in order to get the money for their transportation home.

Another game that season ended in a dispute over the rules before the game could get under way. According to the *Holcad* account, the Westminster team was driven out of Grove City by a crowd of "toughs throwing stones, dirt, eggs, etc."

Westminster boasted its best football team to date in the fall of 1899. The new coach, Samuel M. Zeigler, instituted serious practice sessions and taught the team clever plays, with the result that it won all six of the games he coached. Zeigler left before the season was over, however, and the team lost its last two games, but still won the Northwest Pennsylvania College League championship. The 1905 team, coached by Jack Lang of Pittsburgh, dominated opponents, winning nine of eleven games and outscoring its opponents 310-32.

Basketball arrived at Westminster with little fanfare in 1896, just five years after the first game was played at a YMCA in Springfield, Mass., and just one year after it first surfaced as a college sport. Although the game was invented by a Presbyterian minister and physical education instructor – James Naismith, who made efforts to reduce physical contact – it still was suspected of being a roughneck activity, little better than football. The skeptical

Holcad noted in March, "Basketball has reached Westminster and the Sophs and Freshmen are preparing to demolish each other in this indoor football." Early games featured plenty of air balls; typical was one in which the preps beat the frosh 2-1. "The points were made on fouls, neither side being able to throw a goal from the field," the *Holcad* noted. It was just as well that scores stayed low, for it wasn't until 1906 that the bottom was cut out of the basket (originally a peach basket) used for a goal; until then, someone had to bring out a ladder and retrieve the ball after every score. Backboards came later still. Until 1937, each field goal was followed by a center jump.

Westminster fielded its first varsity basketball team in 1897-98, beating Geneva 21-4 in the first game and compiling a 4-2 record for the season. By 1905, the basketball team was also outstanding, winning the championship of western Pennsylvania with a record of 12-2.

To supply standards for the evolving athletic program, the Board, in June 1898, created a Commission on Athletics composed of three faculty members and two students. The Board also adopted a policy that no student could play on an intercollegiate team unless he was enrolled for the entire year, took at least three courses each term, and earned satisfactory grades.

Fraternities and Sororities

For almost 70 years, from the founding in 1852 until 1920, Westminster College fought a losing battle to prevent or stamp out fraternities and sororities. Following the policy of its parent church, Westminster banned all secret societies. Presbyterians considered such societies, notably the Freemasons with their quasi-religious secret rituals, to be a threat to the community of the church and to the intellectual openness, equality and harmony they sought to establish at a church-related college. The subterfuges used by the fraternities to evade these strictures provide colorful episodes in the Westminster story.

In 1854 some Westminster male students privately organized a secret society first called the "Cross of Hearts" but soon rechristened Pi Rho Phi; its members also belonged to the Kelly eating club. In 1864 the men of the Van Orsdell eating club organized a chapter of Kappa Phi Lambda, a national fraternity initiated two years earlier at Washington and Jefferson College. Controversy swirled around these two fraternities until a ban finally was lifted in 1920.

In June 1866, for instance, four students who had been dismissed for alleged membership in fraternities petitioned the Board to overturn their dismissal. The Board voted to sustain the dismissals but asked the faculty to find

Progressive Feminism: No Clinging Vine

Early Westminster students expressed their opinions on equality of the sexes in *The Student Journal*, published monthly during the late 1850s. Opinions included some male chauvinism and some female subservience, but more representative of Westminster's progressive women students were the views of a coed identified only as "Kate," who took issue with a previous reference to man as the "oak" and woman as the "vine." Man was not superior in intellect, she argued, but achieved more because more was expected of him and more opportunities were open to him. In conclusion she stated, "If every woman would employ the talent given her to some noble end, she would soon refute such slanders, and every demand now made by the strongest advocate for her equality would soon be realized. What is now fanaticism would be simply common sense." ◆

a way to readmit the students. In 1879, the Board reaffirmed its ban on fraternities and sent two trustees to address students on this subject at the opening of the fall term. Students themselves were sharply divided about fraternities. The controversy reached a boiling point in the fall of 1895. What happened at that time was reported later by W. D. Gamble '96. Responding to a questionnaire sent to old grads at the time of the centennial in 1952, Gamble recalled that the controversy started with a hazing incident.

"There was a first year student from West Virginia who was rather a smart alec, and a group of students thought he ought to be hazed. One of this group accosted me on the street one evening and asked me to go to this fellow's room the following evening and get him to go with me to the athletic field which was then back of the old hotel. He said they wanted to have a little fun with this fellow because he was so fresh. I answered that the fellow would not go with me but would suspect that something was in the air because I had only a speaking acquaintance with him. I also advised to let him alone as in time he would get over his freshness. Nothing happened the next night but three or four nights later they captured the young fellow, stripped him and applied shoe polish all over his body. Then the gang caught a Junior on his way home from calling on his girl in the country and rode him on a rail.

"The episode caused one of the greatest stirs in the history of the college. A number of the members of the class of '96 presented a list of about 25 names to Dr. Ferguson and told him that unless these who were, they said, responsible for the hazings were expelled from college, they would leave. Dr. Ferguson asked for proof, and the petitioners said they had no proof but that the names presented were members of one of the sub-rosa fraternities and that they knew they were guilty. In so far as I know, not a single one of those whose names were presented to Dr. Ferguson had anything to do with the affair. I knew, of course, who the ringleader was and some of his followers. Fortunately I was not called to testify."

By the time the petition reached the Board of Trustees its object was not the expulsion of hazers but the elimination of sub-rosa fraternities. Another respondent to the 1952 questionnaire, James A. MacDonald '98, confirmed that the problem started with a hazing incident and then expanded to an attack on fraternities. The Board did direct the faculty that year to "exercise all proper means to rid the college of the fraternities complained of," but the petitioners were dissatisfied with the Board's response and about 20 of them transferred from Westminster to Geneva or Muskingum in protest.

To withstand investigations and interrogations, fraternity members instituted a resourceful subterfuge: They wrote into fraternity bylaws a clause that said if a member was officially asked, "Are you a member of a secret fraternity?" that question itself would dissolve the fraternity and the member could answer negatively without perjury. After the interrogation, the disbanded fraternity would meet and reorganize.

With such tricks, the fraternities not only survived but spun off satellite sororities. In 1905 the girls who were dating Pi's organized a secret sorority, also named Pi Rho Phi, and the girls dating Kaps followed suit in 1913, organizing a sorority they named Delta Tau. Their original constitution stated that the Delta Tau pin could only be worn by men who were members of Kappa Phi Lambda.

It looked like fraternities had met their end in 1907 when the men of Pi Rho Phi and Kappa Phi Lambda signed an agreement at commencement time to permanently disband their fraternities. However, the following year several former Pi's charged that the Kaps had secretly reorganized. As a result 12 students were suspended in February 1908 for belonging to fraternities. The suspended students petitioned the Board for reinstatement, but the Board endorsed the faculty-imposed suspension.

But by 1917, fraternities were gaining acceptance, and students and trustees were negotiating their official recognition. These negotiations were interrupted by World War I, but in June 1920 the Board finally took action to allow fraternities to operate openly. Thus the sub-rosa fraternities and sororities came out of the closet, and within a few years, five fraternities and five sororities were flourishing at Westminster. The sub-rosa Pi's became the Sigma Phi Epsilon fraternity, and the Kaps became today's Sigma Nu's. The Delta Tau's reorganized as the Alpha Gamma Deltas, while the feminine Pi's eventually disbanded as a sorority.

Supervised housing for women finally became possible in January 1885 with the completion of the new Ladies' Hall, a combined dormitory and music building built at a cost of roughly $25,000 for the building alone and almost another $10,000 for furnishings and landscaping. The first governess was Mary Samson of Allegheny City, and professor T.M. Austin directed the new conservatory of music.

Segregated housing for women relieved parental concern about de facto coed rooming houses and opened the door to a double standard of regulation. There was a standing joke on the campus about the girls of the Hall making frequent afternoon and evening trips to the post office to pick up the "male." In October 1904, a new ruling outlawed trips to the post office after supper, and the following April the rule was extended, forbidding the girls to leave the Hall grounds after supper. When 100 new students arrived in the fall of 1891, the Hall overflowed and some young women once again had to room in town.

In the fall of 1889, the College bought "new equipment" for the Ladies' Hall, namely, a cow to furnish milk for the dining room. One October night the cow disappeared, and the next morning, in its place, was discovered a horse belonging to a local minister. The minister had not arranged the exchange, so the animals were returned to their proper places, and the episode remained one of those unsolved mysteries that crop up so frequently in a college town.

Such student pranks were hardly unusual. When the sophomore class in 1877 decided to contribute a boulder instead of a tree to the campus, the boulder, inscribed "Sophomore class of 1876-77," disappeared the first night. In its place the following morning was a mound of earth with head and foot boards indicating the resting place of the class of '79. By the next morning, however, the boulder was again on top of the ground, and it still sits on the campus as a reminder of student activities of bygone years.

Washington's birthday in 1892 brought even more excitement. The town was awakened at 3 a.m. by freshmen marching through the streets and singing. Dawn revealed the freshman flag floating from the cupola of Old Main. A small group of sophomores succeeded in capturing the flag, but escape was cut off by freshmen on the stairway. Juniors joined the frosh in blocking the stairs, and seniors joined the sophs in trying to break through. Then Constable Best arrived on the scene, took the flag and gave it to S.R. Thompson, who eventually returned it to the freshmen.

As the College approached the 50-year mark, awareness of its history began to dawn. Graduating classes presented the College with portraits of Vincent, Patterson and McLean in 1899, 1900 and 1902, respectively. In 1895, the graduating class wore caps and gowns for the first time.

After the Civil War, major national events seemed to have had relatively little impact on college life. To avenge the "Maine," at least two students, Robert Austin McCutcheon and James Frew Grubbs, left campus to join the army in 1898, but that Spanish-American war ended in less than four months. The 1901 assassination of President William McKinley hit closer to home; McKinley's father had operated the original furnace on "Furnace Hill," and the family was well known in New Wilmington.

Illness and death occasionally intruded into the alternately scholarly and rambunctious life of Westminster students. A case of scarlet fever in the Hall caused President Ferguson to close the winter term three weeks ahead of schedule in 1901. After the Hall was thoroughly fumigated, classes resumed for the spring term one week early. The death, on March 19, 1886, of Mary Thompson, 18-year-old daughter of science professor S.R. Thompson and herself a Westminster student, cast a pall over the Westminster community. ❖

CHAPTER 8

Fund Raising and Belt-Tightening:
Financial Perils of the College Business

Starting a college in the 1850s was a risky proposition. We have already noted that fewer than 25 percent of the colleges started before the Civil War lived to see the twentieth century. For Westminster, like many private colleges, the critical ingredient that frequently was in short supply was cash. Our information is sketchy – early financial records, if systematically maintained, were destroyed in the fires of 1861 and 1927. Nevertheless, we can infer from events like the 20 percent cut in faculty salaries imposed in 1855 (see Chapter 4) – the one that caused professors McLean, Harshaw and Lowrie to resign – that Westminster struggled even to meet its payroll. Indeed, Westminster's history has been marked by periods of relative prosperity and bouts of fiscal belt-tightening, a pattern that has recurred up to recent times.

Westminster's first students came largely from farms in western Pennsylvania and eastern Ohio. What wealth their families possessed often was tied up in land, buildings, equipment and livestock – illiquid assets. For these families to finance college educations for their sons and daughters, some form of credit was essential. The simple expedient embraced by the founding fathers was the sale of scholarships. As we have seen in Chapter 2, Dickey, Vincent, McLean, Wolfe and Logue sold approximately $25,000 worth of scholarships during the summer of 1852 – essentially spending weeks on horseback canvassing the countryside, calling on farm families in their homes. By the fall of 1853 the scholarship total had reached more than $80,000. If the average cost of a scholarship was $80, then roughly 1,000 scholarships were outstanding. These scholarships, which covered full tuition but not books, fees, room and board, made Westminster affordable to enough families to ensure a strong start and a steady increase in student enrollment.

Using such scholarships "was a vogue of the times," Ferguson reported in his *The Early History of Westminster College*. We know that it was used by his alma mater, Jefferson College, and by Geneva College.

Scholarships were offered in different forms for different amounts. One, initially authorized at a cost of $30 but soon raised

Robert Gracey Ferguson served the longest term of any president, 22 years, then became a professor and professor *emeritus*. He was known as "Westminster's Grand Old Man."

to $60, entitled a specified individual to free tuition for five years. Another, initially sold for $80, entitled all members of a family to free tuition at Westminster. But by far the most popular – and one which caused problems for the College – was the perpetual scholarship, which could be bought in 1852-53 for $100. It entitled the bearer – and it was freely transferable – to free tuition at Westminster forever. It could be sold, rented, loaned or bartered from one student to another and kept in constant use.

The more than $80,000 in scholarships sold by the fall of 1853 would indeed have put the College in a strong fiscal position if that amount had been collected and invested. But that was not the case. Indeed, in September 1952, Wolfe reported that he had sold $14,110 worth of scholarships but collected only $20 in cash. Few farm families had $100 or even $80 or $60 in ready cash in the 1850s, so the scholarships were sold on credit. Buyers were asked to pay $10 down on the individual scholarship but could buy a perpetual scholarship with no down payment. Perpetual scholarship holders were required only to make semi-annual interest payments of 6 percent – $3 due on April 1 and $3 on Sept. 1. A perpetual scholarship thus cut the cost of tuition from $25 to $6 a year. At that rate, the College did not receive the $100 face value of the scholarship for nearly 17 years, during which time four young people could have used it to earn degrees. Missing an interest payment made the note immediately collectable. Presumably, if the note was not paid the scholarship was no longer valid. Payments were spotty enough to cause Jeffers to observe in his 1877 *History of Lawrence County*, "Much that has been received at different times has consisted of promissory notes, which, on various accounts, have not proved equal to their face value."

As we have seen, the Board voted in January 1865 to discontinue the use of scholarships but was persuaded by financial agent G.K. Ormond to reinstate them at higher prices. Subsequent College catalogs listed prices of $300 for perpetual, $150 for family, and $80 for individual scholarships. Later the cost of the individual scholarship was raised to $100. Terms evidently were tightened as well. The "by note" option was missing from the scholarship form issued in 1868. A note form signed in 1882 included a printed schedule of payments to be filled in by the donor. One such form records that Alex S. Stewart promised to pay $25 on May 1, 1883, 1884, 1885, and 1886.

However, faced with tougher times in 1878, the College offered to rent scholarships to students for $6 a year, according to the catalog for that year, effectively cutting tuition to that amount.

The sale of scholarships finally was shut off in 1888, and the Board launched a campaign to buy back outstanding perpetual scholarships if hold-ers could not be persuaded to donate them back to the College. A report in 1892 indicated that of 698 scholarships that had been issued, 586 (84 per-cent) had been paid in full. Of these, 227 were perpetual scholarships that were still outstanding. Starting in 1904, anyone presenting a scholarship cer-tificate was given a $6-per-year credit on tuition, which at that time was $50 per year. The College continued to grant the $6 credit to perpetual scholar-ship holders into the twenty-first century, but the amount became insignifi-cant long before tuition passed the $10,000-per-year mark in 1988.

To offset the loss of tuition income due to scholarships, the College start-ed charging a contingency fee, which was increased gradually until, by 1892, it exceeded the amount charged for tuition (still $25 per year). The contin-gency fee was raised from $6 to $9 per term in 1892, to $10 in 1895 and then, in 1903, to $20 for the fall term and $15 each for the winter and spring terms. Ministers' children were charged only half the fee. Special fees were charged for music and chemistry courses.

Raising funds from sources other than students was critical. Especially in the early years, before the College had alumni to turn to, those funds were raised in the community and from members of United Presbyterian church-es in the sponsoring synods. As we have seen (Chapter 2), citizens of New Wilmington pledged to raise $10,000 in 1852, when the town was contend-ing with three other communities to be the home of the new college. And in 1861, after the College's main building burned to the ground, New Wilmington raised $8,000 to fund rebuilding and fend off competing offers from other communities.

In 1875 the Board, discouraged by continuous financial problems, appointed a committee to solicit proposals from other localities. The citizens of New Wilmington responded by pledging to contribute about $9,000, con-ditioned upon a Board guarantee that the College would never be moved from New Wilmington. The Board questioned the legality of such a guarantee, but a compromise was reached: The townspeople pledged about $7,000 (later raised to $8,000) on the condition that the money would "be refunded to the donors, or their heirs or a trustee for their use, in case the college should ever be removed." The Board accepted the pledges on these terms and thus prac-tically eliminated the possibility of moving the College from New Wilmington. When a delegation from Mercer met with the Board in 1899 and offered $50,000 plus 25 acres of land if Westminster would move there, the offer was politely declined.

Westminster's faculty for 1896-97.

A financial report issued in 1877 gives us a revealing snapshot of the College's fiscal position 25 years after its founding. Financial assets included an invested endowment of $53,000, plus $25,000 in pledges made prior to 1876 but not yet paid, and $8,000 in pledges from the recent New Wilmington subscription drive described above. The $25,000 still uncollected from older pledges was estimated to be worth only $11,000, so the combination of endowment funds invested or pledged had a value of only about $72,000. Miscellaneous expenses, including fuel and repairs, were covered by the contingency fee — then $4 per term. Because income from the endowment, tuition and payments on scholarships was not sufficient to meet the faculty payroll, it was necessary to borrow about $1,400 annually from the endowment to make up the deficit. This practice of depleting the endowment to meet annual operating budgets, then replenishing the endowment with periodic fund-raising drives, became a familiar pattern.

Since Westminster's founding in 1852, a special fund-raising effort has been made every quarter-century. In 1877, with the College running an annual deficit equal to 2 percent of its endowment, the Rev. W.A. Campbell, a minister from Clifton, Ohio, was picked by the Board to serve as general canvassing agent to raise funds for the endowment. He approached United Presbyterian congregations in Westminster's two sponsoring synods, asking for pledges to be paid in five annual installments. They responded with pledges of about $15,000 a year — enough, if paid, to essentially double the endowment in five years.

Campbell continued as general agent for the College until 1888. During those 11 years, the Ladies' Hall and Conservatory of Music was built. Central

"The Heresy Trial of Morgan Barnes"

The strains implicit in a Christian liberal arts college erupt from time to time, typically when an influential faculty member is suspected of unorthodox religious views. Westminster was no exception. Indeed, Westminster closed out its first half-century with what newspapers at the time called "The Heresy Trial of Morgan Barnes."

At its June 1902 meeting, the College Board received reports that Barnes, professor of Greek (and author of the words to the Westminster hymn), held Unitarian views that conflicted with United Presbyterian doctrine. A committee chaired by the Rev. R.M. Russell (the man who would become Westminster's fifth president in 1906) was appointed to interview Barnes and report at the next Board meeting. That committee report, presented in September, included a written statement by Barnes summarizing his religious beliefs. While the committee recognized some divergence from evangelical orthodoxy in his statement, it found in its discussion with Barnes "every evidence of his being a Christian gentleman with devout reverence and faith, and a deep desire to impress his students with the fact that religion must result in holiness of character." A recommendation to dismiss the charges against Barnes was tabled until the next meeting.

halls and stairways were added to the main building during the summer of 1884, and the gym was enlarged to include a chemistry laboratory and classroom on the south side and living quarters for the janitor on the north side. To finance this $40,000 expansion program, $25,000 was borrowed from the endowment, but the remaining $15,000 was raised from various sources, probably with Campbell playing a key role.

In June 1893 the Rev. J.H. Veazey was named financial agent for the College. As a result of his efforts, all recitation rooms were carpeted and papered during the summer of 1894, and that fall, steam heat was installed in the main building, and central heating replaced stoves in the gymnasium.

As the alumni ranks grew and alumni had time to acquire wealth, efforts to promote alumni giving began to appear. The College catalog for 1877-78 showed that in its first 25 years, Westminster had graduated 355 men and 135 women. These alumni included 230 ministers and students of theology, 42 lawyers and law students, and 68 teachers. On March 27, 1890, more than 100 people, most of them Westminster graduates, showed up for a dinner meeting at the Hotel Schlosser in Pittsburgh, the first recorded off-campus, district alumni meeting. A year later, at a similar dinner meeting, the group organized as the Pittsburgh chapter of the Westminster Alumni Association.

An alumni endowment fund passed the $5,000 mark by June 1892, and, three years later, the record shows that $9,000 had been raised for the endowment of an alumni chair. Occasional bequests helped. In March 1898 Westminster received more than $6,000 from the estate of Josiah Stephenson to establish a scholarship fund to aid worthy pre-ministerial students. For the first time in many years, the College finished 1892 without an operating deficit.

Fund raising, an awareness of history and confident planning for the future all intensified as the world approached a new century and Westminster approached its 50th birthday. In June 1898 the Board created a semi-centennial commission to plan activities and projects in connection with Westminster's arrival at the half-century mark in 1902. An ambitious goal of $200,000 was set for the fund-raising campaign, to be used to replenish the endowment and build a new music building and a gymnasium.

The primary fund-raising duties were handed to the Rev. J.O. Campbell, a Wooster, Ohio, clergyman, with the understanding that a faculty chair of history and political science would be waiting for him at the end of the campaign. The campaign met with some success: A 1901 report indicated that $31,000 had been added to endowment in the past year, bringing the total to $100,000. Two years later, the semi-centennial endowment commission reported that the College endowment had been increased by $51,743.18 during the past three years, raising the total to $141,305.62. Obviously, the numbers don't jibe and it's not clear how the accounting was done, but the total raised fell far short of the $200,000 goal. The music building had to wait until 1907, the gym until 1921, but Campbell took his faculty chair in the fall of 1903. At $141,305, the endowment in 1903 apparently was still several thousand dollars below the level it reached after the W.A. Campbell campaign of 1877, if the five-year pledges were all paid.

In March 1903 the full Board directed the committee to investigate further and submit a new report at the June meeting. The committee made no report in June, but, at the insistence of some Board members, a special meeting of the Board was called in July for further consideration of the matter. Before this meeting, however, Barnes resolved the Board's dilemma by accepting an offer to become Greek Master (and subsequently headmaster) of Thacher School, a prestigious California preparatory school whose students often went on to Harvard and Yale. ◆

Distinguished alumni returned for the official semi-centennial celebration on June 17, 1902. Speakers included, from the class of 1859, J.B. McMichael and J.W. Witherspoon. Joining them were the Hon. S.S. Mehard '69; J.K. McClurkin '73 and John McNaugher and R.M. Russell, both '80. While fund raising fell short of its goals, Westminster concluded its first 50 years with its largest-ever graduating class – 56 – and a total enrollment of 280.

The Rev. J.O. Campbell, director of the College's semi-centennial endowment campaign.

If the founders of Westminster College could have been present for the semi-centennial celebration in 1902, they surely would have been impressed with the progress made during the College's first half-century. Their bold experiment in coeducation had been so successful that the doors to higher education for women were being opened all over the country. The College had been an active participant in the curriculum revolution that had replaced the emphasis on ancient languages with a broader and more utilitarian course of study. The physical plant had grown with the expansion program of the 1880s and the science building construction in the 1890s. The primary goal of educating young men and women for lives of service had been amply fulfilled. A total of 1,314 graduates were engaged in a variety of occupations.

Because Westminster needed more cash to carry out its plans, in the fall of 1904 Westminster's gentle, scholarly President Ferguson took a six-month leave of absence from his on-campus duties to hit the road, primarily in the Pittsburgh area, to raise funds, leaving dean and science professor Charles Freeman in charge of College administration. Ferguson managed to raise $13,566, a significant sum but less than 7 percent of the semi-centennial campaign's goal.

When Ferguson returned to campus in 1905, he submitted his resignation as College president, saying he wanted to be relieved of the increasing burdens of the presidency because of his own increasing burden of years. He was 63. He remained on the faculty as professor of Biblical literature until 1913. He may have been planning to resign before his fund-raising excursion, but that experience no doubt drove home the growing expectation that college presidents act as fund-raisers and public relations agents, in addition to being scholars, educators and administrators. ❖

THE WESTMINSTER STORY
SECTION TWO
1902 – 1952

CHAPTER 9

Building, Borrowing and Fund Raising:
Fiscal and Physical Progress from 1906 through 1948

T
o some degree, the experience of each College president defines the choice of his successor. Robert Gracey Ferguson brought something that had eluded his predecessors Patterson and Browne: stability, equanimity, a significant reduction in factionalism and personality conflicts, an era of cooperation and benign Christian scholarship. Even Jeffers, at the end, ran into "a point of difference" with the Board and left feeling "blue." Ferguson became Westminster's first president to serve more than 13 years (he served 22) and its first to relinquish the office under agreeable circumstances, retiring first from the presidency and then from the faculty at the natural end of his career, apparently beloved by the faculty, students and trustees.

When Ferguson left the presidency in 1906, he left a College of 260 students, 14 faculty members and an endowment in the neighborhood of $150,000. He also left a campus with just four buildings, counting the makeshift gymnasium built in 1878 for $900 as a sophomore class project. His final efforts at fund raising, as we have seen, fell short of expectations and required a six-month leave of absence from his on-campus duties to raise even $13,566. To succeed the somewhat placid Ferguson, the Board chose a man who could be said to embody the new breed of college president, an ambitious and dynamic

The Rev. Robert M. Russell, Westminster's fifth president (1906-15). He conducted a successful campaign for the endowment, which put the College on firm financial ground for the first time.

developer and fund-raiser, a man particularly well suited to representing the College in public – among alumni, the United Presbyterian churches in the sponsoring synods and the captains of industry and finance who might make philanthropic contributions to a College that so far had been more successful academically than financially.

They called the Rev. Robert McWatty Russell, the first Westminster graduate ('80) to hold the office. He had received his ministerial training at Allegheny Theological Seminary and served as pastor of the United Presbyterian Church of Caledonia, N.Y., before moving to Pittsburgh in 1890 to become pastor of the Sixth United Presbyterian Church. If the trustees thought the College needed a go-getter, Russell was not hard to spot. In his 16 years at the Sixth Church, he had attracted more than 2,200 new members and made the church the largest and wealthiest in the denomination. To accept the Westminster presidency, Russell agreed to a salary that cut his compensation nearly in half. Russell, born at Balm in Mercer County on April 6, 1858, was 48 when he was officially inaugurated as Westminster's fifth president in June 1906.

If the Board expected Russell to hit the ground running, they were hardly disappointed. Even before his inauguration (he was offered the presidency in September 1905 and moved into the office and started to work full time on April 1, 1906), he was laying plans for a "Greater Westminster." Back at its November 1905 meeting, the Board made plans to enlarge the physical plant and engaged John C. Olmstead, nationally known landscape architect, to plot a new College campus. On Feb. 26 and 27, 1906, Russell and a committee from the Board visited the College to study three possible sites for future expansion: first, around Old Main (site of the present north-south quadrangle); second, on Furnace Hill, south of Ladies' Hall (now Hillside); and third, in the Athletic Field area in the northwest corner of town. They recommended buying about 200 acres on Furnace Hill, adjoining and extending south from the Ladies' Hall property, advice subsequently approved by the Board. During this February visit, Russell also addressed the student body for the first time and was received enthusiastically. In another sign of outreach, the first annual New Wilmington Missionary Conference was held at the College that August.

Evidence of Russell's fund-raising prowess surfaced quickly. During his first summer on the job, the Ladies' Hall was enlarged and renovated. The work was financed by gifts from members of the Sixth Church in Pittsburgh.

Russell's plan for developing Westminster was anything but modest. Writing in the new *College Bulletin* issued in September 1907, he laid out his vision for the day when the College would stand "in its full glory on Westminster Heights." He wanted to turn over the current campus to the preparatory school and build a new Westminster "of university proportions" on the recently purchased property on Furnace Hill. In the same *Bulletin* he expressed his enthusiasm for a projected trolley line connecting New Wilmington with New Castle, saying: "The friends of Westminster could well afford to subscribe the whole $250,000 worth of stock needed for its building and equipment since every dollar would be returned to the benefit and growth of the College." Meeting in September 1907, the Board appointed a committee to study the matter of the trolley line. Neither vision would ever be realized, but such confidence and ambition did help to energize fund-raising campaigns that were relatively successful.

Russell's $400,000 endowment campaign.

The Ladies' Hall makeover was just a warm-up. At its February 1908 meeting, the Board approved the organization of a "Maintainance and Endowment Association" for canvassing the College's United Presbyterian and alumni constituencies to solicit pledges for annual contributions. The program's goal was to raise $25,000 a year of steady income from 1,850 subscribers who pledged to give between $5 and $100 annually. The record does not show how much actually was raised. This effort may have been superseded by the endowment campaign of 1910. On March 28, 1910, the Board approved Russell's recommendation to apply to the New York Educational Committee for assistance in raising a half-million dollars, $200,000 of which was to go to the endowment.

The following Nov. 5, the bell in Old Main rang loud and long to herald the big news of the year: Westminster had received a challenge gift of $200,000. (Although the gift was officially anonymous, I have always heard that the donor was a New York foundation, perhaps the New York Educational Committee mentioned above.) To get the money, the College had to match the donor's $200,000 with gifts from other sources. The junior class promptly gave Russell 200 pennies to start the other half. The Board met twice that month to organize a campaign to raise the needed amount. It was Westminster's most systematic fund-raising campaign to date. Quotas were set. The Board assigned itself responsibility for raising $75,000. The alumni were expected to raise $50,000. They divided Westminster's territory into geographic districts for local campaigns. Among alumni, class representatives were lined up to solicit their classmates.

Student interest in the endowment campaign ran high; senior girls appeared in chapel in bangs to publicize the campaign. Sunday, April 28, 1912, was designated "Founders' Day" to stimulate church support for the College. By July 1912 about $100,000 had been pledged toward meeting the College's half of the $400,000 goal. Approximately $25,000 had been pledged by 285 alumni, and class representatives were sending out letters to classmates urging further support.

The endowment campaign continued into 1913. On Jan. 23, a big supper was held in the Second United Presbyterian Church of New Wilmington

The Conservatory of Music - later renamed West Hall - was built in 1907. It was destroyed by fire in 1998.

to fire up enthusiasm during the home-stretch drive. Then on March 28 at a victory dinner in the Hotel McCreary in New Wilmington, President Russell announced that the $400,000 endowment campaign had gone over the top.

Expansion of the physical plant

Endowment building was emphasized in the fund-raising campaigns, but some of the money did go to modest expansion of the physical campus, more in the acquisition of land than in the actual construction of new buildings. In addition to the 200 acres bought on Furnace Hill for $30,000 in March 1906, the Board, in April 1907, approved the purchase of land just east of the campus (probably the present site of Shaw Hall and the student union building) for a men's dormitory and authorized proceeding with the building as soon as funds were available. (They weren't. It would be another 50 years before the College built on the property.) The following summer, Old Main was enlarged by an addition on the east end that housed five classrooms and a bigger library. At the same time a porch with colonial pillars was added to the west end.

Probably the most acute growing pains were felt in the music department, which had moved, in 1906, into temporary quarters in the Barnes house, across Market Street from where McGill Library would later be built. Under the energetic direction of professor W.W. Campbell, the music conservatory soon outgrew the Barnes house, so the College purchased the Hope property next door to the south. During the summer of 1907 the College built a new music conservatory on the Hope property, keeping the existing house as the front and extending it west. The completed conservatory contained classrooms, 28 practice rooms, offices, a library, and a recital hall that could seat 150. This building served as the music conservatory until 1961. It subsequently was converted to offices, eventually occupied by the Department of English, the Lifelong Learning Program and the Career Center, and renamed West Hall. It was destroyed by fire on July 31, 1998.

The Science Hall underwent extensive repairs during the summer of 1914, and ten acres were purchased between the "Sharpie" railroad tracks and the campus for a new athletic field. The latter deal was financed through alumni contributions and the sale of the old athletic field.

On March 16, 1915, Russell, then 57, submitted his resignation, to be effective the following June 30, bringing to a close his nine-year administration. He was moving on to become professor of Bible doctrine and homiletics at Moody Bible Institute in Chicago. He stayed in Chicago for four years, until 1919, when he returned to Mercer, where he was active as an evangelist until his death on Aug. 20, 1921. Nothing in the record suggests that his departure was anything but a decision on his part to move on. Still, the campus he left in 1915 was only a modest improvement over the one he inherited in 1906 and a far cry from the "full glory" of a college of "university proportions" glittering on "Westminster Heights" that he had envisioned. I have sometimes wondered if Russell was disappointed that his achievements fell so far short of his aspirations.

However, the nearly $600,000 raised during his administration was enough of an achievement to leave the Board with warm feelings toward their development-minded president. The trustees responded to his resignation with an effusively congratulatory resolution: "For nine crowded years he has labored with energy, courage, and devotion to realize the high ideal of college efficiency and life which has from the first been his guiding star. ... During his administration, and largely through his own efforts, $586,365 has been secured for the college... This testimony would be unpardonably deficient were it to overlook the work done by Mrs. Russell. She has been her husband's wise counselor, loyal supporter, and efficient helper in every work he has undertaken... In receiving from the hands of Dr. and Mrs. Russell the trust committed to them nine years ago, the Board of Trustees places upon record its esteem for them personally and its appreciation for their great work." Russell Hall, a men's dormitory built in 1952 as part of the centennial development program, perpetuates his name.

For nearly a year after Russell's resignation became effective in June 1915, while the College searched for a new president, Charles Freeman, Westminster's dean of the faculty since 1907, served as acting president. Freeman had come to Westminster in 1894 and, with S.R. Thompson, was largely responsible for establishing the natural sciences at Westminster. The erstwhile chemistry professor held A.B., A.M., and Ph.D. degrees from Allegheny College and had completed much of the graduate work for his Ph.D. at Johns Hopkins University. He retired in 1944 after 50 years at Westminster.

The search for a new president ended on March 21, 1916, when the Board elected the Rev. W. Charles Wallace, pastor of the First United Presbyterian Church of Braddock, Pa., as Westminster's sixth president. His acceptance was confirmed at a Board meeting the following April 1, and on May 9 a reception was held for the Wallaces at the former Ladies' Hall, renamed Hillside in 1906, probably at the request of Mrs. Russell. Wallace took up his administrative duties during the summer and was officially inaugurated on Nov. 10, 1916. He was 41 years old. He had been born in Jamestown, Pa., April 20, 1875, and had been graduated from Geneva College in 1899 and from Pittsburgh Theological Seminary in 1904. He had served pastorates at United Presbyterian churches in Colorado Springs, Colo.; Sheridan, Pa.; and Braddock, Pa.

When Wallace took up his duties in the summer of 1916, the "Lusitania" had been sunk by German torpedoes a year earlier and the United States was moving through "preparedness" steps that would lead to its entry into "the World War" the following year. Westminster was drifting toward its own crisis. Thanks to the half-million dollars Russell had raised, relatively little of which was spent on new buildings or ordinary operations, the College was in the best fiscal shape of its 64-year life. The crisis that soon threatened the new Wallace administration was something the College had never faced before: a shortage of students.

The enrollment crisis of 1919 certainly was aggravated by the wave of young men who dropped out of school to enlist in the armed services. Intervening in a European war had been an unpopular notion during the election of 1916, but the tide had turned, partly due to the sinking of several U.S. ships by Germans and to "yellow journalism" accounts of German atrocities published in U.S. newspapers. By the time war was declared on April 6, 1917, patriotic fervor was running high, and many Westminster men, like their peers across the country, were eager to go "over there." The College opened in the fall of 1917 with about half of its normal male enrollment.

For a while, the loss of male students was partially offset by war-related activities. The Red Cross quickly organized first aid classes, which were taught on campus. A unit of the Student Army Training Corps (SATC) was stationed at Westminster and brought about 100 young men from all over the country to town for officer training. The Hotel McCreary was converted to a barracks, and College facilities were used for some of the classroom training. Then the war ended with the signing of the armistice on Nov. 11, 1918. Demobilization of the SATC unit was ordered, and the young soldiers were gone before Christmas. The global influenza epidemic of 1918 struck the U.S. in November and December. There is no record of deaths among Westminster students, but some may have been sick enough to miss the spring term.

The sharp drop in student enrollment, at least partly due to the war and the flu, caused a reordering of building priorities. The Board moved the building of a new gymnasium – the building most likely to attract new students – to the top of the list. At its June 1919 meeting, the Board decided to proceed immediately with the building of a new gym and turned the project over to a committee headed by John Nelson '00, secretary of the Board.

Before Westminster had time to organize its own fund-raising drive, the United Presbyterian denomination decided to launch an ambitious campaign, called the "New World Movement," to raise funds for all its colleges. Westminster was slated to receive $827,000, to be paid over five years and used to build the new gym, a men's dorm, a library, an auditorium and an administration building, as well as liquidate an $82,000 College debt and increase the endowment.

Westminster's sixth president, the Rev. W. Charles Wallace (1916-31).

The old plan to build a new college on the hill had fallen out of favor. The new plan called for arranging the new buildings on a quadrangle that extended south of Old Main. So the prospect of new funds for new buildings sent the Board scurrying to secure options on property south of the campus (the same lots it had short-sightedly sold for a much lower figure back in 1852), and to sell College property south of town, including the manse on South Market Street extension where Russell had lived. By spring of 1920, planning had progressed to the point where the new gym had been assigned a site on the south end of the quadrangle-to-be. Ground was broken on commencement weekend, and the completed building was dedicated a year later, on June 7, 1921. It had cost approximately $145,000 to build and still stands. The red

Old 77. Built in 1921, it was the site of varsity basketball games prior to 1951-52. The Titans won the final 77 games played in the building.

brick structure on the south end of the quadrangle measured 103 by 60 feet and provided a basketball floor with an elevated track on the balcony level, offices, locker rooms, and a place for a swimming pool, which was added in 1926. It would be known to students after 1951 as "Old 77" because the basketball team won the last 77 games it played there. The old gym was torn down and grass planted on the spot where it stood, just east of Old Main.

The very ambitious New World Movement fell short of its goal, and Westminster received less than $400,000 of its scheduled $827,000. That amount covered the $150,000 spent to build and equip the new gym and another $15,000 to add a swimming pool. The rest went to debt retirement and the endowment. The dorm, auditorium, library and administration building would have to wait for the next campaign, which was not far off. In conjunction with the College's 75th anniversary in 1927, the Diamond Jubilee Campaign was launched in 1925-26. Plans for the Diamond Jubilee had been on the drawing board for some time but had been put on a back burner when the New World Movement came along with goals that would have covered Westminster's immediate building and financial needs. Now that campaign was revived, at a time of growing national prosperity. At its October 1925 meeting, the Board approved a plan to raise $1 million, half of it to be used for a men's dorm, a women's dorm and a combination library/chapel/administration building and the other half to bolster the endowment. Reid Kennedy '89 was named chairman of the campaign, and a professional public relations firm, Ketchum Publicity, was hired to provide publicity and organization. Contributions would be solicited from alumni, trustees, faculty, students, United Presbyterian churches, the citizens of New Wilmington and New

Castle, and other friends of the College.

The students enthusiastically set a goal for themselves of $25,000, and in one day – March 10, 1926 – raised pledges for $31,500 and capped off the day with a victory parade and bonfire. The citizens of New Castle took on the task of raising funds for a men's dormitory to be named for favorite son Robert Audley Browne, Westminster's second president and a popular minister and citizen of New Castle for many years before and after his time at the College.

When the Diamond Jubilee campaign closed June 30, 1926, a total of about $365,000 of the $1 million goal had been pledged. The largest amount –$165,000 – came from about 750 alumni. The non-alumni citizens of New Castle pledged to give $60,000, the U. P. Churches in Westminster's three controlling synods committed to giving $50,000. Students, as we have seen, pledged nearly $32,000. The non-alumni citizens of New Wilmington (including College faculty) promised $31,000. The non-alumni trustees came up with $21,000, and the rest came from miscellaneous friends of the College. (Three and a half years later the stock market crashed and the country sank into the Great Depression. Pledges that had not been paid by that time would have been hard to collect.)

Before the College had a chance to begin construction of its new buildings, disaster struck. For the second time, Westminster's main building was destroyed by fire. A College employee noticed the first flames, apparently caused by faulty wiring, at 5:30 a.m. on Jan. 24, 1927, and sounded the alarm. Residents and students helped the local fire department fight the blaze, and fire departments from Sharon and New Castle were asked to send trucks, which arrived within an hour. But by 7 a.m., flames were climbing the walls and had burst through the roof.

Wallace, rousted from bed, raced to the scene. He later wrote down what he saw: "The fire had gained such terrific headway that all the heroism of these various firemen was in vain to save the building. So furiously did the flames rage and so rapidly did they spread as to prevent any attempt to remove contents of the building save a few chairs from some of the first floor classrooms at the rear. Stern authority was necessary to restrain loyal students who sought permission to form a human chain up the fire

Ruins of Old Main. It was destroyed by fire in January 1927, after serving the College for 65 years.

escape to rescue priceless volumes from the library."

At 8:30 a.m., the faculty and students gathered in the United Presbyterian Church across the street from the smoldering ruins. After brief devotions, the faculty withdrew to make plans for the resumption of classes and final exams (the first semester was just ending), and the students passed a resolution pledging their cooperation and support for the reorganizing and rebuilding that lay ahead. The faculty rescheduled semester examinations for the following day, just one day late, and the opening of the spring semester was delayed by just two days. Because Old Main housed most of the College classrooms aside from science and music classes, the faculty and administration had to scramble to find new places to meet. Every available room in the Science Hall, Music Conservatory and gymnasium was pressed into service, and many classes, as well as daily chapel services, were scheduled in the United Presbyterian Church.

Meeting three days later (Jan. 27), the Board decided not to use Diamond Jubilee funds to rebuild Old Main but to meet the emergency with a new campaign to raise money to rebuild Old Main. A committee was duly named. On March 15, the Board approved plans for Old Main Memorial prepared by architect A.L. Thayer, and plans for Browne Hall prepared by W.G. Eckles. Both buildings were to be constructed of native sandstone in collegiate Gothic design and were to be strategically placed within the proposed new quadrangle. The picturesque campus that most people recall when they think of Westminster College was about to take shape. But in 1927, the only buildings standing on the quadrangle were the old science hall, Old 77 and the charred remains of Old Main. When H.H. Donaldson '02 was elected president of the Board in November 1927, it marked the first time a layman had held the office.

Contracts for both buildings were awarded at the June 7 Board meeting. The proposed Old Main Memorial carried a $280,000 price tag, and the College had collected approximately $100,000 in insurance from the Old Main fire. Rather than hold up construction until the balance was raised, the Board authorized borrowing $200,000 so that the rebuilding could begin at once. Help came that same month in the form of a $10,000 bequest from the estate of James P. Whitla '83 of Sharon to be used to replace library books that had burned. On Aug. 6, 1927, the ceremonial cornerstone was laid for Old Main Memorial.

Browne Hall was ready to occupy when students returned in the fall of 1928. Built at a cost of about $155,000, plus $30,000 more for equipment, it provided rooms for about 100 men and dining facilities for about 200. For the first time, Westminster men lived in a dorm, though Browne was converted to a women's dorm in 1931. (The bathrooms still contain rows of stand-up urinals, covered by wooden cabinets.)

Old Main Memorial was ready for business in the spring of

Browne Hall, built in 1928, was named for Westminster's second president.

1929, and officially dedicated the following Oct. 18. The actual cost came to $335,000, not $280,000, plus another $55,000 for equipment, but Westminster got an Old Main with a beautiful chapel that could seat 750, a Little Theatre, 21 classrooms and many offices – a building that remains both useful and the aesthetic cornerstone of the campus today.

As national prosperity soared before the stock market crash and the start of the Great Depression, giving to the College picked up. Trustee J.S. Mack made the first of his historic philanthropic contributions in 1929 by funding the McElwee Ross Student Loan Fund, named in honor of his church's pastor and fellow Board member. The fund provided financial assistance to qualifying students. Another significant gift in 1929 – $150,000 for the endowment – came from the estate of Christina Arbuckle.

Now in declining health, Wallace resigned at the end of the 1930-31 school year and died on Jan. 17, 1934. On March 17, 1931, the Board named Charles Freeman acting president of the College for the second time. He had also bridged the Russell/Wallace transition in 1915-1916. Two months later, the Board mortgaged College property to secure a $400,000 bond issue to provide cash for building and operations in the face of declining revenue and contributions as the Great Depression worsened. To complete Old Main Memorial the College had had to borrow $250,000. Tuition for the 1931-32 school year was cut to $275, including fees.

Deteriorating finances increased the College's dependence on alumni giving and resulted in an emphasis on organization. A new constitution was adopted in the spring of 1931 for the Westminster Alumni Association. Its purpose was "to promote systematic giving for college purposes by members of the Association." S.E. Calhoun, who served as president of the association from 1930 to 1933, was later commended by the Board for revitalizing the association. An alumni quarterly, the 16-page *Westminster Alumni News*, was launched in 1934 with professor R. X. Graham as editor. In November 1938 the *Blue and White Broadcast*, a monthly magazine for alumni and friends of the College, replaced the quarterly *Alumni News*. Wallace Biggs, hired in 1935 to teach journalism and head the news bureau, was picked to edit the new *Blue and White* as well as direct the new radio activities at the College.

Before the year (1931) was over, the Board had elected Robert Ferguson Galbreath Westminster's seventh president and the seventh United Presbyterian minister to hold the post. Galbreath was born at Cabot, Pa., Oct. 7, 1884. He had been graduated from Westminster College in 1907 and from Pittsburgh Theological Seminary in 1910. He had served U.P. pastorates in Romeo, Colo.; Woodlawn, Pa.; and Northside, Pittsburgh, before settling into the pastorate of the Presbyterian Church of Bellevue, Pa., in 1920. He served there for 11 years before accepting the Westminster presidency. He took up his presidential duties in February 1932, at the nadir of the Depression, and was formally inaugurated the following October.

In spite of the national depression, the College was able to pay off the $400,000 bond issue in 1937, leaving the College free of debt and its property unmortgaged. The Board was confident enough of the College's financial health to move forward with construction of a library. Three years earlier, in 1934, the Board had endorsed a feasibility study and hired an architect to draw up plans, and campus events that year raised money for a library fund. After the original library was destroyed in the Old Main fire of 1927, a makeshift library had been squeezed into the museum on the third floor of the science building and shared quarters with the Egyptian mummy and various African artifacts, many of them brought back and donated by missionaries who were graduates or friends of the College.

The new (and current) library opened in the spring of 1938, putting in place another block of the quadrangle. Built at a cost of about $155,000, it was named for Ralph Gibson McGill, a Westminster graduate ('02) and missionary to Egypt. Although many small gifts from alumni and friends helped to finance the new library, a critical large gift came from J.S. Mack, a McKeesport businessman and former Westminster trustee. Mack also provided funds for landscaping the new quadrangle. The final occupant of Westminster's classic quadrangle campus was still missing, but not for long.

Westminster's seventh president, Robert F. Galbreath (1932-46). He guided the College through the Great Depression and World War II.

In October 1939 the Board approved the building of a new dormitory for women and then, in February 1940, launched a campaign to raise $235,000 to build a new dorm and make additions to Browne Hall. When the campaign, once again, fell short and raised only about $100,000, the Board decided to go forward with the construction and borrowed $150,000 from the endowment. The dorm, named Ferguson Hall in honor of Westminster's fourth president, Robert Gracey Ferguson, was completed early in 1941, right on budget at $235,000. It provided rooms for about 220 women. It was built of the same native sandstone and in the same gothic architectural style as Browne Hall, Old Main Memorial and McGill Library, giving the campus a consistent look. It was connected by underground tunnel to Browne Hall. Women moved in during February 1941, leaving Hillside vacant for the remainder of the school year.

A second new dorm built at about the same time was easier to build and finance, thanks once again to J.S. Mack, who in the spring of 1940 offered to pay for construction of a cooperative dormitory (maintained by the residents) for freshmen men. The no-frills project, built for just $35,000, was nearly completed when, on Sept. 27, 1940, Mack died suddenly. The dorm, named Jeffers Hall after Westminster's third president, E.T. Jeffers, was dedicated the following month, on Oct. 28, and Mack's widow attended the ceremonies. Mack's generosity to the College continued when his will was found to include a bequest to the College of $150,000.

Smaller gifts in 1941 provided new band uniforms (from William M. Duff, Pittsburgh trustee) and campus landscaping (from Mrs. Samuel N. Warden '06, another Board member). To encourage continuous giving to supplement the episodic fund drives, the College in 1942 started an Annual Subscription Fund, an updated version of the Maintainance and Endowment Association Russell had attempted in 1908. A Parents' Association was organized in 1941 to foster closer relations with (and greater giving from) that quarter.

The McGills and Westminster: a Four-Generation Association

The McGill family has been intertwined with Westminster for four generations. Among the members of the founding commission was the Rev. John Anderson McGill, then pastor of the Four Mile Church and a representative from Ohio Presbytery. When moved in 1853 to Beaver, Pa., his congregation included a Mack family. The Macks had a son, John Sephus, known as "Seph," who was the same age as McGill's son, Ralph Gibson. The two boys became fast friends. Seph went on to become a successful businessman and philanthropist, while Ralph went to Egypt as a missionary and professor at Cairo Seminary. Then McGill drowned in 1926, while trying to save some children from the Mediterranean.

In 1937, when the College was raising money to build the new library, the campaign stalled far short of its goal. So the College turned to benefactor Mack for help and was not disappointed: He said he would give all that was needed if the College would name the building for his friend Ralph Gibson McGill.

Ralph's two brothers also graduated from Westminster. David M. '00 became a chemist, while Milton Adair '05 became a minister. Ralph's son, Willis A., followed in his father's footsteps, graduating from Westminster in 1933 and serving for many years as a missionary in Egypt and professor at Cairo Seminary. Since his retirement, he has been active in College affairs. He was the first chairman of the Friends of the Library and a member of the Cultural Artifacts Committee, as well as the donor of many Egyptian artifacts.

Willis married Anne McAuley '37 (daughter of the Rev. Harry Craig McAuley '07) and had three sons who graduated from Westminster: Willis A. Jr. '63, a doctor; Jon Gibson '68, an artist; and Gene M. (Kim) '70, a diplomat posted in Egypt. Jon, better known as "Gib," has painted portraits of several Westminster presidents as well as popular campus scenes. ◆

World War II brought a general hiatus in both building and fund raising, but as the war ended in 1946, students and alumni began to raise funds for a student recreation center that would be a memorial to those who had lost their lives in the service. Each group raised about $6,000. On June 25, 1945, the Board approved raising funds to build a science hall to be named for former dean (and twice acting president) Charles Freeman. The College chapel was redecorated in 1947, financed with $3,500 from the Annual Giving Fund, and rededicated at a May 30 ceremony.

A chance to add cheap buildings quickly came along when the U.S. government allocated $65,000 for the erection of army surplus buildings on campus. In March 1947, the Board approved the construction of three of these spartan structures in the area south and southwest of the Conservatory of Music and authorized spending an additional $12,000, if needed, to complete the project. The buildings were erected quickly that year; two of them were ready for use the next fall. One became a College infirmary, and the other housed the art department. The third building, opened in March 1948, housed the College bookstore as well as a student recreation center. It was officially named the Titan Union Building but generally called the "TUB." Students gathered there for refreshments, games and social time until the new student union building was opened in 1958, at which time the old TUB was converted to a building and grounds headquarters.

As alumni giving became more critical to College finances, a full-time alumni secretary, Robert E. Maxwell '37, was hired in February 1946. Postwar euphoria may have contributed to the record attendance at Alumni Day that year. It took three community churches to hold the crowd of more than 500 people who showed up for the alumni luncheon. ❖

——————————————— CHAPTER 10 ———————————————

Accreditation:
The Evolution of the Modern Curriculum

While fund raising, development and erecting new buildings demanded ever-growing shares of the time and attention of the president and the Board during Westminster's second half-century, activity in the classrooms also was undergoing profound changes as modern ideas of a college curriculum evolved rapidly. Through the second half of the nineteenth century, as we have seen, Westminster progressively started with dual classical and English-scientific programs to accommodate different needs of different students and added course work, including laboratory experience, in the natural sciences as biology and chemistry shot forward as disciplined fields of study.

But the academic menu was compact, and a course of study was firmly linked to a degree. Students chose their course of study, followed the curriculum prescribed for that course of study and, if they completed all the courses, received the degree designated for that course of study. There was only a little room for elective excursions. For the most part, academic departments mirrored the structure of degrees and courses of study. A person's degree described rather accurately what he or she had studied.

By 1952, the modern curriculum had largely developed. One degree – a B.A., for example – could cover a host of different courses of study identified as "majors." Westminster's academic menu expanded significantly between 1902 and 1952. Academic departments proliferated as new areas of learning developed. With a few exceptions (notably music), departments corresponded to majors, not degrees. A shifting package of minors, required core courses and electives was built around the new concept of majors.

Curricular diversification in the 1902-1952 period already was taking shape by 1906, the beginning of the Russell administration, when the catalog for the coming academic year (1906-07) split the classical course (A.B. degree group) into two fields of concentration: a Latin-Greek option and a classical-science option. The scientific course (B.S. degree) would offer a choice between a chemistry-biology orientation or a mathematics and physics focus. And the philosophical course (Ph.B. degree), added in 1902, was divided into three paths: education, modern language, and history-political science. A complete four-year course of study was outlined for each of the seven groups, including a core requirement of four semesters of English language and literature for all groups. With this reorganization, the College clearly was moving toward the modern division of the curriculum into majors and specialized departments.

But the curriculum didn't always expand. In an effort to cut an annual operating deficit of about $10,000, the Board in 1915 eliminated the art department, consolidated some other departments and reduced the faculty by four members.

When Wallace became president in 1916, the modern curriculum took another big step forward. The 1918-19 catalog introduced majors, minors, and core area requirements. All students were required to take 12 hours of English, 20 hours of language, 20 hours of science, 14 hours of Bible, and 18 hours of social science and philosophy. They also were required to take 24 hours in a major field beyond the area requirements and 16 hours in a minor field, which could include area requirements. With such a strong allocation of hours to core area requirements, the nineteenth century concept of a prescribed course of study leading to a particular degree still was alive and well, but the trend clearly was toward diversification and greater choice for students.

Once the new curriculum structure was fully phased in over four years, the Ph.B. degree was to be discontinued; the last such degrees were awarded in 1920. In 1926 the requirement of a minor was dropped, and the hours required for the major were expanded from 24 to 30. Specialized departments continued to appear. Senior seminars, thesis requirements and comprehensive examinations for seniors were introduced in 1941, while Galbreath was president.

As Westminster solidified its approach to undergraduate education, it vacillated over what to do with its post-graduate and pre-college programs. When President Robert M. Russell arrived in 1906, he found 67 students enrolled in three years of preparatory work. He conceived an ambitious plan to turn the current campus over to the prep school and build a new college "of university proportions" on Furnace Hill, which he rechristened "Westminster Heights." The 1906 Russell curriculum overhaul expanded the preparatory course to four years, essentially providing a private, campus-based alternative to high school. His dream of expanding the prep school was doomed, however, by the rise of good public high schools throughout the area. In 1911, the Board dropped the four-year program in favor of a single pre-freshman year of essentially remedial study. It was designed to help applicants with only three years of high school or other academic deficiencies. When Russell's administration ended in 1915, all that remained of the prep school were six students enrolled in "sub-freshman" studies. Thus ended Westminster's venture in preparatory education, but the program had met a real need and played an important role in attracting able students to the College during its first 63 years.

To bring graduate education under greater control, the faculty decided in January 1909 to grant the A.M. degree only to college graduates who had completed at least one year of resident graduate work at Westminster or some authorized institution. Then, in 1911, the College catalog announced that the A.M. degree would be discontinued "until such time as the college is better equipped for giving graduate instruction." Master's degrees were not offered again until 1945, when the College introduced a master of science in education degree with courses offered largely in summer school. Over a period of about 50 years prior to 1911, the College had granted 128 master of arts degrees, two master of science degrees and 16 Ph.D. degrees. Prior to 1909, the master's degrees were largely honorary, awarded to those who completed a satisfactory term of employment in public education and who paid the required fee. Writing an "original essay" on a literary, scientific or philosophical topic was added to the requirements in 1882. The Ph.D. degrees often were awarded for graduate work at other approved universities. As colleges across the country came under growing pressure to award their graduate degrees based on a rigorous course of study, Westminster, like many of its peers, bailed out.

Expansion of Vocationalism

Through the first half of the twentieth century, Westminster continued to seek the appropriate balance between being a private, church-related college that provided a strong education in the liberal arts and being a financially vulnerable venture that needed to attract students and prepare them for a world in which they could make a living.

As commerce flourished prior to 1929, demand grew for training that would prepare future business executives and managers. The Depression actually brought increased enrollment to Westminster and heightened concern about post-graduate competition for scarce employment. From 549 in 1927-28, two years before the stock market crash, enrollment climbed sharply to 656 in 1932-33, up almost 100 from the previous year, moved up more gradually to 703 in 1934-35 and 731 by 1939-40, as the Depression waned. Both World Wars brought large numbers of military men to Westminster's campus for training that was sometimes military, sometimes academic. Finally, the post-war G.I. Bill brought a flood of mature men to campus who did not fit the traditional undergraduate mold and required some flexibility on the College's part. All of these factors contributed to an expansion of vocational influences on Westminster's curriculum.

Business administration courses were introduced in 1921, and a separate economics and business department was organized in 1923. Captain William McKee, hired to teach economics and business administration in 1924, became the department's leader until he retired in 1958. The first bachelor of business administration (B.B.A.) degrees were given to seven graduates at the 1931 commencement. The following year, in the depths of the Depression, the expanding business department announced a new two-year secretarial course leading not to a degree but to a "Secretarial Certificate." "Secretarial Science" was expanded to two programs in 1934, adding a four-year degree (B.B.A.) track to the two-year certification program. By 1941, there was a separate Department of Secretarial Science and Commercial Teacher Training listed in the catalog.

A combined English/journalism major had been offered since 1934 when Robert X. Graham was hired to teach journalism and manage the news bureau. Earlier journalism courses may have been offered by Elbert Moses, who took on responsibility for the College's new publicity office in 1919.

Professor C.W. McKee, 1924-58. He developed the economics and business administration program at Westminster.

Within the English department, public speaking and dramatic expression classes were offered after Moses joined the faculty in 1910. His drama classes presented at least two plays a year, and extracurricular junior and senior class plays became a regular part of the College activities. When Moses left in 1923, Mary C. McConagha, famous for her elaborate May Day pageants, took his place.

Albert T. Cordray came in 1928 and by 1932 had built a separate major in speech and dramatic art. (See "Birth of the Little Theatre.") In 1936, speech and drama were spun off into a department in their own right.

In 1939 a new cooperative engineering program was introduced. Students could attend Westminster for three years, then Carnegie Institute of Technology or Lafayette College for two more and receive degrees from both schools. That same year, a civilian pilot training program was introduced. Westminster provided the classrooms, and Wilson Air Field in New Castle housed the planes. When the nation entered World War II, Westminster instituted an accelerated program so that students could graduate in less than three years by attending summer sessions.

Lingering impressions that Westminster was still an "ivory tower" institution were put to flight during the two major wars, which blurred lines between academic education and pragmatic military training. As we have seen, World War I brought 100 U.S. servicemen briefly to campus in fall of 1918 when a unit of the Student Army Training Corps was assigned to Westminster. (The teaching of German, which had been patriotically expunged from the curriculum during World War I, was restored in the fall of 1920.)

On-campus wartime training was more significant during World War II. In January 1943 the U.S. Navy established a V-5 program for training Navy air pilots at Westminster. Cadets were stationed at "U.S.S. Hillside," where they lived, ate and had classes under their own instructors. During the year and a half that the program was operating, about 1,500 cadets passed through Westminster, about 100 at a time, for a short, intensive course.

In August 1943 the 3324th Service Unit of the Army Student Training Program (ASTP) was established at Westminster. About 300 ASTP cadets were stationed in Browne Hall, Jeffers Hall, and the Sigma Phi Epsilon fraternity house. They ate at Browne and attended regular college classes. The civilian enrollment for 1943-44 was down to 63 men and 350 women, but the total enrollment including service men was over 800. College Hall, the old Hotel McCreary at the corner of New Castle Street and Neshannock Avenue, was converted into a recreation center for the service men.

> Westminster's Little Theatre was designed for rehearsals or studio productions of one-act, small-cast plays. A larger theater was planned for the new library building, but plans were scaled back during the Depression, and that theater in Old Main remained the primary venue for Westminster's thriving theatre program until Beeghly Theater opened in 1966. Producing full-length, large-cast plays, including some outstanding Shakespearean productions, challenged the ingenuity of directors, casts and crews for more than three and a half decades. With wing space of only two or three feet, actors entering or leaving the set learned what a tight squeeze was.
>
> I graduated in 1932; Cordray moved on to the University of Michigan in 1946; the Little Theatre became the registrar's office after 1966. Even today I sometimes wonder if, in the middle of the night, the registrar's office is not haunted by the ghosts of directors Cordray, Don Barbe and Bill Burbick and student thespians Bill Hamilton, Jeanne Lewis, Gene DeCaprio, Barbara Cloud, Bill Hezlep, Jackie Walker, Croy Pitzer and a host of others. ◆

When the war ended, a large number of more or less college age men were returned to civilian status, and Congress, for a grateful nation, passed the "G.I. Bill," providing funds for these men, many of them suddenly jobless, to attend college. Like colleges across the country, Westminster bent entrance requirements a bit, scurried to add teachers and classrooms and pressed into service all sorts of housing for the coming ex-servicemen, some of whom were single, others married with families.

What hit Westminster in the fall of 1946 was a record enrollment of 1,316, two-thirds of them men, including 672 former servicemen. In 1943-44, by contrast, Westminster had welcomed just 413 students, 63 of them men. The number of former G.I.s alone who showed up in 1946 exceeded by more than 50 percent the total College enrollment just three years earlier. Dining rooms were converted to cafeterias, meals served in shifts. Classes filled every available classroom from early in the morning until late in the evening. Chapel had to be divided into two sessions. Some men camped out in the gym until better housing could be found.

The G.I. "bulge" came suddenly. There was no time for formal changes in the curriculum or in admission standards, but nevertheless the College flexed pragmatically to accommodate a very large and very different group of students whose preparatory school had been the barracks, the mess halls, the foxholes and the cockpits of World War II. Prior to 1944, Westminster was no elite finishing school, but it was modeled on the prestigious eastern colleges. Formal receptions and dances at which men wore tuxedos and women wore long gowns were regular events on the social calendar. Westminster was consciously preparing young men and women for a post-college life in which good manners would be important.

The G.I. Bill opened America's colleges, including Westminster, to a group of students who formerly would not have been considered by colleges – or probably by themselves – as "college material." For all the curriculum broadening, financial aid, vocational training programs and cooperative dorms, most people who came to Westminster before 1945 were either smarter than average, richer than average or both. The G.I. bulge marked a turning point in the history of higher education in America and at Westminster. Henceforth, both socially and academically, the College would be more democratic, less elite.

Gaining Accreditation

As the American population grew and became more affluent in the pre-Depression years of the twentieth century, an educational establishment developed around organizations like the Association of American Universities (AAU). Academic standards were formalized and measured. Accreditation became a critical mark of quality, important for colleges seeking to place graduates in jobs and especially in graduate schools. Failure to be accredited by the essentially secular certifying agencies – or, even worse, withdrawal of accreditation – became a damaging stigma, a sign that a college was offering inferior education and sending its graduates out with inferior credentials.

When the intellectual W. Charles Wallace became president in 1916, he brought with him determination to move Westminster to the top ranks academically and earn a coveted "Class A" rating on the AAU's list of accredited four-year colleges. Part of his plan involved revising and upgrading the curriculum, which led to the changes introduced in 1918 and described above.

Wallace also planned to improve the faculty with an eye to meeting higher academic standards and raising Westminster's reputation. Prior to the 1920-21 school year, he got the Board to raise tuition from $100 to $150. The additional income was earmarked for substantial increases in faculty salaries so that Wallace could attract the kind of new faculty members he wanted. He was able to raise faculty salaries from $1,500 in 1916 to a flat $2,000 in 1919 and, in 1920, to $2,500 for a full professor, $2,000 for an assistant professor and $1,750 for an instructor. Wallace clearly was shooting for accreditation. The Board in 1920 explicitly authorized the president to give preference in hiring to professors who would meet the standards of accrediting organizations. His plans soon began to bear fruit. Additions to the faculty the following year included professors with Ph.D. degrees from Yale, Radcliffe, Columbia, and Indiana University. These additions probably were a factor in the decision announced in November 1921 that Westminster had won AAU accreditation at the Class A level. With Wallace's departure in 1931 and the worsening of the Depression, the College cut both salaries and operating budgets for the 1932-33 school year.

Accreditation Lost, Then Regained

If accreditation can be gained, it can also be withdrawn, as Wallace's successor, Robert F. Galbreath, was to discover in November 1934, the third year of his administration. Galbreath opened a letter dated Nov. 3 and was stunned to read, "It is with considerable regret that I inform you of the action of the Committee on Classification of Universities and Colleges in removing Westminster College from the accredited list." It was signed by Fernandus Payne, chairman of the classification committee of the Association of American Universities. Galbreath's surprise is evident in his response to the letter: "We of Westminster College were amazed and distressed by the action of your committee. In view of the fact that no intimation of dissatisfaction with our standards and work was given beforehand nor any opportunity for a hearing or defense, we are astonished at the summary action."

The AAU review of Westminster that led to the loss of accreditation evidently was sparked by a letter to the AAU from W.W. Campbell, a Westminster trustee and former head of the music conservatory, written shortly before his term on the Board expired in March 1934. That letter requested such a review. When he learned of Campbell's letter, Galbreath informed the AAU that Campbell's request was unofficial and personal but that Westminster would welcome a review. A few days before the AAU Committee on Classification met, Rylander Dempster had visited the College briefly but had given no indication that he felt there were significant problems.

AAU reported its action to other accrediting agencies. Officials of the Middle States Association of Colleges and Secondary Schools assured Galbreath that they would take no action against Westminster without a full investigation. The American Association of University Women, however, without any further investigation or even any notification to Westminster, removed the College from its approved list and made public announcement of the action at its annual meeting.

McGill Library, completed in 1938, was named for Ralph Gibson McGill '02, who died as a missionary in Egypt.

Galbreath reported in correspondence to AAU that these actions were being used against Westminster by competing colleges and were also undermining the confidence of students and prospective students in Westminster, especially those who were concerned that the loss of accreditation would jeopardize their admission to graduate schools.

However legitimate the action may have been, accreditation was lost. The College's reputation had been damaged, and there was nothing to do about it but address the AAU's criticisms and requalify for accreditation as quickly as possible. Regaining accreditation became one of Galbreath's major objectives for the next three years.

That meant addressing nine areas of inadequacy cited by the AAU in correspondence that had followed the sketchy letter announcing the withdrawal of accreditation:

1. Inadequate library facilities. (Westminster had lost its library when Old Main burned in 1927 and had, by 1934, cobbled together a temporary library of 7,000 volumes in the museum on the top floor of the old science building. By the fall of 1937 when Westminster's accreditation was reinstated, the collection had grown to approximately 16,000 volumes and the new McGill Library was nearing completion.)

2. Excessive indebtedness. (In June 1937, the Board Finance Committee reported that the $400,000 bond issue of 1931 and the mortgage on College property had been paid off, leaving the College free of debt.)

3. Too much control of the College athletic program by the Alumni Advisory Committee. (The committee was dismissed, causing lasting resentment of Galbreath by some alumni.)

4. "Uneven" training of the faculty. (In 1934 several instructors had only bachelor's degrees. By 1937, all faculty had master's or doctor's degrees.)

5. Conditional admission of unqualified students. (In 1934, some students were being admitted conditionally without adequate documentation of their qualifications. This practice was abandoned immediately.)

6. Poor performance by Westminster graduates in graduate schools. (Data were compiled to show that Westminster graduates were doing above-average work in graduate school, contesting the AAU's charge. Nevertheless, Westminster continued its efforts to provide even better preparation for graduate work.)

7. Admissions field representatives were paid on a commission basis. (Straight salaries were substituted for commissions.)

8. One faculty member – John D. Lawther – was paid two salaries, one as coach and one as teacher. (Lawther was told to choose between coaching and teaching and elected instead to leave Westminster.)

9. Low entrance requirements. (This criticism also was disputed, but Westminster did raise entrance requirements.)

After three years of focused efforts to regain accreditation, Galbreath, in November 1937, received the anticipated letter. It stated, "I am glad to inform you that at its recent meeting the committee on the Classification of Universities and Colleges voted to replace Westminster College on the approved list of the Association of American Universities." The letter was printed in the *Holcad*, and the good news spread to the rest of the Westminster family.

Tenure Policy

Although the AAU's nine complaints did not include the absence of a tenure policy at Westminster, one of the letters from AAU officials did request information on the College's "provisions regarding tenure." This request may have prodded the Board to adopt the College's first tenure policy in the spring of 1936. The new policy phased in longer-term contracts based on faculty rank, leading up to permanent appointments for full professors, five-year contracts for associate professors and three-year contracts for assistant professors. Instructors continued to receive one-year contracts. A conventional, modern tenure plan was adopted by the Board in March 1941, dividing the faculty into permanent and temporary instructional staffs. After six years of service, faculty in the top three ranks would become tenured if recommended by their department chairman, the dean and the president, and approved by the Board.

(Granting tenure was becoming standard practice among accredited colleges and universities by the 1930s. It reflected a growing feeling that teachers needed "academic freedom" to perform their duties and should be insulated from ideological pressures brought by politicians or board members. It was soon to play a role in a fierce conflict, based on ideological pressures, between Westminster's faculty and Board.)

Growth of a Separate Administration

In addition to higher academic standards for faculty and protective policies like tenure, the relative position of the faculty within the College community was transformed during Westminster's second 50 years. The change was a result of increasing institutional complexity and the growth of a separate administration. The nature of Westminster College as an organization was evolving. When Ferguson retired as president in 1906, the resident College was essentially a faculty and student body. The College was tightly focused on education and spent very little of its modest payroll on people who were not teachers. All the presidents through Ferguson were active members of the teaching faculty, chosen at least as much for their scholarship, Christianity and teaching skills as for their administrative abilities or their effectiveness in public relations and fund raising.

In fact, the presidential duties through Ferguson probably more closely resembled those of a contemporary academic dean than a contemporary college president. There was no separate administrative staff prior to 1906 – no registrar, no business manager, no development staff, no alumni secretary, no admissions department, no buildings and grounds department, no dean of men or women, no dean of the chapel, no residence directors, not even an academic dean. All those positions became essential during the twentieth century as Westminster, like other colleges, evolved into a complex institution. Instructing students became one of several critical missions. Increasingly, strategic management of the College passed from the faculty to a group of key administrators.

The faculty came to be perceived as a collection of academic specialists, to be judged by their credentials (degrees, academic publications, professional awards) and their teaching skills. Although they continued to serve on institutional committees, management of the College – at Westminster and at colleges generally – was passing to a group of professional administrators, always under the ultimate control of the Board, of course. And increasingly, conservative Board members and even some administrators began to perceive the faculty as a mobile, fractious and expensive but indispensable group of self-interested specialists whose primary allegiance was to their academic discipline and whose religious and political beliefs were likely to be heterodox.

Some details about the evolution of a professional administrative staff will be covered in Chapter 12, but academic life at Westminster from 1902 to 1952 already was being affected by changes that were making the faculty more specialized, more professional and less engaged in the growing nonacademic activities of the College. ❖

CHAPTER 11

Wallace's Feuds and Their Consequences

Many of the achievements of W. Charles Wallace, Westminster's sixth president, have been recounted in the past two chapters. Chapter 9 dealt with the New World Movement and Diamond Jubilee Campaign that together raised nearly $765,000; recovery from the Old Main fire of 1927; plans for the current quadrangle; and the construction of Old 77, Browne Hall and the current Old Main. Chapter 10 recounted the modernization of the curriculum, the raising of academic standards and the achievement of "Class A" accreditation. Wallace left a distinguished record but one that reveals little of the animosity that swirled around this provocative and controversial personality.

He was bright, self-assured and relentless in the pursuit of his goals – a near genius in scholarship, intellect and pulpit performance, but deficient in diplomacy. Some found him inspiring; others considered him egotistical and overbearing. But once he formulated plans and identified goals, he forged ahead with little regard to whose toes he stepped on. And he stepped on some very sensitive and important toes, provoking resentment and stirring up protests that dogged his presidency and created implacable enemies on the faculty and Board. Controversy led him on two occasions to submit his resignation. He had a knack of being right and at the same time offending people.

Professor W.W. Campbell. Starting in 1906 he developed an outstanding music program at Westminster. He was later involved in a bitter conflict with President Wallace.

The first important set of toes Wallace stepped on belonged to W.W. Campbell, Westminster's music czar. Campbell was a Westminster graduate who received a music degree in 1890 and an A.B. in 1891. He returned to his alma mater in 1906 to build a "College of Music." He pushed expansion so successfully that the following year the College built a state-of-the-art Conservatory of Music (later West Hall) for him in 1907. Since 1913, his program was known less grandiosely as the "Department of Music," but Campbell was an empire builder, and this set him on a collision course with Wallace. There is no written record of their conflict or an account by either man of why Campbell resigned in 1919, but I have heard reports that I believe are reliable that Campbell wanted to run a semi-independent "College of Music," however it was called, and Wallace's ambitious agenda called for an integrated College that he controlled and could rebuild.

Campbell stayed in New Wilmington and headed the Campbell Lumber Co., which became a successful building supply business. Even as a prospering businessman, he continued to give voice lessons in his home, and I became one of his students for three years (1934-37) and commuted from my home in Sharon for weekly lessons. (For much of this time, a young woman from Sharon named Anna Mary Shaffer took the lesson just before or after mine, and we would ride back and forth together to our lessons. Soon Campbell had us singing duets. We were married in 1938.) During all of my time with Campbell, he rarely spoke of the College and never mentioned Wallace. However, I do know that Campbell's son, Fillmore, also a Westminster trustee (1954-1978) was outspoken in his contempt for Wallace. (When Wallace wrote and published a 15-page, first-hand account of the Old Main fire, entitled "The Burning of Old Main" by W. Charles Wallace, a campus joke included the author in the title – "The Burning of Old Main by W. Charles Wallace" – implying that Wallace had set the fire himself to collect the insurance money and use it toward a new building. The College did collect $100,000 in insurance. As far as I know, only Fillmore Campbell seemed inclined to take the allegation seriously.)

What we do know from the record is that W.W. Campbell was elected to the College Board of Trustees in 1922, three years after he left the faculty, and continued to be a Board member until Wallace resigned for the second time in 1931. This time, his resignation was accepted by the Board. Then Campbell retired from the Board in 1934. We do know that Wallace's primary goal and crowning achievement was gaining accreditation for the College, which happened in 1921. And we know that it was Campbell, in his capacity as a trustee but acting alone, without any authorization from the Board, who wrote the letter to the Association of American Universities (AAU), shortly before his term ended in March 1934, that caused Westminster to lose that accreditation the following November, in the same year that Wallace died.

The second major incident of toe-stepping came when Wallace, intent on upgrading the faculty in his pursuit of accreditation, decided to make room for some lustrous new names and credentials by firing three members of the old guard in 1921, the same year he was able to recruit new faculty with Ph.D. degrees from Yale, Columbia, Radcliffe and Indiana. He terminated James O. Campbell, James M. Shaffer and James D. Barr. Campbell was the minister recruited in 1901 as financial agent to head the semi-centennial endowment commission. Some of the funds he raised were used to endow the faculty chair he then occupied. Shaffer was another 20-year veteran, hired in 1901 as professor of mathematics and named registrar in 1917. Barr '88 as a student had toured in the popular male quartet, then joined the faculty in 1890 as a Latin instructor. He rejoined the faculty as professor of Greek in 1906, a post he had held for 15 years at the time he was fired.

There was no tenure to protect senior faculty members in 1921, so Wallace had the legal power to remove the three old professors, but doing so violated a kind of gentlemen's agreement that senior faculty were not removed without compelling reasons. The ousted professors had influential friends among the faculty and students, of course, but also among the College trustees. The antagonism of these trustees caused Wallace to submit his first resignation at a meeting of the Board in April 1922. But support for Wallace's initiatives was strong enough at that point that a majority of the Board ultimately persuaded him to stay. The *New Castle News* reported the showdown in a prominent article in its April 4, 1922, edition: "After a discussion lasting more than two hours, the resignation of Dr. W. Charles Wallace . . . was overwhelmingly rejected." The article went on to state that the chief reason for this "vote of confidence" was "in recognition of his services rendered in elevating the standard of Westminster and bringing the school to the front rank." He had brought home the cherished accreditation just five months earlier.

The third set of very important toes on which Wallace trod with disastrous consequences belonged to John D. Lawther, Westminster's reigning sports icon. Lawther, a captain of the football team in 1918, had graduated from Westminster in 1919, then joined the faculty in 1924 as an instructor in education and psychology, in the era when Wallace was building a faculty with strong academic credentials. For the two years before he joined the Westminster faculty, Lawther was high school principal and basketball coach in New Wilmington. In the summer of 1923, he began work on his master's degree in psychology at Columbia University; working summers, he received the degree in 1926. When basketball coach Dwight Dyer quit early in the 1925-26 season, one in which the team won only two of 13 games, Lawther agreed to coach the team. The following year he benched seven returning lettermen to try a new system, using tall men and an innovative zone defense. Thus the "Towering Titans" were born. The experiment proved successful. The team won 10 games that year (1926-27), lost five and tied for second place in the conference. Lawther went on to develop the tradition for outstanding basketball at Westminster. He was named director of athletics and physical education and served as assistant coach for the football team – traditionally a full-time position – but Lawther never relinquished his position as assistant professor of education and psychology. Essentially, he was holding two full-time jobs and being paid two salaries.

Lawther's two jobs apparently brought him into conflict with Wallace, who might well have believed that serving on his highly accredited faculty was a full-time job in itself. Again, there is no written record of what occurred between the two men, but it was widely understood at the time that Wallace had pressured Lawther to choose between his academic position and his coaching and athletic director role and that Lawther, rather than give up either, resigned all posts and left the College in 1930. (I was a Westminster student when this happened; my brother was a friend of Lawther and captain of his original Towering Titans; my father was a friend of Wallace and a member of the Board.)

Word spread like wildfire that Lawther, a College hero in the eyes of many students and some Board members, had been driven off by Westminster's prickly president. Students signed petitions and sent them to the Board, asking for Wallace's resignation. Wallace opponents on the Board, possibly including Campbell, were less public in their opposition but perhaps more effective. Faced with rising opposition and declining health, Wallace presented his resignation to the Board on Nov. 20, 1930. On Dec. 12, it was accepted, to be effective at the end of the academic year.

John Lawther, professor and coach. He developed Westminster's tradition of basketball supremacy, but he left the College after a dispute with President Wallace.

The spring semester witnessed an interesting sequence of three events, all reported in the *Holcad*. In February, Lawrence "Pops" Harrison, who had replaced Lawther as athletic director and basketball coach, resigned. Harrison in his short stint (less than a year) had rebuilt a Titan basketball team that had graduated its top three scorers the year before and was on his way to a stellar season in which the team lost just one game and won the conference and district championships. By March 10, Lawther, who was enjoying a very successful year as football and basketball coach at Freeport High School on Long Island, resigned to accept a position

Wallace Memorial Chapel, located within Old Main Memorial, is a memorial to W. Charles Wallace, Westminster's sixth president.

at Westminster as director of athletics, head football and basketball coach – and assistant professor of education and psychology. By March 24, Wallace had requested and been granted a leave of absence for the remainder of the academic year. Dean Charles Freeman once again was named acting president until a new president could be found. Wallace died Jan. 17, 1934, at the age of 58.

But the story was not quite over. When Campbell's letter to the AAU brought scrutiny from the accrediting agency in 1934, one of the nine complaints that cost Westminster her accreditation centered on Lawther and his dual roles as athletic director and psychology professor. (Lawther himself saw the two fields as interconnected. After he became nationally famous as athletic director and basketball coach at Penn State, he wrote and published books on sports psychology.) This time beleaguered president Robert F. Galbreath had to tell Lawther to turn in one of his hats, and once again Lawther responded by leaving Westminster. This time, although his basketball teams were still winning championships, there was no public outcry for Galbreath's head. The AAU had essentially demanded the change as a price for re-accreditation. The lingering Depression had made giving two jobs to one man unpopular. And Galbreath, a modest gentleman and consummate diplomat, had none of Wallace's enemies to contend with.

During Wallace's 15-year administration, enrollment more than doubled; the curriculum was broadened and liberalized; academic standards were raised, earning the College a class A rating; student government was initiated; fraternities and sororities were recognized; and more than a million dollars was put into new buildings and the endowment. Those buildings included two of the signature landmarks of the gothic sandstone quadrangle – Old Main Memorial and Browne Hall. Wallace Memorial Chapel, where many students attended daily chapel services prior to 1962 and where many College weddings took place, was named in honor of Westminster's sixth president in 1938. ❖

———————————————— CHAPTER 12 ————————————————

Reining in the Faculty:
Post-War Conflict as the Board Asserts Itself

While Westminster, as we have seen, was no stranger to conflict, nothing in the past prepared the College for the nature and scope of the conflict that followed World War II. Earlier battles were essentially personality clashes. While the feuding personalities held ideas and attracted supporters, the struggles were temporary, personal and local to Westminster.

Skirmishes that started in 1944, pitted the faculty against the Board in a kind of civil war that was institutional, ideological and linked to the broad conflict that gripped the United States: liberal vs. conservative; labor vs. management; Democrat vs. Republican; secular vs. religious; Communism vs. the free world; the State Department and then the Army vs. McCarthy. At Westminster, the struggle flared dramatically in the late 1940s, sputtered along into the early 1950s, and broke out again with a vengeance in 1981.

Forces of Change

The battleground usually was over the rights, obligations, loyalties, political activities, personal morality, compensation and level of enfranchisement within Westminster that were appropriate for the men and women who taught her students. Such conflict would have been unimaginable in the early years when the small faculty, dominated by United Presbyterian ministers, was reflexively loyal to the College and the church and fully included in the simple management of an educational institution that had no separate group of professional managers. But a lot had changed since then, and the changes were accelerating.

◆ As Christian colleges and their curricula grew, clergymen-scholars called by God to minister in the classroom gave way to secular specialists expected to meet high standards in their chosen academic discipline. Teachers became more career-oriented, less loyal to any one institution and less involved in non-academic programs.

◆ The post-war economic enrollment boom encouraged by the G.I. Bill forced colleges and universities nationally to scramble to find and keep qualified teachers. In the rush to fill open positions, Westminster, like other colleges, was less able to choose teachers who met all of the standards it would have liked to apply.

◆ The emphasis on academic standards and the expanding influence of accreditation agencies like the Association of American Universities and the Middle States Association of Colleges and Schools meant that academic standards were being set and enforced increasingly by a secular national or regional body, less by local administrations, local boards and sponsoring churches. The value of accreditation in the marketplace gave these agencies a powerful voice in shaping College policies.

◆ The culture of American intellectuals, always somewhat alienated from the world of commerce and the theories of industrial capitalism, began to shift from religious idealism to secular idealism. Many academics were drawn to the politics of the Franklin D. Roosevelt coalition and the New Deal. Some were sympathetic to the ideals of socialism or even communism.

That, at least, was the perception of trustees and some administrators, groups that had also undergone significant changes. Certainly at Westminster the emphasis on raising funds to build buildings and grow the endowment had brought to the Board a growing number of wealthy laymen, shrinking the role of U.P. ministers. Exactly half of the original Board, ministers increased their representation to 21 of 31 seats by 1900 but then declined to just one by 1995. Conflicts between faculty and Board no longer could be resolved on the common ground shared by the U.P. ministers who dominated each group. Both faculty and Board had been secularized but had moved toward opposite ends of a broadly political spectrum.

Growth of a Separate Administration

At the same time, the faculty was losing its influence over the management process. As colleges grew in size and complexity and as activities like alumni relations and fund raising grew in importance, Westminster, like most colleges and universities, developed a separate administrative staff that diminished the role of the faculty in the management of the College.

The professional staff of Westminster was essentially its faculty in the nineteenth century. Even during the Wallace years (1916-1931) when administrative titles like dean and registrar were introduced, these posts were held by faculty members who continued to teach. But within a few years after his 1932 inauguration, Galbreath had three major full-time administrators serving under his direction. Alex C. Burr, Westminster's first full-time academic dean, had the responsibility for supervising academic affairs. Haskell R. Patton, business manager with a staff of four people reporting to him, was responsible for business affairs, and William A. Johns, with the title director of public relations, was responsible for promotion, student recruiting, admissions, and placement.

Specialized roles for faculty and administrators meant that the faculty had both gained and lost clout. A perception within the faculty grew that they were now considered a difficult but important segment of the College that needed to be managed, sometimes with a firm hand, rather than welcomed as members of a cooperative management team. This suspicion waxed or waned, depending on whether the College presidency was held by someone who favored participatory or paternalistic governance. By 1945, the level of distrust between the faculty and Board at Westminster had risen to the point where combustion was imminent.

Opening Shots

Ironically, the first of two major wars between faculty and Board came during the term of Robert F. Galbreath, who shared with Robert G. Ferguson the distinction of being the least confrontational and combative men to hold the office, at least prior to 1967. Gentle, patient and accommodating, Galbreath would have avoided conflict, but conflict would not spare Galbreath. For most of Galbreath's 14-and-a-half-year administration, the pressing issues were regaining accreditation (see Chapter 10) and guiding the College through the stresses brought on first by the Depression and then by World War II. The end of the war brought a new crisis.

The first skirmish was set off by two young history instructors, Irvin G. Wyllie and Neil A. McNall, who wrote letters to their congressman, Republican Louis E. Graham. Wyllie's one-page letter, dated April 4, 1944 (a copy of which survives in the College archives), is scornful and vituperative, without any apparent constructive purpose. He assails the congressman's "singularly reactionary stand" on a long list of current issues, groups him with such "unpalatable characters as Hamilton Fish, Eugene Cox, Howard Smith, and Martin Dies," calls him "a small-time, partisan political hack," and ends with the "fervent hope" that Graham will be thrown out by the voters. It appears to be a broadside directed at a conservative Republican by a liberal college professor. While Wyllie wrote as an individual constituent, a note at the bottom of the letter, apparently added later, identifies him as a Westminster history instructor in the department chaired by Leon Marshall.

When the Wyllie and McNall letters were brought to the attention of the Board, the trustees were not pleased. A special meeting of the executive committee of the Board was called on May 8, 1944, explicitly to deal with the "derogatory" letters from the two instructors. At that meeting, the executive committee drafted a letter to Congressman Graham, apologizing for the incident, assuring him that the two detractors did not represent the views of the College and promising him that employment of the two would "cease at the end of the present school year." Normally, contracts for the following year would have gone out by early May, so dropping the controversial instructors probably would have required withdrawing contracts that already had been offered.

Wyllie, a 1941 Westminster graduate hired in 1943, chose to resign to continue graduate work, but McNall, hired in 1942, would not resign, and students signed petitions protesting his dismissal. He was a Phi Beta Kappa member completing his doctoral work at Cornell University.

The executive committee reviewed the McNall dismissal on June 12, 1944, and again disapproved his appointment for the coming year. As Galbreath recalled in testimony given to a Board investigating committee in April 1945, "I was called to Pittsburgh and told to fire McNall and to do so immediately. After I came home and thought the matter over, I wrote a letter to the executive committee presenting my resignation saying I could not see my way clear to carry out the order." In that letter of resignation, submitted June 13, Galbreath explained that "the dropping of Mr. McNall under present circumstances is precipitating a split in the faculty and an invitation to the A.A.U.P. [American Association of University Professors] to start an investigation." He added that "the strain and bitterness that will inevitably result will be more than either my wife or I can again face."

Two days later, on June 15, the executive committee backed down and authorized a terminal one-year contract for McNall, who left at the end of the 1944-45 academic year. Galbreath was persuaded to withdraw his resignation, but bigger battles were brewing.

In August 1944, just two months after the McNall controversy had been officially resolved, faculty political activity again became an issue when Leon Marshall, chairman of the history department, was elected chairman of the Citizens Political Action Committee of Lawrence County, an affiliate of the National Citizens Political Action Committee, which was associated with the Congress of Industrial Organizations, better known as the CIO. The CIO was a labor organization suspected by conservatives of leftist leanings. The local

Political Sentiments at Westminster

A survey in an October 1936 *Holcad*, with the election rapidly approaching, showed how political sentiment lay at Westminster. Landon would have trounced Roosevelt, 334-105, if only Westminster votes counted, but there were 11 votes for socialist Norman Thomas and nine for communist Earl Browder. Among students, 242 called themselves liberals, compared to only 202 conservatives. There were 17 radicals. The faculty was more conservative but still split, with 29 conservatives and 20 liberals. The fact that the survey was taken at all suggests that weight was being placed on these ideological divisions.

There is no question that students felt the tensions at Westminster. A November 10, 1944, *Holcad* editorial criticized "ungrounded rumors" that were jeopardizing the College's "academic rating," including rumors that Galbreath had "handed in his resignation" and that "some faculty members indoctrinate communistic ideas into their students and demand contributions for political organizations," charges that "have been repudiated by students in their classes," the *Holcad* said. ◆

PACs were organized to solicit support for President Roosevelt and other candidates endorsed by the CIO in the upcoming election.

Marshall's dual associations with Westminster and the CIO alarmed members of the Board, some of whom were prominent Republicans supporting Dewey in the 1944 presidential elections. They evidently leaned on Galbreath, who, in a letter dated Nov. 11 (four days after Roosevelt was reelected to a fourth term), informed Marshall that "with the close of the current college year your contract with Westminster College will not be renewed."

Marshall never denied being a liberal and a Democrat, but he did deny being a socialist or a communist sympathizer. When F.E. Moore, an Elwood City industrialist, wrote to Marshall and Galbreath to protest a PAC pamphlet designed to "keep Roosevelt in power," Marshall replied, on Oct. 31, 1944, "I have not discovered any evidence that would support the charge that the PAC is communistic or unAmerican. If I should discover that it is tending in that direction, I assure you that I will at once withdraw from it."

But Marshall, unlike the two young members of his department, Wyllie and McNall, was a tenured member of the permanent teaching staff, hired in 1930, and could not be dismissed without charges being formally brought against him and a hearing before a faculty-administration committee at which he would be permitted to defend himself against the charges.

Marshall pressed for a hearing, but the Board instead withdrew its dismissal. Marshall then requested and was granted a leave of absence for the spring semester, ostensibly to finish a book he was writing. So he did not teach during the spring semester of 1945, but he was living and writing in New Wilmington and continued to attend faculty meetings and participate in College activities. He continued to be regarded by the leaders of the Board and administration as a troublemaker, the leader of a faction that opposed some key administration and Board policies, and a man who was unsympathetic to the religious principles of the College.

Suspicious that Marshall and other faculty members of his ilk posed a threat to the College and its mission, the Board set up a committee in March 1945 to examine charges against Marshall and other faculty members allied

with him. It was chaired by the Rev. James M. Ferguson, a future
Board president and the son of former president Robert Gracey
Ferguson. The committee conducted a number of interviews and
reported, at the May 26 Board meeting, its conclusion that "his
(Marshall's) conduct has not been such as clearly to justify the
termination of his employment under the present tenure policy
of the Board." But the report also concluded that Marshall's
"general attitudes have not been satisfactory ... toward the religious traditions of the college ... (he having summoned and
presided at political assemblies upon Sabbath afternoons to the
grief of United Presbyterian friends of the College)."

Leon S. Marshall,
history professor
(1930-46).

The report recommended that Marshall's employment and
tenure be continued but that he be stripped of his position as chairman of the
history department, a post not protected by tenure. The Board approved this
recommendation. I don't think there is any doubt that Board members wanted to get rid of Marshall but were afraid that the College could lose its accreditation if it breached its tenure policies.

Some insight into the thinking of the conservative faction of the Board
can be gleaned from a Feb. 27, 1945, letter from Thomas V. Mansell, a 1929
Westminster graduate and Board member since 1938, to James Ferguson,
soon to be named chairman of the investigating committee. In the letter,
Mansell, an attorney and New Wilmington resident, describes "conditions at
the College" as "the worst that they have been for a long time." The problem,
he says, is that a faculty clique led by Marshall "have tried for some time to
run the college and with success have become more bold." Members of this
clique "have openly said that the U.P. church is conservative, anti labor and
all that sort of stuff. They attend the local Methodist Church and talk against
our church. I feel that when they feel that way they should get out. It is their
idea though to reform the college to their way of thinking regardless of what
the U.P. church may want. I say in all sincerity that if that type of person is
to control the college that I do not want my children to go there."

Marshall objected to being stripped of his chairmanship without explanation and in July asked the AAUP to investigate his case. Then, in August
1945, he requested a one-year leave of absence without pay to become a visiting professor at University of Nebraska. His request was granted with the
understanding that the leave would not impair his tenure status. But the following summer, in July 1946, Marshall resigned and circulated a much-pub-
licized three-page letter in which he charged that he was being punished "for

acting on political views opposed by a majority of the Trustees" because of "my part in the election." He was leaving, he said, because "the principles of academic freedom have been violated at Westminster by those responsible for their maintenance." That ended the Marshall controversy but not the war against suspected faculty subversion.

Beyond Marshall, the investigating Board committee that had reported on May 26, 1945, found that others on the faculty were unsympathetic to the religious principles of the College and had gone so far as to join the local Methodist church, a point also made by Mansell in his letter cited above. This was an ideological collision that was at once political, religious and probably economic. The perception among the partisans was that Republicans, business executives and United Presbyterians shared one set of generally conservative values and that Democrats, organized labor and, well, Methodists, shared a different set of values. It may seem strange today to think of Methodists as left-wing radicals, but Galbreath received a copy of a letter from C.J. Herzog, father of a Westminster student, to Methodist Bishop James H. Straughn in Pittsburgh, complaining that the literature of the Methodist Federation for Social Service was "nothing more or less than CIO propaganda." Herzog warned that Christians "must follow the teachings of Jesus Christ and . . . not allow ourselves to be used by communists and other groups who are tearing down the very structure of our great country."

(Although the investigation and complaints appeared to focus on liberal religious views and practices and the word "communist" was rarely uttered in public, there is no question that the Board feared the faculty was being infiltrated by left-wing influences. Mansell's letter refers to Marshall's "pinkish" reputation, and at least one Board member is reported to have referred to the faculty members under investigation as "reds.")

When Galbreath was asked by the investigating committee to identify the "Big Six" (Marshall clique), he named Marshall; McNall; Edward Metcalf, chairman of the chemistry department (hired in 1940); Donald Matthews, chairman of the biology department (hired in 1936); Harold J. Brennan, art professor (hired in 1932); and Michael Radock '42, journalism instructor and director of the news bureau (hired in 1942). Radock chose to leave in 1945.

At its March 1946 meeting, the Board voted to dismiss Metcalf. Taken by surprise, both Galbreath and the College's new academic dean, John Reed Spicer, objected that such action would hurt faculty morale and jeopardize the College's standing with AAUP. The Board again shied away from taking on the AAUP and approved a contract for Metcalf, who then resigned.

Matthews, like Marshall a tenured member of the permanent faculty, requested and was given a leave of absence for the 1946-47 academic year and did not return to Westminster. Brennan left the College in 1948.

(It's interesting to note that at least two of the suspected subversives purged in the mid-40s later returned to the College in good favor. Wyllie, who went on to become chancellor of the southeast campus of University of Wisconsin, was invited back to Westminster in 1965 to receive an Alumni Achievement Award. Radock, who made a career of college and university public relations, was honored by the College with a doctor of literature degree in 1965 and was elected in 1972 to the College Board of Trustees, where he served for eight years.)

While the departure of the subversives may have brought some relief to the Board, it left a legacy of faculty anxiety about academic freedom and kicked off the second extended period of disruption in Westminster's history. Galbreath, caught in the middle of the growing conflict between the Board and segments of the faculty, had already resigned once in protest and had had to use all his influence to stop the Board from moving precipitously against Metcalf and Matthews. When a Board intervenes directly in personnel matters against the wishes of the president, it does not signal strong support for the president. There is little doubt that some on the Board felt they needed a fiercer warrior to battle potential left-wing infiltration and considered Galbreath too sympathetic to the faculty. Mansell, in his letter to Ferguson, observed, "Doctor knows what is right but just doesn't have the courage to carry out his convictions. He will not fight if there is any way out of it."

Galbreath announced his resignation on June 25, 1945, two months after facing down the Board over the Metcalf termination. He was 60. The resignation was to take effect a year later, giving the Board that long to find a successor to its liking. He retired to life as a gentleman farmer on his "Old Spring" farm near Pulaski in 1946 and then served from 1947 to 1956 as pastor of the First Presbyterian Church of New Castle. On Oct. 25, 1957, he was guest of honor for the dedication of Galbreath Hall, a new dormitory for women named in his honor.

Galbreath's administration fell between my graduation from Westminster in 1932 and my return to the faculty in 1946, so I was not on campus during most of his presidency but knew him later as a friend and neighbor and had the chance to read his correspondence. His preference for participatory governance probably was more a consequence of his personality – friendly, unassuming, considerate, reluctant to dominate – than the result of any philosophical or strategic decision.

Tenure Policy

Galled at having to withdraw its dismissals of both Marshall and Metcalf because of tenure policies adopted by the Board in 1936, perhaps in response to questions from the AAU about Westminster's tenure policy, the Board at its May 26, 1945, meeting moved to change that policy so that they would have more liberty to terminate veteran professors. They unanimously adopted changes that would make tenure contingent on three additional requirements:

"(1) an active exemplary participation in the religious programs and policies of the college;

(2) imposition upon one's self by each member of the instructional staff of such limitations of academic freedom as may be suggested by Article VIII [of the College bylaws and ordinances which defined the obligations of the faculty member to the religious principles of the institution];

(3) a loyalty to the College and to the President of the College, by each member of the faculty."

They also added as a reason for removal of tenured faculty "a marked indifference or disrespect or both toward the religious principles of Westminster College as they are stated in Article VIII." This tenure policy remained in effect until 1969.

The Cleland Year

If the Board felt it needed a tougher disciplinarian in the front office to keep the faculty in line, it found its man from within its own ranks. He was H. Lloyd Cleland, director of personnel for the Pittsburgh public schools, and, as a member of the executive committee of the Board and chairman of its educational policy committee, an active participant in the controversies over dismissing Marshall and the other five suspected faculty members. It would be the first time that Westminster's president was a layman. He would have a short and rocky ride.

Westminster's eighth president, born in Monmouth, Ill., April 14, 1890, had graduated from Westminster in 1913. After serving in the army in France from 1917 to 1919, he earned a master's degree from Columbia in 1923, and later received an honorary doctor of pedagogy degree from Westminster in 1942. He had taught school in New Castle, Uniontown, and Bellevue before entering the Pittsburgh school system in 1924.

Cleland was recommended by the search committee, of which he was a member, to the executive committee in February 1946, a meeting at which the faculty petitioned to send a representative to meet with the committee as it considered the choice of a new president. The committee turned down the request, according to its minutes, because, "It was thought to serve no good purpose to have a member of the faculty sit with the committee at this late date."

When the appointment of Cleland was ratified at the March 4, 1946, Board meeting, the move was widely interpreted by the faculty as a signal that the Board was determined to pursue a hard-line policy. If the move was intended to restore order to the campus by asserting the authority of the Board, it backfired. Significant portions of the faculty and student body had lost confidence in the Board, and many teachers, aided by a favorable job market, were voting with their feet. Of a faculty of 52, 26 left that spring or during the following 1946-47 academic year. The departures included the president, the dean and eight department chairmen. Westminster was on the verge of academic meltdown. (During this period, I had returned to the College as a part-time instructor, teaching radio and speech classes, in addition to being program director for WPIC radio station in Sharon, Pa. While I was not actively involved in the controversy, I was an interested observer.)

The embattled
presidency of
H. Lloyd Cleland
lasted just one year
(1946-47).

Cleland felt that he had a mandate from the Board to take charge and rule with a firm hand. His experience in public school administration contributed to an approach the faculty considered authoritarian and heavy-handed and that many students felt was condescending. Strains created by the flood of returning servicemen under the G.I. Bill may have complicated the situation by increasing the faculty workload and forcing the College to hire more teachers quickly, with inadequate review. By the spring of 1947, both the faculty and the student body were presenting petitions to the Board calling for Cleland's removal. Cleland regarded the petitions as insubordination and wanted the faculty spokesmen to be summarily fired, but the Board, in the face of the mass exodus that was occurring, had no choice but to hear their grievances.

Rather than retaliate against the petitioners, the Board appointed a committee to confer with Cleland and to inform faculty and students that their petitions were being given respectful consideration. The committee reported back to the regular meeting of the Board on June 9 that Cleland "did not see his way clear to resign." But given the growing opposition and eroding support from the Board, Cleland bowed to the inevitable and presented his resignation at a special Board meeting on June 20. The Board responded with a perfunctory "unanimous vote of confidence" for the champion it had just sacrificed. Cleland returned to the Pittsburgh public school system where he served until his retirement.

To take charge of this deteriorating situation until a suitable president could be found the board turned to John Orr, professor of Bible, who, for the third time, was serving as acting dean following the departure of Spicer in 1946. Born in Ulster, Ireland, in 1884, Orr had received his bachelor's degree from the College of Wooster, his master's and bachelor of divinity degrees from Princeton and his doctorate from the University of Pittsburgh. He had served

pastorates in Middleport, Ohio, and Howell, Mich., before joining the Westminster faculty in 1928 and becoming chairman of the Bible department in 1931.

John Orr served the College as chair of the Bible department, acting dean (three times), and acting president (1947-49).

Although Orr's stint as acting president was supposed to be a brief one, word of the faculty-Board conflict made it hard to attract a new president, and the search dragged on for almost two years before the big announcement could be made, on March 7, 1948, that Westminster had elected Will W. Orr (no relation) to be her ninth president. John Orr had presided over a two-year truce. The issues that had sparked the conflict between the Board and the faculty remained for Will Orr to resolve. A grateful Board, on June 6, 1948, passed a resolution expressing "appreciation for the loyal and invaluable service rendered the College by Dr. John Orr." They also voted to confer on him the honorary degree doctor of pedagogy. He continued to serve as chairman of the Bible department until his retirement in 1954. ❖

CHAPTER 13

Surviving Two Wars and a Depression

World War I SATC (Student Army Training Corps) Unit in front of Hotel McCreary, later College Hall.

L
ike most Americans, those living on Westminster's campus between 1902 and 1952 found their lives dominated by two world wars and a great depression. Probably more than the Civil War and certainly more than the Spanish-American War, World War I and especially World War II had a palpable impact on campus life.

The first declaration of war on April 6, 1917, triggered a massive mobilization of men into the armed forces (and the first national draft), as well as a host of support activities. By the time fall term opened that year, male enrollment was cut nearly in half as many men enlisted or left for industry where critical manpower shortages and high wartime production goals required a larger workforce.

More Westminster men left for the service during the summer of 1918, but their places were taken by a unit of the Student Army Training Corps (SATC), which brought in about 100 men at a time from all over the country for officers' training, using the old Hotel McCreary (College Hall) as a barracks. When the armistice was signed on Nov. 11, 1918, the unit was quickly disbanded and all the would-be doughboys were gone by Dec. 13.

The poignant transition from boys to men in a dangerous world was brought home on Alumni Day in 1921 and the ten-year reunion of the class of 1911. Back in the spring of 1909, the sophomores ('11), including Paul Delbert Graham, had inscribed a boulder and placed it on campus as an emblem of their class. The feisty freshmen ('12), including Charles Scott Woods, had overpowered the sophomore guards, stolen the boulder and buried it. The sophomores recovered the rock the next summer and maintained a watch over it the following year until, weary of the vigil, they buried the stone again themselves in June 1910. Graduation, then war, followed. Graham and Woods were both killed in the war, and in 1921 the rock over which they had fought as boys was exhumed again, fitted with bronze plaques honoring the two men, and solemnly restored to the campus where it remains just north of the west entrance to Old Main.

The end of the war and the influenza epidemic of 1918-19 caused a crisis of sorts at Westminster. Withdrawal of the SATC unit brought College enrollment down to 162, and the flu played havoc with campus activities in November and December 1918. With morale at a low ebb, Dean Charles Freeman called students together at a YMCA chapter meeting on campus and gave them an inspirational talk. The students responded with a "pep movement." At a spirited rally in February 1919, they adopted the slogan, "A New Gym by 1920, and 200 New Students Next Fall!" A student council was appointed to work with the administration to rescue the College. In March the Board appointed its own committee to work with the students and administration for a new gymnasium and increased enrollment. Enrollment bounced back to 305 in 1920 and 344 in 1921, then rose to 481 and 549, respectively, in 1926 and 1927. The new gym (subsequently renamed "Old 77") was dedicated on June 7, 1921 – the same Alumni Day the war memorial rock was dedicated.

The Depression

The Depression was not particularly traumatic on Westminster's campus. Enrollment grew as the alternative of getting a job became less feasible. The Sept. 14, 1934, *Holcad* trumpeted "Records Broken As 700 Enroll At Westminster" in a headline and noted in the accompanying story that 220 new freshmen had pushed enrollment to an all-time high. An adjacent story recounted progress since 1932 under Galbreath: a 26 percent growth in enrollment, higher admission standards "due to the increased number of students seeking admission," more dormitory rooms and more faculty with Ph.D. degrees. To accommodate the tighter budgets of families sending their sons and daughters to Westminster, tuition and fees were cut from $300 a year to $275 a year in 1931. (The annual cost of enrolling at Westminster had risen from $60 in 1907 to $150 in 1920, $250 in 1927 and $300 in 1929. After being cut to $275, it

Student Reflections on the Depression

One gets little sense from College publications during the 1930s that the Depression was a dominant issue on campus. Occasionally an economic anecdote broke the intellectual surface, as in "New Note in Panhandling" in the Jan. 10, 1933, *Holcad*: "On our way home for the Xmas holiday, we had to wait several minutes in the New Castle station, and as we were staring vacantly at various advertisements posted on the walls, we were approached by a novel type of panhandler. He wanted to work, to carry out bags or something. After the donation of a dime, however, he lost interest in the work and began to harangue us upon the injustice of his fate. It seems that he once was prosperous, but that his partner did him dirt. ..." That episode could have happened during any period, and the unidentified author seemed not to connect it to a national crisis. ◆

was raised again in 1944 to $280 and then to $350 in 1946.) Galbreath's administration introduced cooperative dormitories and expanded the student loan funds that made Westminster affordable to a growing number of students during hard times.

A front-page *Holcad* news story on Feb. 16, 1934, reported, "Westminster is negotiating for an appropriation through the Federal Emergency Relief Administration by which students of the college may receive federal aid for their education."

A January 1933 editorial certainly expresses an awareness of both the Depression and growing interest in foreign affairs: "We, for one, while we regret the loss of personal revenue brought on by the depression, can see a glimmering of hope… rising rampant from the wreckages. In days gone by, when every hand on the section gang had his Ford and every college student graduated from college with a millionaire's desires … very few of our youth turned toward the field of diplomacy as a life work."

Hard times were out there, and graduates took jobs as gas station attendants or bowling pin spotters – when they could find them – but college was a good place to concentrate on learning and fun and postpone confronting the grim realities of the outside world.

World War II

The Japanese attack on Pearl Harbor on Dec. 7, 1941, shocked the U.S. like no other event in its history. Such was the emotional impact of America's sudden entry into the war that "both President Robert F. Galbreath and Dean Maxwell R. Kelso caution Westminster men to avoid hasty enlistment," the *Holcad* reported in a page one story on Dec. 12, 1941. "Our government is calling men and arming them as rapidly as possible. To rush ahead of the orderly program now in operation will mean adding to the present confusion," Galbreath warned. Men should stick to their studies until called, he advised.

Predictably, male enrollment plummeted, from 294 in fall of 1941 to just 63 by the fall of 1943, while female enrollment rose from 370 to 451 between the fall terms of 1941 and 1944. The departures weren't just of male students. When Kelso entered military service in 1943, math professor Harold L. Black was named acting dean.

Westminster responded to the war with an accelerated academic program, including two six-week summer sessions that made it possible to graduate in less than three years. The College held its first mid-year commencement on Jan. 26, 1943, so that a large group of Westminster men could graduate before leaving for the service in February. By the time the war ended, over 900 Westminster students and alumni had served in the armed forces.

The *Holcad* converted its fourth page from sports to "Cadet Capers" to report on activities of the military units training on campus, and it regularly printed excerpts from letters from former students and recent graduates stationed all over the world. (See "In Their Own Words.")

Seeing students and good friends go off to war was emotionally wrenching for a college community, as the introduction to the 1944 *Argo* makes clear: "The flash from a photographer's camera broke the darkness, as Dean Kelso read the names of those who were to go. One by one they entered the station wagons, and 28 of Westminster's Army Enlisted Reserve corps left together for the first taste of military life. As the men drove toward New Castle railroad station, there lingered behind the strains of "Ring out the bells in Old Main tower again, ring out a song of Victory." Dedicated to Westminster's soldiers, that 1944 *Argo* noted, "For a time you must put aside your high hopes and ideals, give up everything you had long desired, and condition your minds and your bodies for the terrible task set for you to do, to fight and to kill in every sector of the World… Those of you who are fighting now, our debt to you can never be repaid."

Galbreath spent many hours corresponding with Westminster servicemen. In one of his letters, published in the Oct. 22, 1943, *Holcad*, he recounts, "Sometimes I have written foolishness into my letters to you. I hope no one will think I take lightly the job you are doing so well. You are all too near to my heart and the heart of Westminster for that ever to be true. When I think of Joe Demoise in New Guinea and Felix at Guadalcanal, Perry Black probably in Italy, Harvey Davis in China, Fulton Kissick in North Africa, Chuck Smiley in Hawaii… Bill Reufle in the South Pacific, Danny Mamula in the North Pacific – and all the rest of you both here and overseas – Well, believe me, I just ache with the tragedy of it all and glory in the splendid morale of all of you."

Westminster had her war heroes. One of them, Col. Robert McClurg '42, was awarded five Distinguished Flying Crosses, eight Air Medals and two Presidential Unit Citations as a carrier-based Navy fighter pilot and a member of the elite Black Sheep squadron of Col. Gregory "Pappy" Boyington. In the air, he downed seven confirmed Japanese Zeros and had three "probables," as well as destroying two Japanese bombers on the ground.

Robert L. Hartzell ex-'43, son of Presbyterian missionaries to China and Thailand, won a Silver Star for flying into occupied China to rescue flyers

In Their Own Words

Going off to war unleashed a surge of letter writing. Recent Westminster graduates and those who left college before graduation to go off to war left a strong record of their experiences and feelings in their own words. The following excerpts from their letters were published in the Westminster *Holcad*.

Forrest Rosenberger ex-'44: "I'm in Norfolk, Virginia; the place most dreaded by sailors. It is a city that seems to hate sailors. The trip here was long, the cars typical – coal dust, poor lights, and no sleepers. At first there was conversation about the future and what would come next; then came the games of chance with dice and cards; there was the usual talk of ignorants, the loud babbling of those who haven't enough on the ball to attract attention any other way, and the goodness of the quiet fellow that you like to sit and talk with. During the night I saw a town in the distance; it made me very homesick for New Wilmington and Westminster. I could see Old Main with its white lights and evergreens – and was quite sure it was a pleasant mistake."

Ed Fellabom '43: "As I stand watch out here in the dark, cold night, I keep myself occupied thinking of the fun we had, the crazy things we did, the dances, basketball games, fraternities, and chapel. All those things mean so much more to me now than they did then. Probably I took too much for granted in those days. I imagine that New Wilmington is awfully pretty these days, covered with snow. I'll sure miss the serenading this year." ◆

(For further reminiscences of World War II, see *When Titans Truly Were* by professor of history Eugene G. Sharkey.)

downed during the Jimmy Doolittle raid on Tokyo. Then he added a Distinguished Flying Cross for flying an overloaded, unarmed transport plane through Japanese Zeroes using a hand fuel pump, with two engines out, according to an Oct. 27, 1944, *Holcad* item. He also spent 16 months and flew 25 missions over enemy lines as part of Chennault's Flying Tigers before a back injury grounded him. The dashing six-foot-two Hartzell, whose photograph shows him to look a lot like Errol Flynn, was signed to a movie contract by MGM as soon as he left the service.

The four Evanoff brothers, three of them Westminster alumni, all enlisted in the Navy and captured public attention when two, Harry and Peter ('42), were killed in action. Harry's ship was hit by a torpedo and went down near the Gilbert Islands. Peter, captain of Westminster's 1941 football team, died when his plane was shot down over Formosa in 1944. Peter's death caused the Navy to reassign Fred '50 to a non-combat vessel in Leyte Gulf just two days before Japan surrendered. Michael '46 was not involved in combat.

The shock of losing a friend was always painful. A recuperating Hugh Rawls '49 reports such a shock in an Oct. 27, 1944, letter to the *Holcad*: "I was reminded of Westminster by none other than Jack Sarver, who walked into this ward on a visit to see one of his men. I was very surprised to see him, and we had quite a talk about old times. He told me that Bill McChesney has been reported missing over Europe, and it was quite a shock to me because Bill was one of my best pals at school."

McChesney's story had a happy ending, however, the *Holcad* was able to report on Nov. 11, 1944: "McChesney had been dive-bombing a German airfield in France on his 72nd sortie when his plane was badly damaged and he was forced to bail out. German soldiers found him, and took him to a prison on the Swiss-German border. ... After seven days he and 50 other Americans were put on a train headed for Germany.

"At midnight the train stopped to change engines, and it was there that McChesney, dressed in a French civilian coat that he had been given to keep warm in prison, was able to overcome his guard and escape through the crowd

A World War II ASTP (Army Student Training Program) Unit marching in snow the past Old Main Memorial.

in the station. McChesney was able to contact the French underground" and subsequently made his way back to American lines.

Back on campus, "Westminster's women are doing their share by trying to conserve defense material. Collections are being made of paper and boxes, tin foil, empty tooth paste containers, used camera film rollers, and anything else that has potential reclamation value," the *Holcad* reported on Feb. 27, 1942.

Once again Westminster became a site for military training. During 1943 and 1944, 1,500 naval cadets occupied Hillside, 100 at a time, for Navy air pilot training. At the same time, 300 cadets in the Army Student Training Program (ASTP) were quartered in Browne and Jeffers and the Sig Ep house and attended regular college classes. College Hall, the former hotel the College had been renting and using as a dormitory since 1938, was purchased for $18,000 in 1943, and the lower floor was turned into a recreation center for military personnel. One of the famed Victory cargo ships was named the S.S. Westminster Victory in 1945 in honor of the College's contributions. Students and faculty donated money to provide the ship with a library. Baccalaureate in June 1946 was a memorial service for the 43 Westminster men killed in the war.

When the ASTP unit was withdrawn in March 1944, three months before D-Day, and the Navy training program closed the following July, Westminster was suddenly a civilian institution again. The calm did not last long. September 1944 found the first trickle of discharged G.I.s coming back to college. College Hall was converted to a men's dormitory, even though only 88 men enrolled that

A World War II Victory cargo ship was named the S.S. Westminster Victory in honor of the College's contributions to the war effort.

term, compared to 451 women.

When atomic bombs fell on Japan in August 1945, bringing the war to a sudden end, the flood of returning servicemen began. During the war, most of Westminster's housing had been assigned to women or military transients and had to be reconverted for men. As the 1945-46 school year progressed, women were moved out of College Hall and fraternity houses and doubled up in women's dorms. Second semester registration showed 309 men enrolled and 484 women.

By the time Lloyd Cleland took up the duties of his brief presidency during the summer of 1946, the College faced a serious housing shortage for both the bulge of post-war students and the larger faculty it would take to instruct them. The fall term opened three weeks late that year as the College scrambled to prepare for a record enrollment of 1,316 – two-thirds of them men and 672 of them former servicemen attending college under the G.I. Bill.

Even so, some emergency housing units were not ready, and men had to camp out in the gymnasium. Two of the three College dining rooms were converted to cafeterias; students were divided between two daily chapel assemblies; and scarce classrooms were kept busy through the late afternoon and evening. The record number of new faculty added that fall included 26 full-time teachers and 13 part-time teachers. I was one of the new part-time teachers in that crowd. As some of the G.I.s who were attending more out of curiosity than a serious interest in getting an education dropped out, enrollment leveled off at 1,243 in 1948-49, but the long era of three-digit student bodies was over.

Plans for a men's dormitory were shelved in favor of an emergency program that included buying and leasing additional properties in town and putting up army surplus barracks for veterans and pre-fabricated houses for faculty families. Camp Westminster went up quickly that year but it met the immediate need. The longer-term solution to the growing Westminster would await the 1949 arrival of President Will W. Orr, Westminster's premier brick and mortar developer. ❖

CHAPTER 14

Life on Campus:
Sports and Recreation from 1902 - 1952

Although the world and its serious problems intruded in major ways during the first half of the twentieth century, the campus remained a world of its own in many ways, a society of the young, the gifted, the intellectually engaged and, increasingly, the recreationally inclined, especially those with a taste for intercollegiate sports.

Forging a Campus Culture

The decision to locate Westminster in New Wilmington meant that the huge majority of students, especially in the slow-transportation days of the nineteenth century, would have a resident experience – living and eating away from home, in the town at first and then, increasingly, on campus. As we have seen, the founding fathers first ignored the issues of student room and board and then, in 1885, built the Ladies' Hall (later renamed Hillside) as a residence for women. Men continued to find their own lodgings and make their own eating arrangements.

Things stayed that way until Westminster's leaders redefined "college" to include living and eating in dormitories. Events surrounding the construction of Browne Hall (1928), Jeffers Hall (1940), and Ferguson Hall (1941) are recounted in Chapter 9. Until 1928, however, Hillside was Westminster's only dorm. There were times (as in the fall of 1906, when summer remodeling fell behind schedule) that returning women had to find rooms in town for the first part of the year. Heavy enrollment in the fall of 1920 forced the College to lease the Cummings and Thompson houses. These two houses, along with another old house on lower Beechwood Road known as the Senior Lodge, provided accommodations for 30 women. When women returned in the fall of 1931, they found that sororities had been assigned to College houses around the campus and that Hillside was reserved for freshmen women. The old eating clubs (and sub-rosa fraternity hous-

"Importance of Being Ernest," was the first full-length play presented in the Little Theatre in Old Main (1930).

es) had provided rooms for some men since the 1850s and became acknowledged fraternity houses in 1920. They were never owned by the College. Browne Hall had been built for men but, in light of expanding enrollment and a need to provide supervised shelter for women, it was converted to a women's dorm over the summer of 1932.

As the Depression increased financial pressures on Westminster and her students, cooperative lodges were introduced in 1932. Students were expected to do most of the housekeeping and meal preparation, reducing their board and room costs. Each lodge, typically composed of 10-15 students, inhabited a house in town owned or rented by the College. The program expanded during the next five or six years until 85 women were living in seven "co-ops" and 30 men occupied two such lodges.

The College expanded dormitory facilities in 1938 by renting Wyatt Lodge (the old McCreary Hotel) on Neshannock Avenue at New Castle Street, renaming it College Hall, and using it to house men. The opening of Jeffers and Ferguson and the temporary exodus of men to participate in World War II provided adequate housing for a brief period until the dramatic "bulge" of returning G.I.s.

Social life on campus gravitated toward fraternities and sororities once the College finally gave up its long campaign to eliminate them. The story of sub-rosa fraternities is told in detail in Chapter 7, but the conflict spilled over into the twentieth century. During the 1907 commencement weekend, the College administration and faculty successfully pressured male students to sign a written agreement to disband the secret and forbidden societies that had functioned almost since the College was organized.

But the agreement unraveled the following fall, leading men formerly associated with Pi Rho Phi (subsequently Sigma Phi Epsilon) to charge that the men of Kappa Phi Lambda (later Sigma Nu) had violated the agreement. So in February 1908, the faculty suspended 12 men for participation in the outlawed organizations. Students protested and confronted the Board, at its March meeting, with signed petitions requesting that the 12 be reinstated. However, the Board voted to side with the faculty.

But by June 1917, the Board was meeting directly with student representatives and negotiating an agreement that would accept national fraternities and sororities on campus. Those negotiations were interrupted by events surrounding the war, but in June 1920 the Board voted to accept the Greek letter clubs on campus, and Pi Rho Phi and Kappa Phi Lambda dropped their respective facades as the Kelly and Van Orsdell eating clubs. Within a few

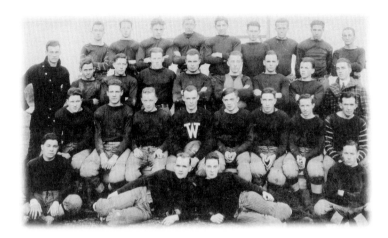

The outstanding 1913 westminster football team, coached by Frank Tinkham and captained by "Tuss" McLaughry, posted a 6-1-1 record.

years there were five fraternities and five sororities at Westminster.

While fraternities were accepted, the faculty continued to oppose all hazing and abolished the rowdy annual flag rush, an old tradition, substituting in 1927 a "Freshman Stunt Day" on the second Saturday of the fall semester. Opening the fall semester with Freshman Week was introduced in 1935.

Competing in Intercollegiate Athletics

During the 1902-1952 period, Westminster's sometimes rocky, sometimes controversial, sometimes illustrious pioneering exploits in intercollegiate athletics settled into a fairly predictable routine with an outstanding basketball program and occasional flashes of brilliance or ineptitude in other sports. The intercollegiate sports program was broadened in Westminster's second half century with the introduction of women's basketball in 1910, golf in 1934, cross country in 1915, swimming in 1926, and soccer in 1946. Organized cheerleading was born in 1911.

The dominant sports, probably in this order, continued to be basketball, football, baseball, tennis and track. The other sports were minor and, while championship teams were occasionally fielded, student and alumni support was marginal and the programs tended to rise or fall (and sometimes suspend participation), depending on the presence of an effective coach or gifted athlete.

Football

After its ungentlemanly beginnings in the 1890s, football instituted rules, gradually improved its image and won acceptance as an intercollegiate sport. But old habits die hard and brawls did not disappear quickly, as we can see from a *Holcad* account of a 1911 game with Pitt: "Wagner, of the Pitt team, resented having been tackled out of bounds by a Westminster man and got into an argument with Weigle, who had previously been ejected from the game. Stevenson, the right tackle of the Pitt team, slipping around behind Weigle, gave him a blow on the side of the head that put him down and out. Coach Gildersleeve, of Westminster, seeing this rushed at Stevenson and handled him rather roughly among other things throwing him bodily over his head. By this time some of the city police on the grounds noted more for their height than their brains – interfered and arrested Gildersleeve; and amid much hooting and jeering by the spectators conducted him off the field. However, he was not long left in arrest as several Westminster alumni quickly got together and secured his release."

Westminster's gridiron teams, after an impressive beginning (see Chapter 7) had settled into a near break-even performance. An industrious *Holcad* sports scribe in 1912 calculated that since the first game in 1892, Westminster had played 137 intercollegiate football games, winning 61, losing 59 and tying 17.

(Readers should keep in mind that prior to World War II, transportation was slow, athletic budgets were relatively small, and teams were not grouped into divisions based on school size. It was not unusual in those days for Westminster to play Pitt and Penn State. In the face of such unbalanced contests, the number of victories or losses was a less reliable guide than it would be today to how successful or disappointing a season was.)

Football flared briefly into distinction in 1913 and 1914 under coach Frank Tinkham and a group of standout players that included "Tuss" and Jim McLaughry, Dan and Butch McQuiston, Ted Buckley, Miz Dart, Mike Wherry and Hub Stewart. The team won six games in 1913, losing only once – to a strong Washington and Jefferson eleven that included a second-team All-American – and tying Carnegie Tech. The 1914 team won five and lost three, but the losses were to Pitt, Penn State and W&J, which that season boasted three All-Americans. Then five Westminster players graduated and another five were expelled for hazing as the College continued its efforts to stamp out fraternities. Tinkham also left. Consequently, the 1915 team won only two games while losing five, coached by DeOrmond "Tuss" McLaughry, who had just graduated the previous June. McLaughry went on to be a celebrated football coach at Dartmouth, Brown and Amherst. He was replaced by Hugh "Tech" Lambie '06 in 1916.

Although the 1916 squad posted only a 2-5-1 record, fans got a thrill when Captain Mike Wherry, a veteran from the 1913 and 1914 teams, kicked a field goal in the final minute for a 3-0 win over Grove City. The Grove City game provided another surge of excitement in 1924 when Phil Reep '25 scored after a long run to lead Westminster to a 7-0 victory. Despite a 1-4-1 team record, Jimmy McQuiston won football fame in 1926 by making a successful 43-yard drop-kick field goal against Waynesburg.

In spite of the U.S. entry into the World War on April 6, 1917, and the drop in enrolled men, Westminster played football in the fall of 1917, chalking up a 2-7 record. (Spring sports had been cancelled earlier that year because of the war.) A year later, the war was over, but the 1918 team had won three and lost two when the final two games of the season were cancelled because of the global flu epidemic, which killed more people (21 million) than the war (11 million). World War II, however, caused Westminster to cancel its football season for three years, from 1943 through 1945. Nevertheless, Westminster posted an impressive 5-1 record in 1944 when an unofficial touch football team dominated squads from neighboring colleges.

Varsity football returned after the war in 1946 with a 3-1-4 season. Perhaps the most significant event in the history of Westminster football went largely unnoticed that year. It was the arrival of a soccer coach who introduced that obscure varsity sport in a 1-6 season. The following year, however, his soccer team went 6-1, his cross country team was 8-1 and his swimming team was 11-1. His name was Harold Burry, and together with his student, protégé and successor, Joe Fusco, he would establish a football dynasty that would make Westminster an admired and feared NAIA Division II power during much of the 1952-2002 period. But that story will have to wait until Chapter 18.

Basketball

Westminster's basketball dynasty arrived sooner, built by four distinguished coaches: John Lawther, Grover Washabaugh, Charles G. "Buzz" Ridl and Ron Galbreath. Basketball greatness was hardly anticipated in 1909 when, after a 4-6 record, men's basketball was dropped as an intercollegiate sport for six years on the grounds that it interfered with scholastic work. Men played only intramural games during those years, even though Westminster women continued to play teams from other colleges. Men's varsity basketball returned in 1915-16 when a fledgling team went 0-4, then won two and lost two the next season, then improved the following year to 8-6. New coach and athletic director Dwight Dyer led the team to a 9-8 record in 1923-24. The following year, an upset victory over Princeton provided a bright spot in an otherwise undistinguished 7-10 season. That team was captained by Bill

Cleary, a four-sport letterman and one of Westminster's best all-around athletes. Then, two games into the 1925-26 basketball season (and after a 2-6 football season), Dyer resigned.

To complete the season, Westminster made a convenient and, as it turned out, auspicious decision: It turned the team over to John D. Lawther '19, a young psychology professor who had been a Westminster athlete (football, basketball) but whose only coaching experience had been guiding the local New Wilmington high school basketball team from 1922 to 1924. He had been hired that fall not to coach but to teach education and psychology. The season dragged on to a miserable 2-11 record. But Lawther had ideas, and his ideas impressed people at the College enough to give him another try during the 1926-27 season.

His key ideas were to rely on tall men and a new zone defense. Not all the returning veterans were impressed with the young coach's innovations, so he benched seven of eight returning lettermen and sent out the original "Towering Titans," so named by *Holcad* sports writer, Irving L. "Bud" Mansell. They included captain Hugh Gamble, Tudor Lewis, Chuck Ayers, Bill Crowell, and Sparky Connor. The five proved to be the best team Westminster had put on the floor in many years, winning 10 out of 15 and tying for second place in the conference.

In the next three seasons, Lawther's teams won three conference championships with records of 17-3, 15-2 and 14-2. Then came conflict with President Wallace over Lawther's dual positions as psychology professor and basketball coach and his departure from Westminster to coach at Freeport High School on Long Island.

In 1930-31, Lawrence "Pops" Harrison coached the team he inherited from Lawther to a 13-1 record and both conference and district championships, but he was unable to hold his job when Wallace was forced to resign.

The 1926-27 Westminster basketball team, the original Towering Titans.

Lawther was brought back in triumph, events discussed in more detail in Chapter 11. Lawther's 1931-32 team posted a 16-2 record and repeated as conference and district champs. The 1933-34 Titans won 22 and lost four to repeat as conference champions. Their top scorer, Wes Bennett from Akron, was also the top-scoring basketball player in the nation that year. The following year, the team won 19 and lost just three.

The tall (6-foot-4) ambidextrous Bennett was tough to guard because he could dribble and shoot equally well with either hand, and he shot one-handed in an era when most players needed to set up and shoot with both hands. He also had a patented no-look, over-the-head-shot that he made with some regularity while facing the opponents' basket. He remains Westminster's most distinguished athlete, twice an All-American (1934 and 1935) in an era when no distinction was made for the size of the college or university. In 1934, he was named College Player of the Year, putting him on the same list as later greats Bill Russell, Elgin Baylor, Oscar Robertson, Bill Bradley and Lew Alcindor.

Lawther was a shrewd psychologist and tough disciplinarian, Bennett recalled, who was famous for pioneering the use of a zone defense at a time when virtually everyone else played man-to-man. In practice, Lawther would flood the floor with eight to ten offensive players that his five defenders had to face from their assigned zones, according to Bennett. Lawther, about 15 years older and 20 pounds lighter than many of his players, liked to practice with the team. One day, the players in fun started to play a little rough and gave their coach a few hard knocks, Bennett recalls. Lawther took it and said nothing, but the next night, practice lasted four and a half hours. "We knew he was evening the score," Bennett reported.

Such was the fame of Lawther and Bennett that when New York sports promoter Ned Irish staged the first basketball games to be played in Madison Square Garden to see if this college sport could attract an urban crowd, he invited four teams – Notre Dame, New York University, St. John's College and Westminster – to play two games on Jan., 29, 1934. The games were played before 16,138 fans, the largest crowd ever to watch a basketball game. In the opener, Westminster beat St. John's, 37-33, when Bennett "unloosed the works," according to the *New York American*'s sports writer, and scored eight of his 21 points in a late rally. NYU beat Notre Dame 25-18 in the seond game. Bennett graduated after the 20-6 1935-36 season having scored 1,168 points, a school record that endured until 1956. Irish went on to organize the New York Knicks, and Madison Square Garden went on to do rather well as a bas-

That Dream Season

Among many outstanding Westminster basketball teams, the 1940-41 Titans, coached by Grover Washabaugh, clearly were historic. They capped a 20-1 season by being invited to the national college basketball championship play-offs, the Metropolitan Intercollegiate Tournament held at Madison Square Garden in New York City. There was no segregation yet between large university and small college teams, and only eight teams were invited to compete, so Westminster's championship prospects were roughly equivalent to reaching today's NCAA "Great Eight."

That starting team – comprising Stan Wasik, center, Lee Fox and Charles "Buzz" Ridl, forwards, Joe Spak and Dale "Smokey" Dunmire, guards, with Fred Miller, critical sixth man – built up momentum over a season that saw plenty of blowouts, several close games, a number of come-from-behind rallies and just one loss. Potential disaster struck on Feb. 15: Ridl, the team's leading scorer from the 1939-40 season, seriously injured his ankle and was ineffective for the rest of the season. But this was a team that refused to quit and rallied to win the rest of its games and end the regular season with a 20-1 record.

In their next-to-last regular season game played March 3, the Titans trailed Slippery Rock 51-43 with two minutes on the clock. Their MIT prospects were fading. Then, with 45 seconds to play, they snatched back the game, scoring "six machine-gun-like points," according to the *New Castle News* sports writer. It was, the reporter concluded, "a scintillating display of superb playing under pressure. Despite the fact that they trailed, the Titans moved around methodically, never once losing their heads. It was the combined effort of five fighting athletes that earned Westminster one of its proudest triumphs." It was enough to bring a coveted invitation to Madison Square Garden.

ketball venue. Bennett went on to play professional basketball for three years with Firestone and Goodyear teams, earning $400 a month for six months a year. Fifty years later, Madison Square Garden remembered that historic night with a halftime celebration that was broadcast on CBS.

After a year in which George W. Roark coached the team to a 14-7 season, Grover C. Washabaugh arrived in the fall of 1937 to coach football and basketball and direct physical education. Washabaugh's greatest success came with his basketball teams, which posted winning seasons routinely. The 1940-41 team, which went 20-1, was a standout. (See "That Dream Season.")

By 1942, with players preparing to leave for the armed services, the team went 12-7. Although football was suspended during World War II, basketball play continued, after a fashion. The 1943-44 team consisted of four freshmen and a sophomore with a medical discharge; they won 11 and lost 8. The following year, with performance still skewed by wartime manpower shortages, the Titans were the top scoring team in the nation, en route to a 14-5 record and another district championship. As servicemen returned and the G.I. bulge began in 1946-47, Westminster went 20-4 but placed just third in the district.

By the time Washabaugh turned over the basketball coaching duties to Ridl in 1956, he had amassed a career record of 289-118. Most impressive was his string of 77 consecutive home-court victories between 1945 and 1951 that caused the College, in 1951, to rechristen the gymnasium where those games were won as "Old 77."

Minor Sports

Although baseball became Westminster's first intercollegiate sport in the 1880s, its local popularity waned in the twentieth century. A 16-inning 5-4 victory over Grove City in 1910 was the occasion for a bonfire celebration in a season when the team went 11-7 and won the western Pennsylvania championship. But such excitement was rare. The *Holcad*'s sports scribe in 1912 counted 88 victories and 73 losses in the 161 intercollegiate baseball games Westminster had played since 1885. After the baseball team had another losing season without a regular coach in the spring of 1924, Westminster's athletic council decided to drop the sport, which did not return until 1950. (The athletic council itself was an endangered institution. Formed during the 1922-23 school year and composed of representatives from the trustees, alumni, faculty and students, the athletic council was an effort to incorporate the sports programs separately from the College. The council was responsible for hiring the graduate manager of athletics as well as the coaching staff and for handling all athletic receipts and disbursements. In 1934, this separate sports kingdom caught the frowning eye of the Association of American Universities (AAU) accreditation examiners, who faulted the College for letting alumni take such an active role in managing the athletic program. Consequently, it was disbanded.)

The swimming and cross country teams, reinstated as varsity sports in 1938-39 after long absences, won fleeting glory in the 1941-42 school year under second-year coach Joe Ferris. The swimmers won all nine meets and broke pool records everywhere they went. The cross country team won all eight meets and took first in the Tri-State meet. Track returned to the varsity ranks in 1941 after a seven-year lapse.

There were other occasional bright spots. Tennis stole the show in 1924, when the netters won eight matches and lost only one incomplete match to Pitt. The 1927 tennis team won a conference championship after a 5-1 season. When the Westminster track relay team won a national meet in 1902 and word was telephoned back to campus, students celebrated with a parade and bonfire. The 1931 track team won three dual meets and placed second in the conference meet. The cross country team won a conference championship in 1927-28, and the golf team won the mythical district title in 1947 with 12 wins and two losses.

Expanding Cultural Activities

While sporting events probably drew the biggest crowds, other cultural and recreational activities flourished. The invigorated drama program (details in Chapter 10) brought an ambitious array of productions. The 1929 season included two programs of one-act plays staged in the aptly-named Little Theatre and two full-length productions, *The Cat and the Canary* and *Minick*,

---

In the first round of the tournament, Westminster faced powerful Long Island University, 22-2, which played a national schedule that included LaSalle, Duquesne, Michigan State and DePaul. Westminster lost, 48-36. Long Island went on to win the national championship. Westminster came home, its dream season over.

But another dream season was distinctly possible. Ridl, Fox, Wasik and Spak were just juniors, Dunmire and Miller only sophomores. The entire team would be back for the 1941-42 season. But just as that season was getting under way in early December, bombs fell on Pearl Harbor, and the young athletes were distracted by the war they were about to enter. They sputtered to a 12-7 season. The dream was indeed over. By September 1943, Dunmire was dead, killed when the "flying fortress" he was piloting crashed during a training run. But Ridl '42 would return to Westminster in 1949 and go on to win many more games as a coach than he did as a player. (See Chapter 18.) ◆

that were presented in the larger Community House. But in the spring of 1930, *The Importance of Being Earnest* and *The Honeymoon*, both full-length plays, were staged in the Little Theatre, and, from that point on, the Little Theatre became the home of nearly all Westminster plays, regardless of cast size. That curtain came up on memorable productions of *Hamlet*, *Macbeth* and *Othello*, as well as classics of the stage by Ibsen, Shaw, O'Neill, Miller, Williams, Wilder, Hellman and other leading dramatists.

Literary and journalistic activities continued to grow. The student literary magazine *Scrawl* and an annual poetry-reading contest were introduced in the spring of 1939. The *Holcad*, started back in 1884, converted from a monthly literary and news magazine to a weekly newspaper in April 1914, under the leadership of editor Ralph Miller. In 1934, on its 50th anniversary, the *Holcad* adopted a five-column four-page tabloid format with a rotogravure supplement. A campus radio broadcasting studio opened in the fall of 1938. The programs aired three days a week at first, then six days a week over a New Castle station.

Musical activities also expanded. A College band was organized to perform at pep rallies and home games in 1930-31 and two years later donned new uniforms, a gift from William M. Duff, a trustee from Pittsburgh. During the summer of 1915 the College male quartet toured the country in their Studebaker Six, appearing in 70 concerts. The Senior Sing, an informal evening of singing on the south steps of Old Main on the evening before May Day, was inaugurated in the spring of 1920.

May Day grew during the College's second half-century into a significant spring festival. The first May pole dance, held on the Hillside lawn May 30, 1907, probably with the support of Mrs. Russell, started a May Day tradition that grew beyond the crowning of the May Queen and the winding of the May pole into an elaborate pageant that was presented on the athletic field. These May Day pageants, directed by Mary C. McConagha, became annual events that attracted many visitors. But in 1931, as the Depression deepened, the expensive pageants were scaled back to the older traditions of crowning the queen and winding the May pole, rites which survived until 1989.

Movies became a popular form of entertainment during the 1920s and 1930s, and Westminster students felt the allure of the silver screen. As early as 1918, a student motion picture bureau was organized to provide Saturday evening movies. Then, in 1935, the College started showing weekend motion pictures in the Little Theatre. After these limited showings, students welcomed the opening of New Wilmington's first regular motion picture theater in November 1941.

Amid major wars and a devastating depression, student interest in national political leadership deepened and led to the College's first mock convention in April 1936. Reflecting their natural political leanings, the students staged a Republican convention in the gymnasium and renominated Herbert Hoover. In April 1940, the second Mock Republican Convention adjourned, deadlocked, after 17 ballots, without selecting a nominee, although Ohio Senator Robert Taft was leading the field. No convention was held in 1944, but in 1948 students once again acted out the political process and nominated Wisconsin Governor Harold Stassen as the Republican candidate.

Religious life, of course, played a part. Evangelist Billy Sunday stirred the campus when he visited in the fall of 1910 and held revivals in New Wilmington and New Castle. The fall of 1947 saw the beginning of annual off-campus retreats for College religious groups.

Students also found time to pitch in for worthy causes. To observe the statewide "Good Roads Day" on May 26, 1914, male faculty and students formed road gangs while the women provided picnic lunches. In February 1947, Westminster students sponsored the first "Shares" campaign to raise funds for welfare and mission purposes.

A student government association was formed in 1917 to participate in making and enforcing rules of conduct, then formally organized as a student council with a constitution in May 1920. In March 1934, a senate replaced the campus committee as overseer of the rules and regulations for women students.

Student financial aid received a significant boost just months before the stock market crash. J.S. Mack, McKeesport philanthropist and Westminster trustee, funded the McElwee Ross Student Loan Fund during the 1928-29 school year, named in honor of his minister and fellow Board member.

Bit by bit, the color and tradition that students would associate with Westminster were introduced. The first College-sponsored dance was held in the gym on Homecoming evening in 1927. Homecoming grew into an Autumn Weekend festival on Oct. 17-19, 1947, when the student and alumni councils combined Homecoming activities with a Dance of the Year and special Sunday services. The carillon chimes were added to Old Main tower in the spring of 1935, another gift from Pittsburgh trustee William M. Duff. Students got an on-campus hangout in March 1948 when the "TUB" (Titan Union Building) was opened. That low-cost (Army surplus) precursor to the Student Union Building now houses the physical plant department. ❖

THE WESTMINSTER STORY

SECTION THREE

1952 — 2002

CHAPTER 15

Iron Orr

There was a strong sense in 1949, as Westminster approached the dawn of its second century, that it had turned a page and was anticipating its future. The selection of Will W. Orr as the College's ninth president ended a difficult two-year search for the right man to lead the troubled College. Behind were the painful leadership conflicts between a majority of the Board and the administration that had prompted Galbreath to resign and had forced the Board to rescind its abortive experiment with the more authoritarian Cleland presidency. Mistrust between the Board majority and factions of the faculty remained from the awkward removal of Marshall, Wyllie, McNall, Metcalf and Matthews, events recounted in Chapter 12. What lay ahead nobody knew, but there was a strong feeling on all sides that the future arrived with Orr.

With relief and enthusiasm the College community embraced that future, most conspicuously when Orr, his wife and three children were met at the Ohio-Pennsylvania border on their arrival and escorted by motorcade to a welcome in New Wilmington. WOW (Will Orr Welcome) Day had been proclaimed for April 27.

Will W. Orr, president from 1949-1967.

The new president had been born May 4, 1904, in Charlotte, N.C., and received his bachelor's degree in 1926 from Associate Reformed Presbyterian Erskine College in Due West, S.C. After a year as a high school science teacher (Statesville, N.C.) and principal (Sardis-Carmel school in Charlotte), he enrolled at Pittsburgh-Xenia Seminary, graduating in 1931. After eight years as pastor of the First United Presbyterian Church of Beaver Falls, Pa., he moved to Des Moines, Iowa, in 1939 to become pastor of the Westminster United Presbyterian Church. Church membership increased from 600 to 2,300 during Orr's ten years there, and his "youth club" program won national recognition. He had received an honorary doctor of divinity degree from Sterling College in 1939, and was to receive a doctor of literature degree from Carroll College in June 1949. He was elected to the Westminster presidency by the Board at its March 7, 1949, meeting.

Orr's presidency would last for 18 years and leave an indelible mark on the institution. He would revive its strong religious culture. He would be spectacularly successful in raising funds for the College and building much of the physical College we know today. And he would, to a considerable degree, end the factional bickering by providing strong, decisive leadership that would unite the College community, although not without occasional clashes of principle and personality.

Essentially Orr resolved conflicts at the College not by compromise or negotiation or building a collegial community, but by winning the war to reassert central authority and conservative principles. In Orr, the Board had indeed found its man. He consolidated power in a very personal way and delegated responsibility reluctantly. He was a staunch United Presbyterian, a spellbinding pulpit evangelist much in demand as a speaker at churches, graduation exercises, and spiritual retreats. Largely by force of personality, he faced down what conservatives regarded as the threat of spreading secularism and liberalism and established a strong moral and religious culture at the College.

He had the iron fist the Board wanted but also the velvet glove that Cleland had lacked. He would charm enemies when he could, crush them when he could not, but he would brook no opposition from a fractious faculty, although even Orr could not turn back the clock and remove the shadow of the AAUP and its censuring powers. He was also politically conservative. On the wall of his outer office hung an autographed portrait of J. Edgar Hoover, a leader Orr admired.

The Orr revolution was not entirely bloodless. How it was accomplished is the subject of this chapter. (I was a high-ranking member of the Orr administration for 16 of its 18 years and intimately involved with Orr in alumni and fund-raising activities. I counted myself among his supporters, but I also saw his faults. People tended to see him with either a halo or horns. My experience convinced me that neither quite fit.)

The honeymoon feeling of WOW Day gradually dissipated over the next few years as Orr was preoccupied with the centennial fund-raising campaign of 1950-52 and with building alliances with wealthy and influential individuals outside the immediate College family. Faculty and students began to grumble that their busy new president had little time or respect for their concerns. Tangible evidence of student irreverence surfaced as the centennial pageant – with a script written by me and music by Bible professor and musical theater buff Joe Hopkins – went into final rehearsals with its large student cast in May 1952. It took its title, "Hail, Hail to Thee," from the College alma mater. Scenes from the production were parodied by students in a chapel program as "Hail, Hail to Me by Will W. Orr." When the pageant was presented on May 31, the ushers opened packages of printed programs and discovered that the page dedicating the pageant to Orr and containing his picture had been cut out of all the programs. Orr was so upset by the slight that he left without seeing the performance. We never discovered who had done the cutting but suspected it was the work of disenchanted students.

Grumbling among the faculty also was growing. The most serious complaint was that Orr was polarizing the faculty, seeking out and rewarding a coterie of teachers whom he considered loyalists and ostracizing another group he regarded as critics. He was suspected of using promotions, raises and committee assignments to create allies who would stand by him out of personal loyalty. His administrative style also was controversial. He had a way of making important decisions himself, then convening a committee to work out the incidental details. Some welcomed this opportunity to participate, but others considered it a charade and waste of time. On his part, Orr was inclined to believe that faculty members who criticized his policies, programs or leadership style were disloyal. A few teachers were conspicuously loyal and a few voiced their criticisms boldly, but most became cautiously discreet out of concern that any hint of criticism might bring retaliation.

Problems with the faculty erupted during the 1953 commencement weekend when a rift opened between Orr and the man he had chosen to lead the faculty, academic dean William Vander Lugt. Vander Lugt had followed Orr from Iowa (where he was chairman of the philosophy department at Central College in Pella) to Westminster in the summer of 1950. But in the months prior to June 1953, reports began to circulate that the dean and the president were at odds. The executive committee of the Board went on record in an open letter to trustees, faculty, students, alumni chapter chairmen and "patrons," dated July 11, reporting "a certain dissatisfaction on the part of the Dean, and the growing tension between him and the College President." Orr and the executive committee framed the conflict as a "loyalty" issue.

William Vander Lugt, academic dean from 1950-53.

Vander Lugt blamed Orr for overruling the senior students' request to have Vander Lugt as their baccalaureate speaker, ostensibly on the grounds that he was not an ordained minister. Orr, who walked into Vander Lugt's office while he was meeting with *Holcad* editor Bob Pellet, blamed the dean for instigating two editorials that subsequently appeared, criticizing the administration for inconsitent enforcement of the drinking prohibition and for its handling of the baccalaureate incident. But these were more symptoms than causes of the rivalry that had developed between the two strong-willed men.

At Orr's request, a group of trustees met with the two men following commencement exercises on the evening of June 8. A year later, on May 20, 1954, Clyde A. Armstrong recalled that meeting in his comments to two AAUP representatives investigating reports of dissension at the College. "He [Vander Lugt] shook his finger at Dr. Orr in the meeting before us. He first accused Dr. Orr of not having been a good friend of his. ... He then said that Dr. Orr had lost the confidence of the students, that the students cringed in chapel when he spoke. He said that Dr. Orr talked too much about the trips that he was making on behalf of the college, that the students were sick of it; they did not want to hear any more of it; that he himself cringed in chapel when Dr. Orr got up to speak."

But by the end of that meeting, according to the executive committee report, "the Dean voluntarily pledged to the President his loyalty and support, and in certain particulars offered apologies." Orr pressed his advantage the next day, handing Vander Lugt the following letter:

> "You have admitted before a committee of the Board disloyalty to and failure to cooperate with the Administration and the Executive Committee of the College. This offense is over a long period of time, and is looked upon as a most grave matter by the Board.
>
> "You have solemnly pledged and promised that, if you are continued in the employment of the College, you will give me and the Executive committee your one-hundred per cent loyalty and cooperation.
>
> "This pledge may be more than you are capable of delivering. You promised this when you came to the College. There is a great deal that you must undo if you keep your promise. Whether or not you remain at the College will depend on the degree and the extent of your willingness to undo many of these things."

Orr asked the dean to sign or initial the letter as an acknowledgment that it represented the previous night's agreement. Whatever reconciliation had been accomplished in that meeting fell apart when the dean read the letter and fired off a brief written resignation: "I will not sign such a pledge. You have my resignation effective today (June 9) or July 1, whichever you prefer." Orr's letter subsequently found its way into the hands of students and was circulated widely by them. About 100 students who already had gone home for

Mack Manse,
the president's home,
was built in 1951,
one of the many
buildings to spring
up during the
presidency of
Will W. Orr.

the summer, roughly 10-15 percent of the student body, returned to campus and drafted a letter, which was read to the president over the phone, asking him to reinstate Vander Lugt.

Stunned faculty members moved quickly to try to salvage their dean and make peace between the two leaders. They persuaded Vander Lugt to withdraw his resignation, but Orr replied that the resignation already had been accepted and could not be withdrawn. On June 25 the executive committee unanimously backed the president's decision that the dean's resignation was irreversible and installed John Forry, an English professor, as acting dean. In a letter written on June 29, 1953, Delber McKee, then a young, non-aligned history teacher, expressed a prevailing mood of dismay: "The usefulness of the President has been seriously curtailed whether he is in the right or wrong." He speculated about Orr's successor.

Vander Lugt was gone but not silent. Eight times he wrote directly to the AAUP, urging an investigation. "Academic freedom and democratic practices will not be realities on Westminster's campus so long as Dr. Orr and the Executive Committee of the Board control the College," he charged in letter dated July 10, 1953. Once the investigation occurred and the report was filed, Vander Lugt wrote again on February 14, 1955, to praise the report and predict that it would be used to "protect the college from the blind and arrogant spirit of Dr. Orr and the Executive Comm."

One of the faculty members who had tried most aggressively to reconcile the president and the dean was J. Wiley Prugh, an idealistic young minister who had joined the Bible department only the previous January. Prugh became concerned about the religious atmosphere on campus. When he met twice with Orr in late April 1953, he shared his misgivings and tried to offer constructive suggestions, according to an account Prugh wrote the following July. Orr heard him out, perhaps led him on, and later remarked that it was quite presumptuous of a young instructor who had just arrived to think he knew more about how to run a college than a president who had been there four years. Prugh was a critic.

Prugh also discussed his concerns with Vander Lugt. At one point just before his resignation, when Vander Lugt was being officially questioned by Orr and the group of trustees on June 8, the dean said, "If you want to know where the real problem is at the College, ask Wiley Prugh." Now that Vander Lugt was gone, Orr and the executive committee did just that, at a special meeting of the executive committee in Pittsburgh on June 30. Prugh was grilled for an hour and a half by attorneys on the committee about his role in rallying faculty and student support for Vander Lugt. Prugh insisted that he was a peacemaker, not a partisan, but he refused to name other faculty members who shared his concerns. When pressed for details he could not clearly remember, he admitted to being "confused." He insisted that he wanted only to improve relations between the faculty and students and their president and agreed that if "it would be in the best interests of the college for him to surrender his contract for the year 1953-54, he would do so." The committee quickly and unanimously agreed that his departure was just what the College needed, characterizing Prugh as a "badly confused young man." Whatever real critics Orr had on the faculty got the message: The Board was solidly behind its man.

Prugh was highly regarded in United Presbyterian circles, where news of his dismissal caused the Presbytery of First Ohio to request each of Westminster's three controlling synods to conduct an investigation, but no action was taken. On campus, Donald McKee, a young political science instructor, resigned in protest on Aug. 14 and sent a copy of his resignation letter to the *Pittsburgh Post-Gazette,* which quoted from it in an Aug. 20 news item. McKee said he had been told by the Board president that "what the college administration does is no concern whatsoever of the faculty."

The faculty received another jolt a year later, when Orr removed Mary Purdy as chairman of the English department and replaced her with George Bleasby. Purdy, who had been a professor and department chairman since 1936, was considered by Orr to be one of his principal opponents. Like Marshall in 1945 (see Chapter 12), tenure protected her teaching position but not her chairmanship. Unlike Marshall, she was 63 years old and had little choice but to continue teaching for two more years until she could retire in 1956. She had been a popular teacher, and as word of her demotion spread, a host of current and former students rallied to her support. Some students who had gone home for the summer returned to campus to protest.

The Vander Lugt-Prugh affair and several other faculty terminations led to complaints being filed with the AAUP, which on May 20, 1954, sent two representatives, professors George P. Shannon and Warren C. Middleton, to Pittsburgh for informal, exploratory conversations with Orr and one or two Board officers. What they encountered was Orr, the full executive committee, court stenographers to record the session and pro-administration faculty members waiting in the halls to be called as witnesses. Shannon and Middleton expressed concern that faculty-administration tensions might undermine academic goals but found no basis for bringing charges against the College. In fact, a comment by Shannon – that the safest course when dropping an untenured faculty member was to "state no reason" – provided Orr with a tactic he would use for the rest of his administration. Whenever pressed to defend a decision to not rehire a faculty member, he would say that it was AAUP policy to "state no reason."

The March 1955 dismissal of Thomas F. Cummings, a young chemistry professor hired in 1952, caused further reverberations among the faculty, students, churches and alumni. Cummings had good academic credentials: an undergraduate degree from Massachusetts Institute of Technology and a nearly completed Ph.D. from Case Western Reserve University. And he was a United Presbyterian deacon and elder. He also had a strong Westminster pedigree. His great-grandfather was J.B. Cummings, who joined the Westminster faculty in 1856. Both his grandfather, Thomas F. Cummings '84, and father, James B. Cummings '19, had long, distinguished careers as ministers, missionaries, and educators. His wife, Mary Eliza Stewart Cummings '48, was the daughter of Harris Stewart '04, another distinguished minister, missionary, and educator, and she was the niece of Elizabeth Stewart '03, who taught modern languages at the College for 28 years (1921-49).

Another aunt (and retired missionary), Mabel Stewart '11, protested to the Board president, in a letter later circulated among alumni, that Cummings was dropped as a "reprisal for his sympathy with Dr. Vander Lugt, Dr. [J. Oliver] Collins, Wiley Prugh, and Dr. Purdy, and his courageous standing up for what he and many others knew to be right." (Collins was a chemistry professor, hired in 1948 and dropped in 1953.)

The dismissal of Marilyn Strub as student editor of the *Holcad* in the fall of 1954 raised another controversy that spilled over into the public press when allegations of censorship were raised. Under Strub's predecessor, the *Holcad* had criticized the administration, and Orr was known to resent barbs aimed at him by editors of the student newspaper. Bleasby appointed a new member of his English faculty, Charles Cook, as *Holcad* adviser and directed him to work closely with the editor to improve the quality of the content. Strub took this to mean control the content and refused to work with Cook, so Bleasby removed her as editor. A fact-finding committee appointed by the student council found no evidence of censorship, and a student publications committee was established to provide a hearing before future editors could be dismissed. Cook remained faculty adviser to the student newspaper for many years, and *Holcad* editors continued to criticize Orr and his administration.

The cumulative weight of the Vander Lugt, Prugh, Purdy, Cummings and Strub controversies between 1953 and 1955, many of which had received attention in Pittsburgh, New Castle and Sharon newspapers, had raised concern among alumni. A number of alumni had written and circulated letters criticizing the administration and Board and calling for an investigation. The letter writing campaign itself was fanning the flames and encouraging the impression that something was seriously amiss at Westminster, especially when such letters were cited in the public press. Unlike faculty, alumni could not be dismissed. Moreover, alumni support was critical to Orr's strategy for building the College.

The mounting pressure for an investigation and the stream of unfavorable publicity forced the alumni leadership to take action. Harvey Moore '26, president of the Alumni Association, and I convened a group of alumni leaders – essentially the officers and directors of the Alumni Association and the presidents of the local alumni clubs – on April 23, 1955. The group decided to appoint a committee to investigate the charges and report back to the larger group prior to the June 4 annual meeting of the Alumni Association, just six weeks away. The committee consisted of Henry Herchenroether '42, chairman; Moore; Jack Hudson '48; John Kerensky '49; and Perry Reeher '36.

Among the widely circulated letters that the committee was asked to investigate was one from Margaret Duff '19, who had been dropped from the Westminster faculty in 1954 after six years in the English department. She complained about "the policy of secrecy and suppression of information" that was causing the "loss of students and of promising young faculty members who seek employment elsewhere." In a later letter to "alumni and friends of

Westminster," Duff enclosed, with permission, a copy of Stewart's letter, cited above.

Another letter came from Robert Carey '50, director of the news bureau and journalism instructor at Westminster from 1952 to 1954. A copy of that letter fell into the hands of a *Pittsburgh Post-Gazette* reporter (who insisted he had not received it from Carey) and resulted in a story in the April 13, 1955, edition. Despite the headline, "Westminster President Under Fire by Alumnus," most of Carey's criticisms were directed at the Board – charging that it was unwieldy in size and self-perpetuating, that it contained no teachers, and that the faculty had access to the Board only through the College president.

In addition to these public, partisan letters, the committee also had a file of personal letters from alumni I had received as alumni secretary. Because the committee was charged with conducting an unbiased investigation in a short period of time, I thought they should have the benefit of all available evidence. I stipulated and was assured that the letters and the identity of the letter writers would remain confidential.

The committee met on Saturday, May 7, at Herchenroether's office in Pittsburgh and, by registered mail, invited a substantial group of letter writers, faculty, students and members of the administration, including Orr himself, to appear and give evidence that would support or refute the charges, which the committee consolidated into four:

- ◆ "The Administration and Board of Trustees has a policy of secrecy and suppression of information concerning college affairs";
- ◆ "There is a lack of academic freedom and fair treatment of students and Faculty unless they are willing to agree with the Administration";
- ◆ "Faculty members have been dismissed from the Faculty in reprisal for sympathy with Dr. Vander Lugt, Mr. Prugh, and Dr. Purdy," and
- ◆ "The Board is inefficient and unwieldy because of its size… and it is self perpetuating."

Strange Enemies: Two Mislabeled Letters

Nine letter writers were identified by name in the report of the alumni investigating committee, and the "charges" in their letters were specifically labeled as false and hostile to the College. I was surprised to discover that I was personally responsible for supplying two of those letters. The first letter writer cited by the committee was Lucy Dimon Smith '44, a young woman who had written only to me and whose letter had been given to the committee in confidence. The letter simply expressed concern over stories she had heard about troubles at the College and asked if they were true. The second letter writer, Mary L. Vartanian ex '44, was equally innocent. Their letters were treated just the same as the widely circulated letters by Mabel Stewart, Margaret Duff and Elizabeth Curry Morgan '40.

Henry Herchenroether, the investigators' chairman, later told me that Armstrong, the vice president of the Board, had contacted him and tried to impress on him the importance of putting an end to the criticisms that were proving so damaging to the College.

Years later when I had a chance to read a transcript of the testimony heard by the investigating committee, I saw that none of the critics had chosen to appear and put their testimony on the record; only supporters of Orr had testified. The four faculty members who did appear were Orr loyalists whose support he had used on other occasions. Because four of the five investigators were lawyers, they may have justified their decision as based on the evidence that was presented by witnesses. ◆

When the committee met on campus the following Wednesday, May 11, to hear testimony, only members of the administration and four reliably supportive faculty members – Bleasby, Forry, Robert F. Galbreath Jr. and Samuel H. Sloan – showed up. Orr generally did not record his private thoughts about the controversy swirling around him. However, he did speak with candor before the alumni investigators, and a written transcript was kept of that meeting, so we do have, in his own words, a record of what he thought he had to contend with:

"In the junior and senior class you will find people have been worked on. This is a battle of the minds. It is unfortunate. I don't wage it. I don't talk with students. I do not incite students to evil thoughts and animosities. I am too busy. If I had nothing to do I couldn't stoop to that level. Therefore, I make no effort to win the popularity of the students. I attempt to do my job as best I can. There are a group of people at Westminster who make it their business to incite. One of them [history professor Martin Ridge] was the main speaker this morning at Honors [Convocation]."

He also ran down a list of the professors he had terminated and his reasons for doing so: "Lathrop – a total misfit in this kind of college. Ralston – drinking. Carrier – 98 percent A's and B's. John Reed – as fine a Christian man and as poor a teacher. Schuster – department head positively refused to recommend her. Dr. Stag – a total misfit in every sense of the word. The kindest thing I can think about the lady was that she was a mental case. Hetzler – staff reduction (four men in the physical education department to three men.) Faddis – art – should never have been given a contract at Westminster. Harvey Mercer – Bob Galbreath positively refused to recommend him for another contract. Elizabeth Duff – poor teaching. Ingleright – 89 percent A's and B's. I hired Ingleright."

Word that the administration was being investigated by the alumni stimulated support for both Orr and his critics. Some of the Orr critics among the alumni proposed their own slate of candidates for the two alumni representatives to be elected to the Board of Trustees, setting up a contested election. When the day of the Alumni Association meeting arrived, the luncheon was a sellout; alumni who couldn't get tickets for the luncheon waited in the halls to attend the post-luncheon meeting.

The investigating committee didn't present its findings to the leadership group that had appointed them until 11 a.m. on June 4, just an hour before the luncheon. I had no advance knowledge of the report's contents and had to miss the 11 a.m. meeting, where it was first presented, to attend to luncheon details, so I heard the ten-page, single-spaced report of the investigating committee for the first time when it was read at the business meeting. The committee report completely vindicated the Orr administration and not only dismissed the charges in the letters as false but identified the letter writers as enemies of the College. The leaders of the alumni, like members of the Board, had closed ranks to present a united front in defense of their beleaguered president. (The Board had earlier given Orr a unanimous vote of confidence at its March meeting.)

The report concluded, "…we find that the charges as contained in the various news articles and circular letters written by or attributed to alumni or former faculty members are not substantiated by the facts as found by us and in many cases seem to be statements of intentional mistruths which could have been meant only to injure the College or individuals connected with the College. The fact that the letter writers failed to appear and produce any facts to substantiate their charges supports this conclusion."

In any case, the alumni investigation report had the effect of immediately terminating any open criticism of the administration and Board and brought to an end a power struggle that had been going on for about 10 years. The authority of the president, solidly backed by the Board, was accepted as supreme. The AAUP report, delivered April 18, 1955, was hopeful. Noting that "Westminster College history has been marked by internal dissension for at least fifteen years," the investigators concluded, "…present indications are hopeful. The administration clearly is united. The dissident group in the faculty appears to be bitter and determined, but only a small minority. There is no superficial evidence of student unrest." The accepted reign of an effective, paternalistic president brought stability the College sorely needed after its near meltdown in 1947, and the stability Orr brought no doubt contributed to the College's strong growth, the subject of the next chapter.

Curiously, when the cease-fire ended that had marked the two-year acting presidency of John Orr and a board-administration alliance again squared off with the faculty, the issue no longer was cleansing the College of suspected leftists. Indeed, political views, religious practice and personal morality appeared to play no role in the Vander Lugt, Prugh, Purdy and Cummings cases. Internal politics replaced national politics. The Cold War continued, but the McCarthy era ended early in the Orr administration. Orr never played the "Red scare" card.

Diversity suffered, but less than one might expect. In fact, Orr was bent on building Westminster into an academic institution of the first order and directed his department chairmen to hire the best teachers and scholars they could find. In the booming post-war economy when enrollment at Westminster and elsewhere grew rapidly, qualified teachers with Ph.D.s were scarce. In the scramble to land them, Westminster continued to get her share of free spirits, political liberals and agnostics. Many did not stay long, but in the seller's market of the 1950s and early 1960s, college teachers could teach and speak out with the confidence that another good job would be waiting for them if the one at Westminster did not last. Students during the Orr administration, including my two older children, found academic freedom to be alive and not seriously impaired.

Consumption of alcoholic beverages became a frequent flash point. Orr vigorously enforced the uncompromising position that had been spelled out in the College catalog only since 1949. (Earlier references were brief and general.) It banned the use or possession of "intoxicants in any form" by students "whether they are on campus or away from it … in any place, public or private, while they are enrolled at Westminster College." Violations meant expulsion or suspension, which happened in the 1960s to a couple who had wine with dinner in Youngstown and then admitted as much when questioned by College authorities. They were suspended for the remainder of the term – an unpopular punishment.

Orr was not inclined to bend to the more liberal view American society was taking toward drinking but went along with a softer policy the Board introduced in the 1963-64 catalog. The new policy banned the use or possession of all intoxicants but only on College property or while students were under the jurisdiction of the College. It also broadened the range of punishments to include "disciplinary action, suspension, or dismissal." Students home for the summer or Christmas vacation were returned to the jurisdiction of their parents.

The drinking policy for faculty and staff was not spelled out in writing, but when candidates for positions interviewed, Orr customarily explained the College's drinking policy and asked, "Would this be a problem for you?" The usual response – "No, sir. It would not." – was interpreted by Orr as a commitment to total abstinence. Faculty members known to drink significantly increased the chances that they would be denied tenure or not have their contracts renewed, but, in keeping with the College's "state no reason" policy, drinking problems were rarely cited in dismissal cases.

Drinking was generally acknowledged to have played a role in the decision to dismiss Dan Wilson, an assistant professor in the English department in the spring of 1963. Wilson, who had taught six years and was up for tenure, admitted to Orr that he drank beer at home and sometimes served it to student guests. When Orr notified Wilson on March 6 that his employment would terminate at the end of the current academic year, Wilson pressed for a terminal one-year contract. One section of Westminster's tenure policy, which had been changed to conform to AAUP standards, gave him that right, while another section stipulated that a one-year final contract was required when a full professor or associate professor was denied tenure but not an assistant professor or instructor.

When the College balked at giving Wilson a terminal one-year contract, he appealed to the AAUP, which investigated and found in Wilson's favor. When the College still refused to offer a one-year contract, the AAUP criticized the College's action in a report published in the summer 1965 *AAUP Bulletin.* Of all Orr's skirmishes with AAUP, this one probably came closest to bringing official censure on Westminster.

Objective evaluations of the Orr administration are hard to come by, but we have one from the committee that gave Westminster its regular ten-year evaluation on behalf of the Middle States Association of Colleges. In their 1961 report, they were duly impressed by the president's dedication. "The president has more than given his life to the College. It is his life. Only a man of his boundless energy and of his complete dedication could have achieved what he has in the past decade and survived."

Yet the visitors found that Orr's paternalism had taken its toll on faculty morale. During Orr's first 11 years, faculty meetings "show a steady decrease in the frequency and the average duration," they noted, as the meetings became "largely informational," an occasion for announcements of decisions already made by committees or department heads working closely with the president. Committees, the examiners noted, were "appointed and advisory. There are no elected faculty committees with power to study academic problems and policies and with authority to take the results of their deliberations to the faculty for consideration and appropriate action." Faculty were left with more than "the usual amount of discontent" at being excluded from academic decision making, the report concluded.

Like all presidents, Orr answered to the Board. To make certain he would not be dominated by a powerful, entrenched Board, as Galbreath and Cleland had been (and to keep dead wood from accumulating), Orr, before accepting the presidency, had insisted that Board members could serve only two consecutive four-year terms and then must rotate off the Board. In practice,

The Rev. James M. Ferguson '97, son of former president Robert G. Ferguson, served as president of the Board of Trustees from 1948 until his death in 1957.

Board turnover was less than complete because the 52 Board members represented five different constituencies; 12 were elected by each of the three controlling synods and eight each by the alumni and the Board itself. A member could not be re-elected more than once by the same constituency but was eligible for election to a new term by a different constituency. By changing constituents, some trustees did serve continuously for many years, but Orr appeared not to object to this arrangement. Until late in his administration, I know of no serious differences between Orr and the Board. He led the College, and they supported his policies and decisions.

Orr enjoyed strong support from the two presidents of the Board during most of his tenure. The Rev. James M. Ferguson, son of former president Robert Gracey Ferguson, held the post from October 1948 until his death on Oct. 20, 1957. Ferguson '97, recently retired from the ministry in 1948, spent a lot of time advising Orr, who didn't always listen. (Ferguson reportedly advised against bringing in the assertive Vander Lugt as dean.) Ferguson was succeeded by Clyde A. Armstrong '19, a Pittsburgh attorney and Board vice president, who served even more aggressively as Orr's advocate until he retired from the post, against Orr's wishes, in October 1964.

That Board rotation arrangement was upset by the May 1958 merger that combined the United Presbyterian Church of North America with the Presbyterian Church U.S.A. to form the United Presbyterian Church U.S.A. Before the merger, three U.P. synods elected a majority of the Board. After the merger, church ties were weak and the church elected no trustees. Twenty of the 28 trustees were elected to four-year terms by the Board itself, the rest by the Alumni Association. With only two constituencies instead of five, perpetuating membership became more difficult, and a nucleus of Board members who felt that continuity was essential saw that the two-term limit was dropped when amendments to the College charter were approved in 1959. Orr felt that the Board had reneged on its commitment to him to limit Board terms. The change reduced the president's control over who joined and who left the Board. The Alumni Council chose to keep the rotary system for its elections to assure that some new blood would occasionally enter the Board.

Clyde A. Armstrong '19 served as president of the Board of Trustees from 1957-64.

Orr had vigorously opposed the church merger, partly because it might dilute the conservatism of the smaller U.P. denomination but largely because it would dilute church support for the College. Pre-merger, Westminster was the only college supported financially by three U.P. synods, including two of the strongest, spanning the Middle Atlantic states and New England. The merger made it one of six Presbyterian colleges supported by a single, albeit larger, Pennsylvania synod.

Thus did Orr consolidate power and unite the College behind his strong leadership. If he had collected power for power's sake, his contribution to Westminster's history would have been modest and temporary. But he was a builder who used the power of his office and the force of his personality to build the College in ways that permanently transformed it, accomplishments that will be recounted in Chapter 16. ❖

CHAPTER 16

Bricks and Mortar:
The House that Orr Built

Freeman Science Hall, completed in 1952, is named for Charles C. Freeman, who served the College for 50 years as chemistry professor, acting dean and acting president.

Will W. Orr's legacy was distinctly tangible; he was a builder. It is no accident that during his 18 years at the helm, second only to Ferguson (22 years) in longevity, the physical campus more than doubled as he broke ground and raised funds for one building after another. When Orr arrived in New Wilmington, he found the classic quadrangle, surrounded by six buildings: Old Main, the old Science Hall, McGill Library, Browne Hall, Ferguson Hall, and Old 77. Up on the hill, Hillside and Jeffers Hall provided two more dormitories, and a music conservatory (later West Hall) sat across Market Street from the library. Two Army surplus buildings west of the campus had been pressed into service as an infirmary and student union, and six old College-owned houses near campus served as sorority houses.

While he was president, the campus grew with the addition of the Freeman Science Hall; Memorial Field House; Russell Hall; Galbreath Hall; the Walton-Mayne Student Union Building; the president's manse; Brittain Lake and Anderson Amphitheater; Shaw Hall; the Arts and Science building, with its Orr Auditorium and Beeghly Theater; Eichenauer Hall; and a large addition to McGill Library. In addition, 21 faculty houses were built south of Russell Hall in Gateway Center. Orr had a passion for physical buildings and a talent for finding wealthy donors who would help pay for them.

He left the College with a modern, serviceable physical plant, built at a small fraction of what such buildings would have cost had the College waited until the 1980s or 1990s to build them. Measured in brick and mortar, he exceeded in 18 years all that his predecessors had built in nearly 100 years. Since his departure in 1967, the College has added just two freestanding buildings – the Hoyt Science Resources Center in 1974, and the Remick Admissions House in 1999 – although several major additions and renovations have been needed. Orr presided over the College during the great postwar economic boom, which brought a measure of success and prosperity to Westminster that it had never known. Orr's ability to expand the campus was critical to attracting students and faculty to the College and accommodating the academic and extracurricular activities that flourished.

There is no question that his fund-raising prowess contributed greatly to the wealth of the College or that Orr's penchant for buildings channeled most of those funds to the physical plant instead of the endowment. That relatively thin endowment contributed to a concern about the College's financial viability after 1978, concern that touched off the College's third major crisis.

Growth of the Physical Campus

Built simultaneously or in quick succession were:

◆ Russell Hall, approved for immediate construction by the Board on Oct. 24, 1949, just 10 days after Orr was officially inaugurated and six months after his arrival. Construction was under way by the summer of 1950. Built for slightly over $500,000 (and partly financed by a loan from the College endowment), it was first occupied by freshmen men on March 22, 1952. It housed 139 men and had a dining hall that could feed 275. It was named for Robert McWatty Russell, Westminster's fifth president.

◆ The Memorial Field House, also approved on Oct. 24, 1949. Actual construction, authorized by the Board in April 1950, began the following summer and was largely completed a year later, in August 1951. It was used for the first time as a dining hall for the New Wilmington Missionary Conference, which had built and equipped a kitchen for the building. The College used it for the first time on Oct. 12, 1951, for the convocation that officially launched Westminster's centennial celebration. It was formally dedicated on Dec. 15 as a memorial to those who served and died in the two world wars, just before its debut as a sports venue, hosting a Westminster-Geneva basketball game. Completed at a cost of $250,000, it could seat 3,500 for basketball games and up to 5,000 when used as an auditorium. An additional $75,000 was spent to build new football and baseball fields and a new track during 1950 and 1951.

◆ The president's manse, built for $50,000 on Furnace Hill during the summer and fall of 1950, was occupied by the Orrs on Jan. 16, 1951. It was named Mack Manse for former trustee and longtime benefactor J.S. Mack, whose Mack Foundation contributed $40,000 for the residence.

◆ The Freeman Science Hall, approved in principle by the Board Oct. 24, 1949, as part of the centennial building campaign, with actual construction authorized on March 7, 1952. Built for $328,000, it was located just south of the old Science Hall and connected to it. It was ready for classes in the fall of 1952 and formally dedicated on Oct. 14, a memorial to Charles C. Freeman, who in his 50 years at the College (1894-1944) was a science professor, academic dean and twice acting president.

◆ Brittain Lake, dammed and graded south of the new football field in the summer of 1951. Originally about five acres but enlarged to 15 acres in 1956, it was named for trustee J. Frank Brittain, whose gifts financed the project. On the west shore of the lake, the New Wilmington Missionary Conference built Anderson Amphitheater, an open-sided auditorium, as the main assembly hall for its annual conference. Built in 1958 for $70,000 on land leased from the College, it was to be available for College use during the rest of the year.

◆ The Walton-Mayne Student Union building east of the Science Hall was approved by the Board on June 1, 1957, completed within a year, and dedicated on May 31, 1958. It provided recreational facilities, a snack bar, meeting rooms and five guest rooms and housed the College bookstore. It replaced the ramshackle Army surplus building that had served as the TUB (Titan Union Building). Almost half of the $320,000 cost of constructing it came from a $150,000 posthumous gift from Mrs. Jessie B. Mayne, who had inherited the estate of her brother, W.D. Walton, a Westminster alumnus ('95) who had died in 1953.

◆ Galbreath Hall, named for former president Robert F. Galbreath, who attended the Oct. 25, 1957, dedication ceremonies, was built for a cost of $1,140,000 and included a food service complex with two large dining rooms, as well as dormitory rooms for 166 women. One dining

room was named for trustee and benefactor John Duff, who had recently been killed in an automobile accident, the other for Samuel Wilson McGinness '01, who also had died recently. Most of the funds came from an $803,000 Federal Housing Administration loan. The Board approved plans for the building in January 1955 and students moved in two years later.

Russell Hall, Brittain Lake, and Memorial Field House were competed in 1951-52 as part of the College's Centennial Campaign.

◆ Gateway homes, ultimately 21 of them, were under construction by the summer of 1957 and built as funds became available through 1966. The attractive houses overlooking Brittain Lake were built for a total cost of $450,000 and helped the College attract badly needed faculty during its expansion.

◆ Shaw Hall, named for benefactor Walter C. Shaw, included rooms for 160 women and an infirmary dedicated to Shaw's wife, Virginia. Ground was broken on Sept. 13, 1958, and the building was completed in January 1960, ahead of schedule, at a cost of $519,000. Women were moved from Hillside to Shaw at the beginning of the second semester.

◆ The Arts and Science Building got tentative Board approval on June 1, 1958, but with the stipulation that it would be a "pay-as-you-go" project, built in stages only as funds were raised. The section housing the music department was built first and occupied in January 1961. The old music conservatory was turned into a classroom annex. When funds ran out, construction stopped in November 1960 but resumed the following April and continued until the auditorium was completed. On March 8, 1961, Westminster dedicated the building, which so far had cost $1,600,000. The auditorium could seat 1,750, enough to accommodate the whole student body, so the dual chapel programs were consolidated and moved from Wallace Chapel to the auditorium; compulsory attendance was dropped from five times to three times a week. On June 1, 1964, the Board approved construction of the sec-

Galbreath Hall, named for former president Robert F. Galbreath, was completed in 1957. It included dorm rooms for 166 women and a food service complex with two large dining rooms.

ond phase, to include the classroom wing, quarters for the art department and Beeghly Theater, named for Leon A. Beeghly, a Youngstown industrialist and contributor to the College. Building the second stage cost $950,000 and dedication ceremonies were held in October 1966.

♦ Eichenauer Hall, a new dormitory for men, was approved for construction by the Board in the spring of 1965. Built along Market Street south of Russell Hall for a cost of $930,000, it was occupied in September 1966, and housed 260 men. It was named for John B. Eichenauer, a former trustee and benefactor.

♦ A new addition to the north side of McGill Library, roughly doubling its size, was completed in 1966 at a cost of $530,000.

All told, 12 major building projects were begun and completed during Orr's presidency at a total cost of $7,567,000. College sports programs, except for swimming, now had modern, state-of-the-art facilities. The art, music, and speech and drama departments had spacious classrooms, practice rooms, rehearsal rooms, an art gallery, and a well-designed, well-equipped theater. The science departments had new classrooms and laboratories. Student food service had been overhauled with new dining rooms and new, well-equipped kitchens. Westminster now had two places – the Field House and the auditorium – where large, inclusive events could be held. The four large dormitories that were added, two for men and two for women, provided adequate on-campus housing for a large majority of the resident students. Students had a modern, attractive union building where they could bowl, dance, eat or talk. The library had been enlarged and modernized. Attractive living quarters were provided for the president and 21 new faculty families.

Older buildings that were still serviceable were renovated. Orr and his Board and administration had built the house that Westminster was to occupy for decades to come. With few exceptions, the buildings had been well designed for their intended uses, and nearly all College activities were well housed by the time he left in 1967.

Fund Raising

The buildings were the fruit; the labor, largely unseen, was the fund raising. Like many colleges at that time, Westminster recognized the growing role of "development," an amalgam of fund raising, alumni relations and public relations, by creating an executive position under the president to coordinate those activities. I was promoted from alumni secretary to that newly created position in 1960.

To the extent that this reorganization eliminated duplication of effort and saved Orr time by having fewer people report to him, everything proceeded smoothly. But he vetoed my proposal to build a long-range giving program based on the organized solicitation of repeated gifts from alumni, trustees and friends. He also showed little enthusiasm for a deferred giving program (major gifts through trusts and bequests). He didn't like to see giving deferred. But, with the help of Sharon attorney Harvey Moore, the former Alumni Association president who was now a member of the Board of Trustees, we eventually launched such a program in 1963, and it has paid off.

The pressure pattern in Orr's fund raising was forged at the very beginning of his administration. In 1949, Orr walked into a college on the brink of its centennial celebration. The Board already had set ambitious objectives for a centennial building and fund-raising campaign but left it to the new president to organize and conduct the campaign. Thus Orr found himself under immediate pressure to raise large amounts of money before he had time to become acquainted with his new post. The challenge played to two of Orr's strong points: an ability to move quickly and a gift for raising money. The successful centennial campaign made Orr the "man-of-the-hour" in the eyes of the Board, the alumni, and the general public. He went on to play the hero in a succession of fund-raising sagas.

Like he did with so many aspects of administration, Orr personalized fund raising. Although we traveled together frequently to alumni activities, I never saw him close one of the major contributions he would bring in with some regularity. Those were one-on-one occasions. I heard him talk about some of them. I know that he was not intimidated by wealth nor shy about proposing large gifts. He said that his brashness got him figuratively thrown out of a few high places, but much of the time he prevailed. No doubt his own sincere dedication to the College was infectious, and his offers to name a dormitory or dining hall or lake or theater after a major donor clearly were effective.

Other Growth

It is appropriate to emphasize Orr's role as a physical builder, but he was actively working to build enrollment and the academic and extracurricular programs as well. Enrollment, which had run between 500 and 700 during Galbreath's administration, swelled temporarily to over 1,300 during the "G.I. bulge" of 1946, then ebbed to about 800 by 1953. Then it climbed steadily until 1967, when there were more than 2,000 total students – 1,400 under-graduates and 600-plus graduate students, nurses and special students. The full-time faculty likewise hit a peak of 84 in 1946, dipped to 67 by 1952 and stood at 106 in 1967. Faculty salaries increased by 164 percent during Orr's administration, bringing Westminster from near the bottom to near the top of its peer group and making it possible to attract better qualified teachers. The increase was funded largely by tuition increases of 220 percent.

Graduate and summer school programs were expanded. A new core cur-riculum revived the College's traditional liberal arts emphasis. So did the demise of vocational programs like the two-year secretarial course. Probation standards were raised so that only students who were on track for graduation could continue to enroll. Titan sports teams dominated the West Penn cham-pionships, and football and basketball teams often won national honors. The revival of religious emphasis sent approximately 200 graduates into church vocations during the Orr years and created the full-time position of dean of the chapel.

Orr's Leave of Absence

The problem with a personalized, high-powered administration is that it eventually wears out the driver. That happened to Orr. As stress took its toll, Orr turned to prescription barbiturates for relief. He increased the doses to a high enough level that Dr. Frank McClanahan, the College physician, came to me privately to discuss the problem and his fears for Orr's health. He may have talked to others as well. Orr's behavior, always intense, became erratic enough to attract some attention and concern.

The Board intervened in September 1963 and insisted that Orr take a leave of absence for the 1963-64 academic year and enter a treatment center at a discreet distance from the campus. The official explanation, offered by Board president Clyde Armstrong, was that Orr had over-extended himself and was suffering from exhaustion. When word got back to a few of us that Orr had left the treatment center after only a few days, we were alarmed, but he had simply taken personal control of his rehabilitation, which he managed quite successfully. During his absence, academic dean Charles Saylor was acting president. Orr returned to campus in April 1964 rested, relaxed and in better shape physically and mentally than he had been for years. He received a hero's welcome. A special assembly held in Wallace Chapel celebrated the achievements of his first 15 years.

And Retirement

Then, in June 1966, Orr surprised many of us by announcing his resignation, effective as soon as suitable arrangements for his departure could be made. He actually left the College the following January but technically terminated his employment in June 1967, taking the spring semester as a leave of absence. He was 63 when he left. We expected him to serve until he was 65 and had completed 20 years as president.

No reason was given for the timing of his departure. I had left the administration for the classroom by this time and was out of the loop. But two events might have been factors in his decision. In 1959, the Board, against Orr's wishes, revoked a policy of rotating Board membership that would have broken up the continuous service of a group of trustees who considered themselves indispensable. Orr had insisted on a rotation policy before accepting the presidency. (For a fuller discussion of how church union disrupted old patterns of Board membership, see Chapter 15.) Orr may have felt that his leadership over the Board was eroding. (And, of course, he couldn't forget that the Board had sent him on an involuntary leave of absence.)

The second event was the resignation of Armstrong as president of the Board. Orr relied on Armstrong as an important partner and friend. He had prevented Armstrong from resigning on several occasions by saying, "If you resign, I'll resign." But Armstrong finally did resign in October 1964 and was succeeded by Judge John L. Miller, the Board vice president. I think Orr probably missed Armstrong and his solid support. Rather than see his powers decline, Orr chose to go out at the peak of his success.

As his departure date approached, accolades mounted. His achievements were celebrated at a student assembly, a faculty and staff dinner, a Board dinner, an alumni luncheon, and a Rotary Club dinner. The Board, at its June

1967 meeting, named the new auditorium the Will W. Orr Auditorium and made Orr the College's first president *emeritus*. He retired to Melbourne, Fla., where he organized a new church, the interdenominational Community Chapel by the Sea. Until his death on Jan. 29, 1994, he would return to the campus occasionally, once, in June 1975, to receive an honorary doctor of divinity degree and give the featured baccalaureate address. ❖

The House that Orr Built

The map below shows the campus of Westminster College as of October 2001. The silhouettes represent buildings and facilities built before or after the Will Orr administration. The remaining buildings and facilities were begun and completed during Orr's 18-year tenure as president (1949-67).

ACADEMIC BUILDINGS

1. Old Main
   Tower Room
   Wallace Memorial Chapel
2. McGill Memorial Library
   Miller Board Room
3. Thompson-Clark & Charles Freeman
   Science Halls
4. Patterson Hall
   Art Gallery
   Beeghly Theater
   Orr Auditorium
5. Hoyt Science Resources Center
   Information Systems
   J.S. Mack Science Library
   Phillips Lecture Hall
6. Memorial Field House
   Natatorium and Fitness Center
   Buzz Ridl Gymnasium
   T.V. Mansell Education Wing
7. Old 77

RESIDENCE HALLS

8. Ferguson Hall
9A. Browne Hall
   McGinness Dining Room
9B. Galbreath Hall
   Duff Dining Room
   Lindley Dining Room
10. Shaw Hall
   Student Health Center
11. Jeffers Hall
12. Eichenauer Hall
   Down Under
13. Hillside Hall
14. Russell Hall
   Russell Dining Room

ACADEMIC BUILDINGS

15. Physical Plant Buildings
16. Anderson Amphitheater
17. Walton-Mayne Union Building
   (TUB)
18. President's Home
19. Thompson House
20. Henley Pavilion
21. Remick Admissions House

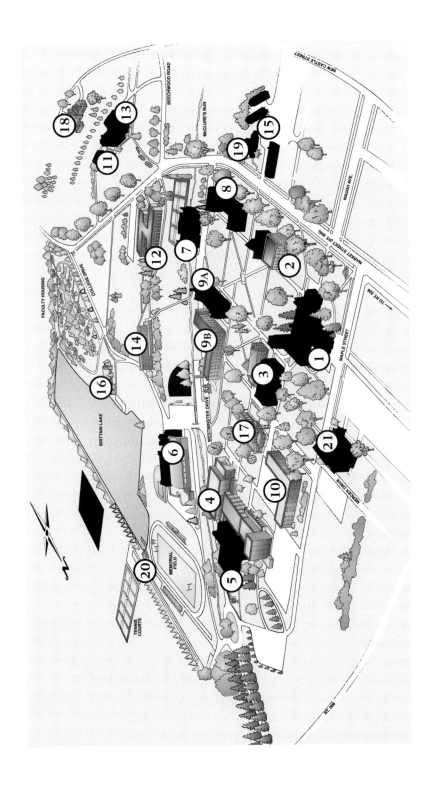

CHAPTER 17

The Perpetual Money Machine:
Funds Raising Turns Pro

Patterson Hall
(named for the Rev.
James Patterson,
Westminster's first
president) and its
Beeghly Theater
(named for benefac-
tor Leon Beeghly)
was a "pay-as-you-
go" project, built in
stages as funds
were raised.

Westminster's third half-century started with a fund-raising bang that reverberated and expanded into a long preoccupation with financing the College. The course of higher education in the second half of the twentieth century made Westminster, like virtually all of its private, liberal arts peers, an expensive institution to operate. It placed growing fiscal pressure on fund-raisers to supplement student tuition and fees for operating income as well as capital projects and endowment building. Fund raising grew from a series of discrete campaigns into a perpetual activity. And it evolved from being largely a personal quest driven by a high-powered president (Will Orr) to being an institutionalized program managed by a staff of development professionals. However, the pressure on the president to be an effective closer and "star" who enjoys a good rapport with wealthy contributors has not abated.

It was concern about the fiscal condition of the College and the perception in some quarters that fund raising was not keeping pace with growing operating expenses that was in a large measure responsible for the major turmoil of the College's third 50-year period. That unrest saw a procession of six presidents, interim presidents or designated presidents over a seven-year period, including a controversial corporate CEO (Robert Lauterbach) with a financial agenda who installed himself for a year in the College president's office.

The College, in 1949, was approaching its centennial in disarray. A major fund-raising drive clearly was in order. Indeed, a centennial expansion program had been authorized by the Board in 1938 but kept on a back burner until the future leader of the College could be found. After years of depresion and World War II austerity, a booming post-war economy was driving up enrollment and putting severe strains on the College's limited physical resources. A leadership vacuum persisted after the Board's "Red scare" tactics prompted the resignation of Galbreath and efforts to install Cleland as a tough executive backfired, events covered in Chapter 12. Galbreath was effective at building College morale during the Depression and war, but he was no high-powered fund-raiser. It is doubtful if fund raising could have flourished under any president during that period of national emergencies. The embattled Cleland was consumed by internal politics during his brief tenure. Then the interim administration of caretaker John Orr maintained calm, but postponed tackling long-term needs. Fund-raising efforts had essentially collapsed.

As a result, Will Orr, in 1949, stepped into a fund-raising campaign – the largest in the College's history to date – that was seriously behind schedule and could easily have become a debacle. Orr rose to the challenge in a pattern that was to mark his presidency and hit the road in search of wealthy contributors. In October 1949, 10 days after Orr was inaugurated, the Board approved three building projects, already on the drawing board, that would form the core of the centennial campaign: the Freeman Science Hall, Russell Hall and Memorial Field House. In October 1950, those projects, along with a president's manse and a $100,000 addition to the endowment, were consolidated into the official Centennial Campaign, with a stated goal of $1,245,000. The campaign had a chairman (John B. Lewis '20), a director (Bible professor Joseph M. Hopkins '40), and an alumni coordinator (alumni secretary Paul Gamble '32), but it was Orr who assumed leadership of the campaign and personally solicited most of the large gifts.

Orr didn't quite start from scratch. Contributions for construction of the Freeman Science Hall had accumulated to the sum of about $160,000 by the time Orr arrived. Students and alumni already had raised a little more than $12,000 for a Student Union War Memorial. Those funds, along with the war memorial concept, were transferred to a higher priority in February 1950 – the Field House construction fund – subject to the donors' consent. Once student solicitors secured pledges for another $10,000 in a hasty campaign, the Board voted in April to proceed immediately with construction of the Field House.

The Centennial Campaign gave birth to the Annual Alumni Fund (now Westminster Fund). The new alumni secretary (Paul Gamble, hired in July

1949) was asked to develop an annual alumni fund that would bring in at least $25,000 a year. Shortly thereafter, he was given the responsibility for soliciting alumni for the Centennial Campaign. To avoid launching an annual fund that would compete with the campaign, the two were combined initially. The campaign would solicit pledges from alumni to be paid over a three-year period, and the first $100 of each cash payment would be credited to the Alumni Fund for that year. Thus the Centennial Campaign helped to jumpstart the Alumni Fund.

Goals for the first year (1949-50) were to collect $10,000 from 1,000 alumni donors. To stimulate alumni giving, competition among the classes was inaugurated in February 1950. By June, 1,191 alumni (33% of all living alumni) had given $30,654 in cash ($20,000 from Centennial Campaign contributions credited at the $100 limit). The following year 1,145 alumni (36%) made cash payments totaling $73,461. Centennial payments peaked in 1951-52 with a total of $100,253 from alumni (31%). Then, as Centennial payments ebbed, the total dropped to $66,255 in 1952-53, to $60,214 in 1953-54, and bottomed out the following year at $52,031 from 1,176 donors (25%). From that point the fund grew every year until in 1959-60 alumni gifts totaled $198,140 (including gifts of all sizes) from 2,300 donors – 43 percent of the alumni body. Within ten years the Annual Fund had become firmly established as a significant but somewhat erratic source of College income that far exceeded the original $25,000 goal.

In other phases of the Centennial Campaign, the town of New Wilmington was tapped and responded initially with pledges for more than $50,000; the amount later topped $62,000. Support from the College's church constituency was promoted through a series of dinners scheduled in the 20 presbyteries that made up the three controlling synods that elected Westminster's Board of Trustees. The Sixth United Presbyterian Church of Pittsburgh, one of the largest and wealthiest in the denomination, provided generous support for the construction of Russell Hall, which was named for their former pastor and the College's former president. (Details of the buildings that resulted from the

Centennial Campaign are covered in Chapter 16.) The Centennial Campaign did not reach its $1,250,000 goal by the time of the centennial observance. It passed the million-dollar mark on year-end gifts at the end of 1952 and continued until the centennial goals had been funded. In reality, the campaign never stopped. Orr had impressed the Board with his skill and dedication, and he had a list of building projects that still needed funding. So he kept raising funds to complete one building after another, events also covered in Chapter 16. And he was routinely successful. Some projects took longer than others; some required a degree of debt. But the money was raised and the buildings built.

During the final year of his presidency (1967), Orr reached a cherished goal when annual gifts to the College topped $1 million for the first time. Not all of the funds raised were for brick and mortar, however; income from a 1955 grant of $216,500 from the Ford Foundation was used to increase faculty salaries. The Mack Foundation in 1959 established a fund to provide faculty study grants – up to two months salary for teachers working on advanced degrees. That summer nine of Westminster's faculty got grants. The grants continued through the 1960s.

When Earland Carlson assumed the Westminster presidency in 1967, his initial priority was bringing participatory governance. (See Chapter 19 for details.) But the need for fund raising now was constant. After a year or two of preparation, in June 1971, Westminster launched the 125 Fund, the most ambitious fund-raising campaign yet. This time the goal was $5.5 million, to be used to build the first phase of a science resources center, a natatorium and expanded physical education facilities. Additional money was slated for the endowment as well, to maintain a prudent ratio between physical facilities and endowment resources. The campaign's name anticipated the College's 125th anniversary in 1977. Lauterbach, then vice president of the Board, was named general chairman. Harry Shoup, director of development, worked closely with Carlson. Ketchum Inc. of Pittsburgh was hired to work behind the scenes to develop a large campaign organization to solicit trustees, alumni, foundations, corporations, and other constituencies. It was the most elaborate, expensive and professional approach the College had yet taken to fund raising.

Neither program suited the best long-range interests of the College, and we didn't want the Alumni Association competing with the College for contributions. The solution, which was getting results at other colleges, was to mount an annual alumni giving fund, asking graduates to give as much as they could each year rather than pledge a multi-year obligation. To eliminate the association's dues, we agreed to give them $2 from each alumni gift received, with the understanding that they would return unneeded funds to the College. For several years, the College transferred that money to the association, which then transferred most of it back to the College. Then the association folded its program into the growing College alumni program and ceased to exist as an independent organization.

The impetus to organizing alumni giving at Westminster can be traced to Armstrong's disappointment with the pledge system he had introduced. Writing in the April 1949 *Blue and White*, just before Orr's arrival and about two months before I was hired, Armstrong said, "Unless and until we can have a competent and energetic full-time secretary acting as such for both the Alumni and the Annual Giving Fund, we will continue to lose both valuable time and financial support." ◆

All those resources paid off. By the end of 1973, more than $5.74 million had been pledged, and more than 80 percent of that amount had been collected. They had beaten the goal by nearly a quarter of a million dollars. Lauterbach in particular emerged with a reputation for effective leadership.

The money raised covered the cost of the science building ($2.7 million) and physical education facilities ($2 million), which were built debt-free. Ground was broken in August 1972 for the Hoyt Science Resources Center, named for Alex Crawford Hoyt, a trustee *emeritus* and major donor. The building, occupied in January 1974, housed the chemistry and mathematics departments, a science library and a computer center. It was located just east of the Arts and Science building (later renamed Patterson Hall in memory of Westminster's first president). Construction of the new physical education facilities adjacent to the Field House got under way in the summer of 1974 and was completed in the fall of 1975. This expansion program included a new natatorium, which provided excellent facilities for swimming classes, the swimming team, and recreational swimming. It also included a gymnasium area, two handball courts, locker rooms, and extensive remodeling of older facilities. Olympic Gold medalist Micki King was featured speaker at the February 1976 dedication of the natatorium.

Annual alumni giving continued to rise. The 1976 Annual Giving Fund set new records with $178,355 in gifts from 3,611 alumni – 21 percent more money and 26 percent more givers than the year before. Fiscal responsibility and effective fund raising allowed Westminster to operate with balanced budgets through the 1970s, at a time when many private colleges had been forced by declining enrollment and rising costs into deficit spending and shrinking endowments.

The Hoyt Science Resources Center was completed in 1974. It was named for trustee *emeritus* and major donor Alex Crawford Hoyt.

By its 125th birthday, the College had come a long way since two professors and twenty-some students gathered in the "old Seceder Church" to launch a pioneer venture in coeducation, with faith as their principal asset. Westminster in 1977 had about 1,600 undergraduate and 300 graduate students. A full-time faculty of 113 plus an administrative staff of 24 and support staff of 110 gave the College an annual payroll of approximately $3 million and an annual operating budget in excess of $6.5 million. College buildings were valued at more than $34 million; all physical assets, including land and equipment, came to about $45 million. The endowment stood at $7 million-plus.

Earland I. Carlson, Westminster's 10th president (1967-81).

In the fall of 1978 Carlson was sidelined with a serious illness. In mid-December he underwent cancer surgery in Pittsburgh. His release from the hospital was followed by a period of recuperation at home. During his sick leave academic dean Philip Lewis served as chief administrator of the College, a role he previously had filled during Carlson's sabbatical leave in the spring of 1974. Lauterbach, who had become president of the Board following the death of Judge John Miller in July 1978, also assumed a more active role in administration of the College during Carlson's leave. Lauterbach was instrumental in starting plans for another fund-raising campaign. Carlson, who had recovered from his illness, assured the Board that he was in good health and ready to make a total commitment to the campaign. In March 1981, the Challenge '80s fund-raising campaign was publicly announced, with a goal of $12.8 million, of which more than $500,000 already had been pledged.

With the upheaval that followed Carlson's sudden resignation the following October and Lauterbach's dramatic takeover (events covered in Chapter 19), the campaign was moved to a back burner. But the machinery that had been set up continued to operate, and during Allen Splete's presidency in the spring of 1984 the Challenge '80s campaign concluded with pledges of $13.1 million, surpassing the goal by $300,000. Once again, Lauterbach, as campaign chairman, had delivered. Large gifts helped. Seven-figure contributions included a $1.1 million bequest from the estate of Katherine Stewart Armington in 1983.

Eventually, the national decline in private college enrollment that marked the 1970s caught up to Westminster. From 1,600 in 1977, it fell to 1,150 in 1986. The decline brought a reduction in tuition revenue and an increase in financial aid as Westminster had to compete for its share of a shrinking pool of students. In March 1984, the Board responded to the fiscal crunch by freezing salaries of faculty and staff, just a month before Splete succeeded Lauterbach as president. Enrollment began to recover in 1987 and reached

The Natatorium in Memorial Field House was completed in 1975.

1,385 by 1990. Gifts, which in the 1987-88 fiscal year totaled $2.4 million, helped to offset some of the tuition loss, and the alumni giving base continued to broaden, with 33.5 percent of all living alumni making gifts in 1991.

After Oscar E. Remick settled in as Westminster's president in 1987, it was inevitable that he would be called upon to lead a fund-raising campaign. After several years of behind-the-scenes cultivation and solicitation of special gifts, during which time $14 million had been raised (including a $1.1 million gift from Scott and Theresa Beck in 1990), "A Heritage for the Future; A Campaign for Westminster" was publicly launched Oct. 19, 1991, at a black-tie dinner dance in Pittsburgh. Former Board chairman and Pittsburgh banker Robert F. Patton was to serve as chairman of the fund-raising drive with a goal of $35 million. Included in the original plans were a new administration building, a football stadium to be named for the late football coach Harold Burry, scholarship funds, and an addition to the endowment.

After a strong start, a campaign that was scheduled for five years was extended to six. Raising money for bricks and mortar was particularly difficult. Major donors were more interested in funding student scholarships, faculty chairs and the endowment. No major buildings came out of the campaign, but by June 1997 it had raised $35.25 million, the largest amount for any campaign in Westminster's history. The funds covered the renovation of Wallace Memorial Chapel, expansion of the Field House, and funding student scholarships and professorships to the tune of $7 million. A $2.5 million gift from the McCune Foundation helped. Alumni gave $11.8 million to the Annual Fund during the six years of the Heritage for the Future campaign, with a strong participation rate of 40.2 percent. ❖

CHAPTER 18

The Curfews Crumble:
'Liberation' and Sports on Campus

I n Westminster's third half-century, student activism collided with the College's long history of regulating student life. The regulations crumbled. From daily compulsory chapel to the ban on drinking alcoholic beverages to male-free women's dorms and strict curfews for resident women, Westminster conceded that it could no longer act in a parental role to the assertive generation of students who enrolled in the 1970s and 1980s. With some regret, administrators concluded that the founders' determination to prevent students from "frequent[ing] taverns, groceries and places of idle amusement and vice" and to keep the combustible sexes apart, at least after 10 p.m., no longer was feasible.

Most of the liberalizations occurred during the 1967-81 Carlson administration when the president was implementing his style of participatory governance and encouraging all of the Westminster constituencies, including students, to share in the institutional decision-making.

President Carlson meets with students during a period of student unrest.

The dress code and compulsory chapel were among the first to fall. A student protest occurred in May 1968 when a crowd of students dressed in shorts entered the library to protest that ban. In the fall of 1968, the Carlson-appointed self-study committee dropped the dress code entirely on the grounds that "Westminster College believes that the student is capable of assuming responsibility for his appearance."

Compulsory chapel had become the object of informal protests; students played cards, read and talked to neighbors while guest speakers strained to be heard. In September 1969, at the recommendation of the self-study committee, the attendance requirement was dropped. Henceforth, worship services would be held two mornings a week in Wallace Chapel, but attendance was voluntary. The self-study committee also issued a statement of "Student Rights and Responsibilities" and established a judicial board to assure due process for students charged with violating College rules. These changes were approved by students, faculty, and the Board in the spring of 1970.

But those measures failed to satisfy student leaders, who, in March 1970, dissolved the student government to protest its lack of authority over student affairs. By the next fall, a task force of 12 students elected by the student body, three faculty members, and five administrators had agreed to a new student association. It included a representative senate responsible for recognizing student organizations and allocating monies from student activity fees.

The new Student Association wasted no time in addressing the issue of visitation. In February 1971 the group proposed a policy that would permit limited visitation by men and women students to each other's dorm rooms at designated times. The Board, at its March meeting, appointed a committee composed of trustees, administrators, faculty and students to study the matter. Then, at its June meeting, the Board rejected the visitation proposal on the grounds that it posed problems with "such areas as admissions, alumni relations, development and institutional image, the concern for personal privacy, the problem of security, and physical arrangements within the Westminster residence halls." Instead, the Board offered 11 rooms on the lower floor of Eichenauer Hall as meeting rooms where "small student groups" could be assured of privacy. Students referred to them as "fornication rooms."

A year later, in the spring of 1972, the Board did approve limited visitation rights very similar to those the Student Association had proposed, and those hours of visitation were extended in 1975. In 1989, over the objections of some parents and alumni, the Board removed the 1 a.m. visitation curfew on Friday and Saturday nights, so male and female students were free to spend the entire night in each others' rooms. That policy continues, with visitation barred from midnight to 11 a.m. on weeknights on open visitation floors. Somewhat more restrictive hours apply to a shrinking number of limited visitation dorm floors.

The anti-war demonstrations that wracked many college campuses in the late 1960s and early 1970s were muted at Westminster. Students organized Peace, Inc., staged a few peaceful local demonstrations and sent about 70 members to a Vietnam Moratorium demonstration in Washington, D.C., in November 1969.

Westminster's one taste of radical student demonstrations was provoked by allegations of racism. A white student secretary working in the admissions office reported to the Dean of Women and student government members that she had heard athletic director and football coach Harold Burry make racist remarks in a private conversation with secretary Lila Newman. The report of Burry's alleged comments spread like wildfire and polarized the campus. Some students and faculty mobilized to combat ugly racism, while others rallied to support Burry, a sports icon who enjoyed famously good relations with his African-American athletes and who was personally responsible for bringing racial integration and more African-American students to Westminster than anyone else.

Dissatisfied with Carlson's written promise of "a thorough inquiry into the incident," dissident students occupied Carlson's outer office on May 14, 1971, and refused to leave when it was time to close the office. (Carlson was in the Washington, D.C., area on business at the time.) College officials prepared to seek a preliminary injunction to force the students to leave, but the students left of their own accord before action could be taken, and legal steps were abandoned.

However, a mimeographed underground paper fanned the flames, falsely reporting that "At this time the Administration is filing for a permanent injunction against any student gathering which opposes Administration policy." Those reports appeared on May 14, the same day that William Kunstler, the famed defense lawyer for the radical left, was scheduled to give a speech on campus. Kunstler took up the issue and urged students to stand up for their rights, attracting further publicity to the incident. When Carlson returned to campus, he met with concerned students and the confrontation ended.

Whatever investigation Carlson conducted was done privately, but Burry went on his own to a student government meeting, asked to be heard, and encountered tough questioning. A special faculty meeting was convened on May 19, 1971, specifically to deal with this incident. The "prosecution" was led by sociology professor John Bush, the faculty's only full-time African-American, and Bush was widely perceived to be rushing to judgment before hearing the evidence. (Burry's explanation was that the girl had misinterpreted his account of some of Archie Bunker's racial comments.) The result was that faculty support swung to Burry and the episode quickly faded as a cause célèbre.

Westminster was not spared the ultimate nightmare of student freedom run amok. After a party at the Sig Ep house on Sept. 26, 1981, a freshman woman reported that she had been gang raped by a large number of men. The men insisted that she had participated willingly. The question of consent was clouded by allegations that she was high on drugs at the time. No criminal charges were ever filed, and the woman and her alleged attackers were never publicly identified, but the incident shocked the College and the community, even though complaints of wild, noisy parties in fraternity houses already had frayed relations between "town and gown." On Oct. 2, with Carlson and Dean of Students William M. Wright in attendance, state and local police raided the Sig Ep house and seized small amounts of marijuana and drug-related paraphernalia. Five Sig Eps were later charged with possession. On Oct. 5, Sig Ep alumni, legal owners of the house, voted "to close the house for an indefinite period of time because of the fraternity's inability to operate in a manner acceptable to the board." By Oct. 9, the building was empty and boarded up and did not reopen for two years. Other fraternity houses were subsequently inspected in unannounced visits, and two fraternities were cited for violating the College ban on liquor in fraternity houses.

The Greeks banded together to protest these intrusions by campus authorities and boycotted Homecoming activities on Oct. 24, but their protest was overshadowed by the spreading news that Carlson had been forced to resign the day before, reportedly after having been given an ultimatum by Board president Robert Lauterbach to get the fraternities under control or else, events that will be described in Chapter 19. Ironically, when Lauterbach quickly succeeded Carlson, he held cordial conversations with fraternity leaders. The raids stopped, and, in March 1982, the Board officially lifted the ban on drinking in fraternity houses.

Discipline became an issue again in May 1997 when five members, all graduating seniors, trashed the Sigma Nu house. The five escaped criminal prosecution by agreeing to pay for the damage they had caused – an estimated $28,000 – but the College placed the fraternity on disciplinary probation for three years because of the incident.

Race Relations

The national preoccupation with civil rights and race relations during the 1952-2002 period was reflected in a small way on Westminster's campus. Westminster's anti-slavery founders had boldly declared in the first College catalog that "No person will be refused admission because of Color, Caste, or Sex," but in fact few African-Americans attended before the first black athletes arrived in 1952 and 1953. As the civil rights movement grew in the 1960s, Westminster, like many colleges and universities, made a commitment to recruiting more African-American students and faculty members. But competition for qualified blacks was intense, and Westminster, as an overwhelmingly white college in an entirely white community, was only modestly successful. By the late 1960s black enrollment was running from 25 to 30 students – about 2 percent of the student body. The Black Student Union and SHARE (Society for Human Awareness and Racial Equality), a mixed-race group, promoted racial equality and looked after the interests of black students.

In the fall of 1969 Westminster was able to attract two African-American faculty members, former football star Harold Davis in physical education and Bush in sociology. Davis, who coached the basketball team, stayed just one year before returning to his old job at Xerox Corp. Bush, an outspoken militant who had pushed for action against Burry over the alleged racist remarks, did not have his contract renewed after the 1973-74 academic year. While integration was welcomed, interracial dating, at least prior to 1967, was not. Women students of the 1955-65 era remember freshmen orientation sessions in which Dean of Women Martha Whitehill would explain that the "white birds" and "black birds" were both lovely but should not mix.

In January 1963, the Westminster concert choir ambitiously took its annual bus tour into the Deep South for the first time, travelling as far as Miami. That choir included one African-American member, soprano June Singleton, and the tour had to be carefully arranged so that she would have a place to stay and so that the choir would stop to eat at places where she would be served, according to Clarence Martin, director of the choir at that time. A few minor incidents of discrimination occurred, but the event that stood out from that tour was positive. The principal of an all-black school near Savannah, Ga., invited the choir to give an impromptu concert at his school, and Martin revised the schedule to accept his offer. When it came time for the choir to perform the suite from "West Side Story," Singleton sang the solo in "There's a Place for Us."

At the end of its first 150 years, Westminster remained as it has almost always been: intellectually and idealistically committed to diversity, but practically a rather homogenous community. Racial minorities were actively recruited, but more than 98 percent of the student body was Caucasian, and the faculty even more so. Only on the Board was the College able to attract statistically significant African-American participation. (There were three in 2000.) The Black Student Union still functioned, and an "Allies" support group was organized for gay, lesbian and trans-gendered students. Voluntary chapel, still held twice a week, usually drew small crowds. Protests typically took the form of chalk statements that appeared on sidewalks overnight.

Drinking still was banned on campus and regulated in fraternity houses (no kegs, punch bowls spiked with grain alcohol, or drinking games), but penalties for violations were mild compared to those that would have been meted out prior to 1970.

Football

After decades of mediocrity (75 wins, 161 losses and 26 ties from 1915 to 1950), the 1953 Titans started a four-year streak in which they won 28 while losing just once and tying once. What happened? Harold Burry, Harold Davis and Billy White had arrived – three legends who ushered in a new era. Burry '35 was the coach who brought consistent winning to Westminster football. When he retired from coaching in 1972, his teams had won 127 times, lost 31 and tied 5 in 20 seasons that included six undefeated teams and one

The 1956 football team, led by Harold Davis (52) and Bill White (10), who played four years on teams that compiled a 28-1-1 record.

national championship. He was succeeded by his protégé and assistant coach since 1968, Joseph Fusco, who, from 1972 to 1990 won 154 times, including four national championships, while losing just 34 and tying 3. Eugene Nicholson, an assistant coach under both Burry and Fusco, kept the tradition alive, winning 64, while losing 25 and tying 2 from 1991-98, including two national title appearances and one championship (1994). It was nothing less than a dynasty.

Westminster's gridiron fortunes changed conspicuously in 1998. The College had decided to leave the declining National Association of Intercollegiate Athletics (NAIA) and join the National Collegiate Athletic Association (NCAA) at the Division II level so that it could keep its athletic scholarships. (Westminster had belonged to both NAIA and NCAA for many years, partly because NAIA sponsored the leading postseason tournaments for small colleges like Westminster. But when NCAA censured Westminster in January 1972 for participating in the NAIA football playoffs, the College dropped its 30-year NCAA membership that fall.)

When Westminster joined the NCAA's Great Lakes conference in 1998, it essentially graduated to a tougher league, reflected in its 3-8 football records for both 1998 and 1999, only the second and third losing seasons since 1950. Westminster also had to travel further, spend more and play unfamiliar rivals, costing the school fan support. In 1999, President R. Thomas

Williamson decided to forego the scholarships and move Westminster from Division II to Division III. As a member of the Division III Presidents' Athletic Conference, Westminster rejoined local rivals Grove City, Waynesburg, Thiel, Washington and Jefferson, and Bethany in 2000.

The Burry Era

Burry had joined the physical education staff in 1943 and coached the soccer, cross country and swimming teams with notable success. He stayed away from football until he succeeded Melvin Hetzler as football coach in 1952 and led the team he inherited to a 6-2 record. But Burry, who was known to say you couldn't make chicken soup without chickens, needed a new level of talent, and he found it, most spectacularly in Harold Davis. (See "The Recruiting of Harold Davis.")

Burry faced another challenge. Davis was African-American. New Wilmington was an all-white town. Westminster's new president hailed from North Carolina. But Burry was on the leading edge of a national trend to recruit black athletes to previously all-white colleges and universities. Judging from *Argo* photographs, William Thompson, an undistinguished football player from New Castle who enrolled in 1952, was the first African-American student to enter Westminster in the twentieth century. Then Davis, White and Perry Kirkland arrived in 1953.

By 1956, Davis' senior year, Westminster's football machine looked invincible, rolling to an 8-0 record and outscoring opponents 344-51. Davis and White were both named Little All-Americans. But there was one bump in the road in Burry's victory tour. Playing Bethany on a high school field in Wellsburg, W. Va., in the season's third game, the Titans went into the fourth quarter trailing 16-13, led by lightly used quarterback Steve Kosko. Davis was on the bench, ejected in the first quarter for fighting with Bethany center Ron Whitt. Fusco, a tackle on that team, recalls that racial baiting provoked the incident, but Davis remembers it differently. "I ran a sweep around the end and was protecting the ball when I went down and

The Recruiting of Harold Davis

The event that put Westminster on the map of football greatness came when Harold Burry persuaded Harold Davis to join a previously undistinguished program. Davis was a star three-sport athlete, the likes of which Westminster had not seen before, certainly not on the football field. His prowess at football, basketball and track at Youngstown North High School had attracted national attention and recruiters from major universities. Burry had to challenge Ohio State, Minnesota, Pitt, UCLA and other football powers for this quarterback on whose skill he intended to build his football program.

Competition for Davis was intense, but Burry had important allies in Emanuel and Lulu Davis, the quarterback's parents. They were strong Christians who liked the idea of their son attending a church-related college close to home. "Coach Burry really recruited my parents," Davis recalled in 2000. "The other coaches would come in and talk nothing but football. Coach Burry would talk about the classes, the daily chapel programs, the small community and the Christian influences as well as football, and that got my parents on his side." Mrs. Davis was so partial that she would call Burry when rival coaches were coming to talk with her son. Burry would scurry over to Youngstown to defend his interests. "He ate a lot of meals at our house," Davis noted.

When Davis decided to go to Kent State, he called Burry and gave him the bad news, but Burry said that was fine and kept coming to visit and talk about education and wholesome influences. Eventually Davis gave in to parental pressure and chose Westminster. But that August, when Davis played in a North-South all-star game in Canton, Ohio, (sharing the quarterback role for the North squad with Len Dawson, the future NFL Hall of Famer), scouts from the big universities were out in force, recruiting aggressively. When Burry saw what was happening, he quickly found a job for Davis in New Wilmington as assistant athletic director for the New Wilmington Missionary Conference and arranged for him to live the rest of that summer with the William "Pinky" Carson family. He was hiding his treasure from the other coaches to prevent any last-minute burglary. ◆

rolled out of bounds. One Bethany player wouldn't get off me and kept punching me, so I punched him back, which was a mistake. I fell for the oldest trick in the book; they sent in a third-stringer to start a fight and get both players thrown out of the game." But Burry's conditioning program and on-field adjustments eventually paid off; Westminster uncorked a 27-point fourth quarter and won the game 40-16.

The annual sports team records are available to readers in Appendix B. As the record shows, winning football seasons became routine, district championships commonplace, and national championships and perfect seasons never far away. Westminster had never had an undefeated regular season prior to 1953. After that, it had 11. All those storied seasons and thrilling games inspired William J. McTaggart, professor of English *emeritus* and sports public address announcer, to write *Winning: 100 Years of Westminster College Football* (1994). Readers wanting more details about Westminster football through 1993 can read about it there or in his detailed account of the 1988 team, *That Magical Season*.

Basketball

Basketball expanded and matured rapidly after World War II; never again could Westminster or any other small college team expect to achieve the level of national recognition the Titans reached in 1934-35 and 1940-41. (See Chapter 14.) But Westminster basketball was consistently competitive and often exciting. Coach Grover Washabaugh's teams won 77 consecutive home-court games over several seasons; the gym in which those games were won was renamed Old 77. When Charles G. "Buzz" Ridl, a star of the 1940-41 team, took over head coaching duties from Washabaugh in 1956-57 he raised the level of competition and excitement. Ridl was not just winning games; he was filling the Field House with fans eager to watch the exploits of 5-foot-9-inch Chucky Davis, a flashy ball-handler from Uniontown, who could put on a show in the manner of the Harlem Globetrotters. By Davis' senior year (1959-60), the basketball Titans won 24 games and lost just three in the regular season, so they packed their bags in March for a trip to Kansas City for the NAIA tournament and a game the players and fans would never forget.

Three victories brought the Titans to the semifinals where they faced the reigning champion for the past three years, top-seeded Tennessee A&I. The tall, flashy Tennessee team was averaging 92 points a game, but the Titans set the pace that night, and it was exceedingly slow. "We all agreed how to play the game; hold the ball for the good shot," Ridl told reporters after the game. At halftime, Westminster led, 22-18. The second half was even slower, with the Titans controlling the ball for just under 15 of the 20 minutes. Then, with three minutes remaining, Tennessee scored on a foul shot for its first lead of the game, 38-37. The disciplined Titans played for the final shot. For three long minutes they passed the ball around. Then, with nine seconds to go, the ball went not to Davis, whom Tennessee was guarding closely, but to Ron Galbreath, who got open at the top of the key. His jump shot rimmed out, but the ball landed in the hands of 6-4 teammate Don McCaig, who put it back up for the final two points.

They had upset the champion, 39-38, but with that game the Cinderella team's magic had run out; they were blown away in the final by Southwest Texas, 66-44. The daring ball-control strategy Ridl chose could not be duplicated today. Under pressure from television broadcasters, college officials in the 1970s adopted the shot clock rule that requires teams to shoot within 35 seconds. "The shot clock takes a lot of strategy out of the game and makes it harder for teams with less firepower to pull an upset like we did," according to Galbreath.

The 1961-62 Titans, led by Little All-Americans Galbreath and Warren Sallade, were perhaps the best in a series of outstanding Ridl-coached teams. They played to a 26-3 season record, were picked by both the Associated Press and United Press International as the number one small college team in the country, and advanced to the NAIA finals in Kansas City, where they were routed by a towering team from Prairie View A&M of Texas led by future pro star Zelmo Beatty. The five starters on that Westminster team – Galbreath from Wampum; Sallade from New Wilmington; the Douds twins, Bill and Bob, from Fredonia; and Lou Skurcenski from Zelienople – all came from class B high schools within a 40-mile radius of the College. Ridl was named

A Game Like None Other

Although 1956 and 1977 were perfect football seasons in their own way, perhaps there was no more storied season than the undefeated, national championship season of 1988, and no game more breathtaking than its Dec. 10 finale against University of Wisconsin-LaCrosse, played on Westminster's snow-packed field in below-freezing temperatures.

Quarterback Joe Micchia was battling the flu, but with seconds remaining in the first half and trailing 7-0, he let fly a 17-yard pass into the outstretched fingers of Dave Foley in the end zone to tie the score. Trailing 14-7 with 3:35 to go in the second half, Micchia again hit Foley in the end zone to tie the game. Westminster's defense held, giving Micchia the ball on his own 15-yard line with 2:38 remaining on the clock. The Titan drive seemed to stall on Wisconsin-LaCrosse's 33-yard line. It was 4th and 10 with 13 seconds remaining when Micchia took the snap, spotted Foley racing down the left sideline and heaved the ball. As McTaggart, who was announcing the game, tells it, "He strained forward, keeping his balance, and felt the ball at his fingertips. He pulled it in and fell into the end zone, where the fans collapsed atop him." He had stayed in-bounds. There were no penalty flags. They had won. Press reports the next day recorded Fusco's reaction: "I've never been in a game like that, not in a national championship game, not with an ending like that." ◆

The 1961-62 basketball Titans were rated the number one small college team in the country.

NAIA Coach of the Year that year, and the Westminster and Grambling University teams were picked by the U.S. State Department and the Amateur Athletic Union to make a six-week goodwill tour of South America the following summer.

Women's Varsity Sports

True to its coeducation principles, Westminster moved quickly to include women's sports. But the record also suggests that women's sports were not taken very seriously except by those who participated. Support for women's sports took a big step forward when Marjorie Walker and Carolyn Bessy arrived in 1962 and moved into Old 77, abandoned by the men's basketball team in 1951 when the Field House opened.

The two women were hired to teach women's physical education and to coach intercollegiate coed teams in basketball, field hockey, tennis and volleyball, each team playing four to six games a season. They also taught an education course in health and phys ed for elementary education majors and supervised intramural programs in basketball, badminton, table tennis, softball, swimming and volleyball. In addition, they trained the cheerleaders, Mermaids and Titannaires (drill team). And they baked cookies, drove teams to away games in their own cars and scrubbed shelves, Walker recalled in 2000. She and Bessy were mistaken on at least one occasion for cleaning women.

Financial and institutional support for women's intercollegiate sports programs nationwide necessarily surged when Title IX of the federal Education Amendments became effective in July 1975, requiring parity between men's and women's varsity sports programs. The Keystone Conference was organized in 1975. Women from Westminster, Allegheny, Geneva, Grove City, Thiel, Mercyhurst, Behrend, and Villa Maria competed in four varsity sports – basketball, volleyball, tennis and softball – until the conference was dissolved in 1985.

As Walker recalled in her remarks at a ceremony dedicating the Marjorie A. Walker Recreation Center in Old 77 in February 2000, "In the mid-'70s we convinced Dr. Burry and Dean Lewis that jackets should be awarded to varsity athletes, cheerleaders and Titannaires. There are people sitting here tonight who still harass us because we didn't even buy them socks in the '60s and early '70s."

Men's football and basketball grabbed the headlines and the crowds, but the performance in other sports was good enough to bring Westminster the newly organized West Penn Conference's all-sports trophy for eight consecutive years from 1958-59 through 1965-66.

Political activities

Westminster continued its tradition – the third-oldest in the nation – of holding a mock presidential nominating convention every four years, usually for the party that did not currently occupy the White House. A convention has been held every presidential election year since 1936 except for 1944, when World War II disruptions squeezed out that extracurricular activity. As Republicans, students nominated Dwight D. Eisenhower in 1952 and 1956. Then, as Democrats for the first time, they nominated Adlai Stevenson in 1960. Pennsylvania Governor David L. Lawrence delivered the keynote address.

Westminster's long tradition of holding a mock presidential nominating convention continued into 2000, when student delegates nominated Ariz. Sen. John McCain.

Back in the GOP fold, students came up with Henry Cabot Lodge in 1964 but chose a Richard M. Nixon-Charles Percy ticket in 1968. As Democrats in 1972, students picked a George McGovern-John Lindsay pairing, then went with Jimmy Carter and Henry Jackson in 1976. In 1980, as Republicans, they bypassed Ronald Reagan in favor of a Gerald Ford-George Bush ticket, with Sen. Mark Hatfield providing the keynote address.

In 1984, as Democrats, they nominated Gary Hart and Jesse Jackson after hearing from Sen. Joseph Biden. It was a Michael Dukakis-Al Gore ticket for the Democrats in 1988. Dukakis showed up in 1992 to deliver the keynote, while students nominated Paul Tsongas and Barbara Roberts. In 1t996, after an Alan Keyes keynote, students came up with a Lamar Alexander/Colin Powell ticket for the Republicans. In 2000, student delegates to the 16th mock convention heard political commentator Robert Novak give the keynote speech, then nominated John McCain and Clint Eastwood.

Hamlet, presented in Old 77 in 1958.

Cultural and social activities

Students were two days late returning from Thanksgiving vacation in 1950 when a record snowfall dumped almost 30 inches on the town.

In November 1954 the Little Theatre celebrated its silver anniversary with a revival of *The Cat and the Canary*, a mystery thriller that had been presented 25 years before during the Theatre's first season. After the Beeghly Theater brought a larger stage and more sophisticated equipment in 1965, the music department collaborated with the theatre department on ambitious productions of popular musicals like *Man of LaMancha* (1972) and *Fiddler on the Roof* (1976). In January 1968 WKPS-FM, the College's first licensed broadcasting station, started daily operations at an FM frequency of 88.9 megahertz. Westminster's outstanding concert choir toured Europe in January 1974.

To add to the on-campus social life, students in January 1989 organized "Down Under" in the basement of Eichenhauer Hall as a non-alcoholic pub and more spacious alternative to the Student Union for dances, concerts and film presentations. ❖

—————————— CHAPTER 19 ——————————

Taking Back the College:
The Board Seizes Control

Three times in Westminster's history, once in each half-century, tensions and mistrust between the Board and the faculty or administration boiled over, causing a leadership crisis and a certain amount of turmoil in the operation of the College. In each case, a president perceived to have strong ties to the faculty (Patterson in 1866, Galbreath in 1946, and Carlson in 1981) left under pressure from the Board and was replaced immediately by a member of the Board (Browne, Cleland and Lauterbach). In each case, the successor had a troubled administration and needed to give way to a new president before stability returned.

In 1952, Westminster entered its third half-century still recovering from the Cleland upheaval. (See Chapter 12.) Both the collegial Galbreath and the authoritarian Cleland were gone. With Will Orr, the College was firmly in the hands of a strong president whose leadership and agenda were accepted and respected by both the faculty and the Board. With some grumbling, the faculty bowed to a regime in which it was their duty to teach and leave the broader management of the College up to the president and his administration. Through a painful process, the Board had chosen its president and recognized that it must support him. And Orr had the will and political skills to unite the College. Dissident faculty periodically were purged or left of their own accord, but Orr wanted to recruit a distinguished faculty and improve their compensation, so many teachers thrived in a circumscribed role during the Orr administration. Orr also had considerable influence over who served on the Board. It was a monarchy, generally benevolent, but it restored stability and ultimately quite a bit of harmony to the College.

The Hon. John L. Miller '23 presided over the Board from 1964-1978.

However, Orr did not resolve potential conflicts between the Board and the faculty; he froze them during a period when his personality could dominate both groups. After he retired in 1967, some old bones of contention began slowly to thaw.

A new direction, one favoring participation and cooperation among the various College constituencies, was apparent the moment new Board president John L. Miller organized a search committee to choose the College's president to succeed Orr. It included Miller as chairman, seven other trustees, a representative of the Alumni Association, and four members of the faculty including one chosen from the local chapter of the American Association of University Professors – a group long regarded as anathema by Orr and many trustees.

Other faculty members helped to screen the many prospects and probably influenced the choice of Earland I. Carlson, the first Westminster president to have both strong academic credentials and extensive experience in higher education. Except for Cleland, all the others had come directly from pastoral ministries. Carlson, 42, came from a position as vice president for academic affairs at Millikin University, Decatur, Ill., another Presbyterian college, so he was stepping into familiar territory. He had earned M.A. and Ph.D. degrees in history from the University of Illinois and had taught history at North Park and Colorado Colleges before returning to North Park as academic dean, then moving on to Millikin.

Carlson moved quickly, once he assumed the office in August 1967, to introduce participatory governance with active faculty involvement. The Board still contained many members who had strongly supported Orr's paternalistic approach, but there was no question that Carlson had the full support of Miller. In fact, one of the complaints sometimes voiced against Carlson was that he could not make significant decisions without first consulting Miller.

Within three months of taking office, Carlson initiated an inclusive self-evaluation program that produced a new faculty constitution adopted by the faculty Jan. 30, 1969, and approved by the Board the following March 7. The constitution clarified the legislative and advisory responsibilities of the faculty and established 16 standing committees with faculty members to be elected by the faculty instead of appointed by the president, as had been the case. Eight of the committees included student members elected by students. Twelve committees included administrative staff who served by virtue of their offices. The College was reorganizing to bring faculty, administration, and students into a closer working relationship.

In its new constitution, the faculty claimed a broad advisory role, allowing its members to "(1) participate in the definition of policy concerning its professional status, (2) assist the administration and Board of Trustees in selection of major administrative officers, and (3) consult with the administration and Board of Trustees on matters dealing with the long-range educational planning and the growth of the institution." But there was balance as well. Faculty-initiated changes in educational policy would "take effect only after such recommendations have been submitted by the executive committee of the College to the Board of Trustees and approved by the Board," the constitution read.

The professional rights and status of the faculty also were clarified and in some cases strengthened. A third-year review of faculty performance gave teachers a better idea of their prospects for tenure. The AAUP's statement on academic freedom and a clarification of Westminster's policy on tenure and dismissal were approved by both the faculty and Board in the fall of 1969. In 1972, a joint committee on student affairs was established that included student, faculty, administration, and Board representatives. In 1973, an educational policy committee was formed with similar representation.

Then, in 1978, two events occurred that caused a turning point not only in the Carlson administration but also in the College's history. First, Miller died on July 20. He was succeeded by Robert E. Lauterbach '39, recently retired head of Wheeling Pittsburgh Steel Corporation. Then Carlson was diagnosed with cancer and underwent surgery, followed by a period of recuperation. While academic dean Philip A. Lewis filled in for Carlson, Lauterbach also took a more active leadership role at this time. This may have been the beginning of the conflict that developed between the two men. The industrialist was destined to play a major and controversial role in the years that followed. His success in climbing the corporate ladder attracted attention and led to his election to the Board in October 1970. Shortly thereafter he accepted the role of general chairman of the 125 Fund. When that ambitious campaign exceeded expectations (see Chapter 17), and when Lauterbach's personal effectiveness as a fund-raiser for the College became apparent, his stock rose and he was elected vice president of the Board in 1972. His influence in Board deliberations also grew. Since vice presidents traditionally have succeeded to the presidency of the Board, interest in this outspoken, sometimes blunt, steel executive spread throughout the College community. Reports began to circulate of critical comments he had made about the faculty, causing him to be viewed on campus as a potential threat to academic freedom and faculty participation.

(The controversy surrounding Lauterbach generated a wide range of perceptions and a thin written record of facts. Lauterbach did grant the College historian one interview. I am particularly indebted to two trustees, the late Thomas V. Mansell and Fred Rentz, both members of the executive commit-

Robert E. Lauterbach '39, the former corporate CEO, emerged as a controversial figure during his stints as chairman of the Board of Trustees (1978-85) and interim president of the College (1981-82).

tee during the 1980-87 period, for confirming the accuracy of most of the material presented in this chapter.)

When Lauterbach became chairman of the finance committee, the bylaws were changed to give that committee responsibility for the College budget process in addition to overseeing the investment of the College endowment. When Lauterbach became chairman of the Board in 1978, the inner circle expanded to include the finance committee as well as the executive committee, which frequently met together to hammer out major policies that would be ratified by the Board.

Carlson recovered, but he now had a very different Board president to deal with, one reportedly out of sympathy with the democratic reforms that had marked the first ten years of his administration. Members of Carlson's staff privately expressed opinions that he was less in charge of events than he had been before his illness and before the death of Miller.

When Lauterbach was elected to succeed Miller in October 1978, he moved quickly to change his title to "chairman," a corporate touch. More significantly, changes to the College bylaws, passed in June 1979, gave him "access to all college property and records" and authority to "require reports in writing on any college business from any officer of the college." The president had lost his historic role as the only authorized channel of communication between the Board and the faculty and staff.

Also gone from the new bylaws were all references to the academic dean. Among the statements that vanished were the following: "the president and the academic dean shall consult with each other regarding the employment, tenure, changes in rank, and qualifications of the faculty," "the president, in consultation with the academic dean, shall direct and supervise established educational policies of the college," "the academic dean shall oversee the curriculum, instruction, and the academic aspects of the college," and "he [the dean] shall preside at faculty meetings in the absence of the president." The shrinking influence of the academic dean became even more obvious when Carlson was forced to resign in October 1981 and the Board departed from an unbroken tradition by naming Lauterbach rather than Dean Lewis as interim executive.

The struggle over who was in control of the College had reached a point in 1980 where staff turnover, especially in the area of development where Lauterbach had particular interest and influence, became conspicuous. From 1980 to 1987, when the arrival of Oscar Remick (much like the arrival of Will Orr 40 years earlier) finally ended the conflict, the College had six different presiding officers, five vice presidents for development (or its equivalent), five alumni directors and four directors of annual giving.

Eugene Haberman was hired as vice president for college relations and development in April 1980 but left after less than two months, explaining that internal conflict made it impossible for him to do the job. Shortly thereafter, Harry Shoup '39, director of development, and Dick Cochran, director of annual and deferred giving, were suddenly fired and given 24 hours to vacate their offices. Their abrupt dismissal sent shock waves throughout the College community; such treatment of high-level staff was unprecedented. Before leaving town, Shoup warned friends that Lauterbach was grabbing power; he predicted that within a few years Lauterbach would be sitting in the front office running the College. Shoup's comments, which spread quickly across the campus, added to the growing tensions.

Academic dean Phillip A. Lewis served as acting president during Carlson's medical leave of absence, and was later named vice president for academic affairs and dean of the College.

The next fall (September 1980), Paul Yackey was hired as vice president for college relations and development and Dean Lewis was given the title "vice president for academic affairs and dean of the College" to reinforce his position, Carlson explained, as ranking administrator in the absence of the president. The Challenge '80s campaign to raise $12 million was just getting under way, and Carlson assured the Board that he was in good health and committed to seeing the campaign through.

But the Board's commitment to Carlson was running out. It was Carlson's fate to preside over the College during a time of student rebellion. The phenomenon was national if not global, but the new attitudes toward sex, drugs and alcohol posed special problems for a church-related college in a small, conservative town. Accounts of rowdy drinking parties at the fraternity houses were causing growing concern among the faculty and townspeople. (See Chapter 18.) Some trustees grumbled that Carlson was too lenient with students.

He also was under pressure from the Board to be less liberal in granting faculty tenure. A tight job market for college faculty, starting in the early 1970s, had slowed the natural turnover, and colleges across the country were starting to see their percentages of tenured faculty rise. At the June 1980 Board meeting, Carlson asked the Board to reaffirm the current faculty personnel policies. Lauterbach responded that the Board wanted to change the implementation of current personnel policies. A motion that tenured faculty could be dismissed if the Board abolished instruction in their fields was then passed. Members of the faculty were concerned about changes in the tenure agreement without faculty consultation.

At the October 1980 Board meeting, Lauterbach excused the administrators who were present so that the Board could discuss an evaluation of Carlson. Although that evaluation was part of the self-study program, the Board's interest in Carlson's performance was hardly routine. That became evident at the next Board meeting (March 1981), when Lauterbach again excused the administrators so the Board could go into executive session to continue discussing the president. No minutes were kept during the executive sessions. The same scenario was repeated at the following Board meeting (June 1981). For three consecutive sessions, the Board had excused administrators for key parts of its deliberations. Carlson, Lewis, and treasurer James Christofferson regularly attended Board meetings, and other administrators sometimes attended.

The problem of wild fraternity parties came to a head when a freshman woman reported that she had been gang raped on Sept. 26, 1981, during a party in the Sigma Phi Epsilon house. Those allegations and the raid and drug arrests that followed were a major scandal, but no one was prepared for the shock that followed on Oct. 23, when an announcement was issued that Carlson had resigned, effective immediately, and that Lauterbach had been named "chief executive officer" of the College, also effective immediately. Never before had a Westminster president left so abruptly. Even in earlier periods of turmoil, provisions always had been made for an orderly transition. Earlier resignations usually were effective at the end of an academic year or as soon as a suitable replacement could be found. And always before, since the position was established in 1907, the academic dean had filled the role when a transitional executive was needed.

The fact that the College now had a retired steel company executive with no academic or ministerial experience sitting in the front office as CEO left the whole community stunned. Shoup's predictions, once dismissed as the angry words of a fired employee, were remembered with a shiver. In just 15 months, Lauterbach was indeed sitting in the front office and running the College. The CEO title added to suspicions. The College bylaws provided for no CEO. It was a corporate title and implied powers well beyond those normally wielded by a college president, who operated in a culture that was intentionally collegial.

Fears that Lauterbach would attempt to run the College like a corporation appeared to be confirmed when he promptly bypassed channels to bring back Paul Frary, a member of the business faculty who had left that fall. Frary was to start in February, even though the teaching schedule was already made up for the spring term, and he was to become department chairman effective with the fall term.

What brought about the sudden resignation of Carlson, and what was Lauterbach's agenda? Those questions preoccupied the College in the closing months of 1981. Carlson's resignation letter released by the College was brief, stating only that it was prompted by "personal and philosophical reasons" and was tendered "on my own initiative." Minutes of the Board and executive committee meetings shed little light on what was happening. Lauterbach reported to the executive committee at an Oct. 20 meeting at the Duquesne Club in Pittsburgh, with no College personnel present, that he had received an irrevocable resignation letter from Carlson. Following discussion, trustee Dave Fawcett moved that the executive committee recommend to the Board that Carlson's resignation be accepted with regret and that Lauterbach be named chief executive officer to assume the duties of president.

At the regular Board meeting on Oct. 23, Lauterbach presented Carlson's resignation and moved its acceptance. The motion was approved without dissent. Vice chairman Thomas V. Mansell then assumed the chair and moved approval of the executive committee's recommendation that Lauterbach be elected chief executive officer. The minutes record that his motion was approved unanimously with Lauterbach abstaining. No discussion was held. The Board appeared to be living up to its reputation as a rubber stamp for the executive committee.

Thomas V. Mansell '29 was an influential member and officer of the Board for an unprecedented 50 years (1938-88).

Lauterbach later said that he accepted the CEO position reluctantly, but the record shows that he never withdrew from executive committee or Board meetings to permit a free discussion of the situation. Carlson's communications with the executive committee and the Board in regard to his resignation came only through Lauterbach.

What was happening off the record surfaced largely in private but probably reliable comments made by key players at the time. Mansell told me that he had heard Lauterbach telling Carlson in strong terms, amounting almost to an ultimatum, that Carlson was going to have to take decisive action in regard to the fraternity scandal. And Carlson, in a moment of some emotion, reportedly told Joseph Henderson, chairman of the education department, "They wanted me to start throwing out students without due process."

Carlson was a due-process man to the core, which may account for the "philosophical" differences that led to his resignation.

And Mansell, Lauterbach's most conspicuous ally on the Board, privately explained to Henderson, "Carlson gave the College away to the faculty and now the Board has to get it back." Mansell's statement goes a long way toward explaining both the sudden change of leadership and the series of puzzling actions that the Board would subsequently take.

Sharing management with the faculty, a keystone of the Miller/Carlson program of participatory governance, now was viewed by the Lauterbach Board as a threat to the College's mission if not to its survival. Clearly the Board was convinced that it needed to reassert its authority. Yet, as this history shows, whenever the Board has stepped in to exert direct control over the College, the results have been disruptive.

Lauterbach's move into the front office raised immediate questions about how long he intended to stay. Would a search committee be appointed to find a new president? He answered rather vaguely that this would come later. Questions about the unprecedented concentration of power resulting from one person serving as both Board chairman and chief executive officer were also answered evasively. Those who hoped Lauterbach would be a transitional CEO were disappointed when he set out almost immediately to remodel the president's office, tearing out partitions and refurnishing to suit his taste. He also moved into the president's manse. Although Carlson's resignation was immediate, his severance agreement continued his salary through June 30, 1982, but required him to vacate the manse by Dec. 31.

Growing apprehensions resulted in some actions. Shortly after the Carlson resignation, the Alumni Council called a special meeting and drafted a request to the Board that a search committee be formed immediately to look for a new president. The faculty prepared a similar petition, adding that the undue concentration of power in one person should be corrected immediately. At a Dec. 15 faculty meeting Lauterbach announced that he would appoint Mansell as acting chairman of the Board. He also said that he was calling a special meeting of the Board for Jan. 15, at which time, "if everything is in place," he would recommend setting up a search committee with faculty representation.

The faculty was left to wonder what Lauterbach meant by "if everything is in place." At the January 1982 Board meeting, he presented a lengthy report, recounting activities of the past several weeks and expressing his conclusions that the College needed to make significant changes in leadership, control, enforcement of regulations, and governance. To successfully "modify past methods of governing," he would need the full support of the Board, he said, according to the minutes of that meeting. Following discussion Mansell indicated a Board consensus to support Lauterbach's agenda, "leading to proper controls and the reestablishment of administrative prerogatives." Clearly, as it had back in 1946-47, the Board was alarmed that participatory governance had weakened administrative control. Mansell, evidently satisfied that controls were now "in place," named a bona fide search committee, headed by trustee Fred Rentz, that included seven trustees, three faculty members and one alumni representative.

Those who expected Lauterbach to launch a tough financial retrenchment program also were surprised. The population of college-age young people began to decline around 1980, and other colleges had been making plans for an orderly reduction in faculty and staff. During his year in the front office, cost cutting was not a major issue, but he did place a high priority on retrenchment once Allen Splete became president in 1982. ❖

CHAPTER 20

Fiscal Squeeze from the Man of Steel

Major upheavals make it particularly difficult to recruit a new president. Candidates are leery about coming to a fractious institution, of course, and the search committee feels particularly driven to find the "right" person who can take charge, inspire confidence and restore cooperation. The search committee appointed by acting Board chairman Thomas V. Mansell on Jan. 15, 1982, advertised the Westminster presidency nationally that winter, and committee members were pleased when several applications arrived from apparently well-qualified candidates that spring. Lauterbach was dissatisfied with all of the candidates and advised the committee to discard all applications and start over. However, the search committee recommended Allen P. Splete, vice president for academic planning and special projects for 12 years at St. Lawrence University in Canton, N.Y. His résumé showed a wide range of academic, development and administrative experience, including participation in a $30 million fund-raising campaign. The Board was feeling real pressure to put a permanent president in the front office, so the executive committee and then the full Board on July 1, 1982, approved the selection of Splete, who took office in September and was formally inaugurated on April 30, 1983. Splete had earned his undergraduate degree at St. Lawrence, his master's at Colgate University, and his Ph.D. in higher education administration at Syracuse University, where he held several administrative posts from 1965-1970, including executive assistant to the provost and associate dean for academic affairs.

Westminster's 11th president, Allen P. Splete, guided the College from 1982-85.

The arrival of Splete appeared for a while to calm the waters. Lauterbach went back his position as chairman of the Board, and Mansell was once again vice chairman. History cast Splete in the role of rescuer, the man who, like Jeffers and Orr, would right the ship and restore harmony. But Splete either failed to grasp that role or, more likely, was denied the chance by a Board that saw him as its tool, not its leader, and was not yet ready to return management of the College to an academic administrator. Splete made a good impression on people, especially alumni, but he was never in charge like Jeffers and Orr had been and like Remick would be. Instead of ending the turmoil, the two-and-a-half-year Splete administration continued it.

Lauterbach and his supporters on the Board concluded that it was time to give the College a stiff dose of fiscal discipline, and Splete was the knife with which they meant to attack the College budget. The budget squeeze became apparent in the spring of 1983 when contracts for the following year revealed that faculty and staff salaries had been frozen, despite a $700-per-student increase in tuition and fees for the coming year. Then, at its June 6 meeting, the Board rejected the administration's proposed $13.5 million budget. The Board demanded that the budget be cut by another $814,000 and that those cuts come from reduced personnel and programs. Even if the College exceeded its 1,200 enrollment target and received more revenue than budgeted, those funds would go into the surplus column and not be used for operating expenses, the Board stipulated.

Lauterbach did not act alone, of course. He was able to persuade a working majority of the Board to support his policies. Certainly most members of the executive and finance committees, which Lauterbach appointed and which exercised considerable influence, closed ranks behind him on most but not all issues. Members of these committees made it clear that they believed the College faced a crisis and that tough, sometimes unpopular leadership from the Board was needed.

Exactly what that crisis was and what remedy was called for were unclear to many members of the campus community. At one point, it seemed to be a reassertion of conservative moral values, but Lauterbach's removal of the ban on drinking in fraternity houses undercut that theory. A philosophical quarrel with the participatory governance introduced by Miller and Carlson also may have played a role. But increasingly, once the Splete administration began, the Board seemed to focus on a perceived financial crisis and ways to rein in spending to protect Westminster's fiscal health. Faculty bore the brunt of the cost cutting. Some teachers grumbled that the Board was using finances as an excuse to implement an agenda that would put the faculty in its place as hired help.

Did Westminster face a financial crisis? Was that crisis severe enough to justify the controversies that were caused by the medicine prescribed by Lauterbach and his Board supporters? Finally, did their retrenchment medicine work? To answer those questions, we must enter a briar patch called financial statements. Colleges have unusual and highly complex financial statements, but we can isolate just a few key lines to show important trends. (Annual numbers in key categories are reproduced in Appendix C.) Nearly 70 percent of Westminster's educational and general operating income came from tuition and fees paid by students. Another 10 percent or so came from gifts from alumni and other benefactors that are not designated for specific purposes like a building fund. We will track those two sources of income. Another 10 percent or so of operating funds came from endowment income, which reflects investment performance. Smaller amounts came from state and federal grants and contracts, from short-term investment income and from miscellaneous income, all of which we will ignore in the interests of simplicity. (The College takes in and spends millions of dollars annually on room, board and other auxiliary enterprises, but in this period it consistently broke even – actually took in slightly more than it spent – so this was not a factor in the alleged financial crisis and also can be ignored in this analysis.)

The critical expense item to watch is "instruction and research," essentially the cost of paying the faculty and supporting its teaching activities. Because it increased dramatically during these years, we will also track "scholarships and grants," the monies the College actually pays out for financial aid in the form of outright grants. Pay for work done is not included in this line.

And of course we will track the total revenue and the total expenses and the net difference – the critical indicator of whether the College was operating in the red or the black. And finally, surplus operating funds often are added to the endowment, so we will track the annual contribution to (or withdrawal from) the endowment.

During the period from June 1976 to June 1981, the period leading up to the forced resignation of President Carlson in October 1981, the College showed a modest gain of 9.6 percent a year in revenue, on average, and a slightly higher 12.2 percent average annual gain in expenses, led by a 16.2 percent annual boost in financial aid spending. But so delicate was the balance between income and expenses that even this small difference in growth rates all but wiped out the surplus in five years, as it fell from $652,316 to $51,184. The College was on the verge of deficit operations when income bounced back a bit in 1980-81 and the surplus edged back up to $109,435. Lackluster fund raising of private gifts played a part. Paying for Westminster's faculty grew at a 7.2 percent average annual rate, below the growth rate for either total revenue or total expenses.

Then, almost four months into the 1981-82 fiscal year, Lauterbach replaced Carlson. During that year, revenue was up a very healthy 15.3 percent, while expenses also rose more than usual, but at a slightly slower 14.7

percent rate, allowing the annual surplus to double to $214,072, still below the level of three years earlier. Giving was back up above the $1 million mark but now failed to offset expenditures for financial aid, which had equaled half the amount raised by private gifts back in 1976-77. Spending on the faculty was up a surprising 32 percent.

Then Splete took over, two months into the 1982-83 fiscal year, and the battle over financial retrenchment was joined. During the Splete years, the operating surplus started at a very thin $35,721 and grew to a respectable $273,192. Revenue dipped ever so slightly that first year (1 percent), while expenses edged up (0.8 percent), making the surplus perilously thin again. Then both revenue and expenses were up noticeably in 1983-84 but the slightly larger gain in revenue doubled the small surplus. Then revenue actually declined in 1984-85, a rare event, but the College was able to shrink expenses even more, resulting in a healthier $273,192 surplus, the best since 1977-78. Was retrenchment working? The numbers suggest that it was. Spending on faculty actually decreased in each fiscal year during the years of the Splete administration, falling by 4.6 percent over a period when revenue increased by 8.5 percent.

What happened after June 1985 when Jerry M. Boone was named acting president, when Jack B. Hoey replaced Lauterbach as Board chairman, when the confrontation over retrenchment subsided and when the College opened its 1985-86 fiscal year? The first year saw the surplus slip to $62,023 but then begin a rally that led to the College's first million-dollar surplus by 1988-89, the second year of the Remick administration. The decline in enrollment bottomed out in 1986-87 and the return to growth, coupled with rising tuition and fees, brought strength back to revenue, even though private giving remained essentially flat. Average annual spending on the faculty increased by just 5.3 percent during this period, while revenue was rising by 14.2 percent.

The numbers do not indicate a College on the verge of bankruptcy. At no time during this period did the College fail to show an annual operating surplus. The draconian measures Lauterbach and the Board tried to impose are usually reserved for institutions in worse financial shape. Nevertheless, the drift during the closing years of the Carlson administration was clearly toward operating deficits, largely because of a national decline in college admissions. And the changes that avoided those deficits more or less coincided with the time when Lauterbach and his backers were pushing their case aggressively.

Back in the years immediately after World War II when the Board injected itself directly into an effort to control and discipline the faculty (see Chapter 12), the job market made it easy for teachers to move on to other jobs, and nearly half of them did so over a two-year period. When a similar confrontation occurred in 1981-85, the job market for college teachers was tight. The faculty protested their treatment by the Board, but there was no general exodus this time, although turnover on the administrative staff was high.

At that June 1983 meeting, the Board launched a frontal attack on tenure. They moved to cap the percentage of faculty that could receive tenure and to permit open-ended employment of non-tenured faculty. This was a significant departure from the Statement on Academic Tenure that the trustees and faculty had adopted mutually in 1969. On Jan. 16, 1984, Splete asked the faculty personnel committee to prepare a response to the Board. The committee met later that month and agreed to oppose the Board plan. Department chairmen met separately and also announced their opposition. A January 30 memo from the faculty personnel committee to Splete reported that "the faculty does not support the proposal for term contracts," but indicates that the faculty was "willing to consider certain revisions" if the same participatory process used in 1969 to adopt the tenure policy were followed.

The assault on tenure continued. Lauterbach presented a detailed plan for further changes that was approved by the Board on March 13, 1984. The plan included redefinition of tenure, abolishing tenure and use of contracts for specified periods, and a layoff program giving the president authority to reduce faculty in various departments based on declining enrollment. From this point on, relations between the faculty and the Board deteriorated rapidly. Splete was caught in the middle.

Over-tenuring was a real, recognized problem by the 1980s, and many college boards and administrations were looking for ways to preserve turnover and the benefits of fresh blood. During Carlson's presidency, the percentage of tenured faculty had grown from less than 50 percent to nearly 70 percent, and even many faculty members agreed that something should be done about it. Other colleges had adopted departmental or faculty-wide quotas. Westminster's faculty was prepared to consider such solutions, but they wanted a voice in policy changes that would have such direct impact on their job security.

The Board, while insisting that it could act unilaterally, did invite some faculty input. An ad hoc tenure committee, chaired by Robert F. Patton, included three trustees and five faculty members. While the committee searched diligently for a middle ground, the Board and faculty continued to polarize around their own positions. The Board increased tensions by holding up faculty contracts for 1984-85, as well as tenure for four teachers who had passed the faculty and administrative reviews. Unfortunately, very little was accomplished to solve the tenure problem. The faculty, on Nov. 3, 1984, passed a resolution stating that "any unilateral modifications of the content of the Westminster College Faculty Handbook are not and will not be accepted by the faculty of Westminster College."

Meanwhile, Splete was working with faculty committees and department chairmen on a five-year program that would eliminate several staff positions and not replace faculty who resigned or retired. College catalogs show that enrollment declined by about 10 percent and faculty by about 9 percent during the two and a half years that Splete worked on retrenchment. But the Board kept pressuring him to make quicker decisions and deeper cuts.

Everyone knew that tensions were high, but Splete seemed to be struggling to reconcile the two sides. Therefore, it came as a real surprise on Jan. 18, 1985, when the Board announced that Splete had resigned, effective immediately, and would be replaced, also immediately, by Robert Johns, who would serve as interim president for two and a half years. Most people who heard the announcement were unfamiliar with Johns, even though he had attended Westminster from 1938 to 1940 and was the son of William A. Johns, College admissions and placement director from 1932-57. The abrupt departure of Splete, just three and a quarter years after the very similar abrupt departure of Carlson, alarmed many faculty and alumni. Inevitably, many of the faculty suspected the hand of Lauterbach in these developments.

They were right. The Board held its regular meeting at the College on the morning of Oct. 26, 1984, then reconvened in executive session that afternoon at the New Castle Country Club. A quorum (19 of 28) was present, and minutes were kept of the executive session. Lauterbach presented a report from a secret committee that had been set up to evaluate Splete's performance. The report recommended "that we should proceed forthwith with plans for the expeditious removal of the president... that we give the authority and flexibility to successfully carry out the task to the Executive Committee with

'Lack of Confidence' Letter

The Alumni Council made an unprecedented effort to intervene in the perceived leadership crisis with a March 2, 1985, letter to the Board. It included the following points:

"**Leadership.** In light of a current lack of confidence in the Board of Trustees and in the best interest of Westminster, we recommend that other trustees be elected to fill the offices of chairman and vice chairman. We feel that without this action the Board's operations will be seriously and permanently handicapped.

Interim President. We recommend that an interim president be appointed as soon as possible from among those persons knowledgeable of Westminster College's philosophy and operations. Because of the lack of confidence in the Board which now exists, a current trustee should not be selected.

Search System. A search system should be instituted for the selection of a new president. Key College constituencies (including the Alumni Council) should be represented on the search committee." ◆

subsequent reporting to the Board; that our primary purpose is to find a replacement in a confidential manner before advising the president." The Board then approved these recommendations. The trustees kept their secret well; when the axe fell almost three months later, nearly everyone was caught by surprise.

Once the initial shock had been absorbed, attention turned to Johns. People of campus naturally wanted to know whether he was a legitimate college president who might provide critical leadership or an obliging puppet whose strings would be pulled by the Board. His résumé was reassuring. He had served as president of three colleges and vice president of several others. But photocopies of a story published in the Oct. 11, 1982, *St. Louis Post-Dispatch* began to appear within days after his appointment was announced. According to that article, one university had bought out his contract because he proved "difficult to work with." He had been forced to resign from another when charges of financial mismanagement were raised. A third had fired him amid allegations that included "running a one-man show," unauthorized hiring and sexual harassment, the newspaper reported. The Johns appointment was doomed. On Jan. 26, just eight days after his appointment, Johns withdrew and returned all advance compensation given him by the College. The executive committee then hired him as a consultant and asked him to prepare a report about the College's long-range needs.

Some of the faculty who worked closely with Splete had their own doubts about his leadership ability, but the prevailing impression was that he was earnest, reasonable, accessible, well spoken and struggling to do a very difficult job. When an essentially popular president was sacked abruptly, less than three years after he was hired, and his replacement, a man with a tainted past, was forced to withdraw, howls of protest were heard. The faculty, after several meetings, passed a resolution on Feb. 12, 1985, that included a vote of no-confidence in the Board's executive committee, a request that Lauterbach resign as both chairman and a member of the Board, and an appeal that Dean Lewis be named interim president. The Alumni Council met in emergency session on March 2 and drafted a letter sent to all trustees. (See "'Lack of Confidence' Letter.") The executive committee of the Westminster Parents Association also met on Feb. 10 and wrote a letter to the trustees expressing deep concern about recent events at the College.

These unprecedented protests by faculty, alumni and parents created expectations that the March 1985 Board meeting, which included the election of Board officers, might prove decisive, but the same officers were reelected by a 16-8 vote with one abstention, and no change of strategy was indicated. Reports began to circulate that the eight trustees elected by the alumni supported the prevailing sentiment of their constituents that a change in leadership and direction was needed but that the 20 trustees elected by the Board felt that they should stand firm against all pressures to undercut their authority and their agenda.

At that March meeting, the Board did try to name Lewis acting president until an interim president could be found, but the dean instead submitted his resignation, effective June 30. No search committee was authorized, but, after considering a number of prospects, the ad hoc committee of faculty and Board members recommended, and the Board approved, the appointment of Jerry M. Boone as interim president at its June 3 meeting.

What the Board expected Johns and then Boone to accomplish as interim presidents was unclear. Many thought the Johns report would contain the Board's blueprint for retrenchment. Suspicions on campus grew when the Board decided to keep the Johns report under wraps, but the Board may have had a different reason for not releasing the report: It basically supported the faculty position. The November 1983 proposal of the faculty personnel committee that the Board had rejected was called "sound and, although parts of it may be difficult to implement, every reasonable effort should be made to consider it in making adjustments in the number of personnel," the report concluded.

Following the Boone appointment, Lauterbach stepped down as chairman of the Board and was replaced by Hoey, a business executive (president of the People's Gas Company, Pittsburgh) whom Lauterbach had recruited. Hoey shared many of Lauterbach's fiscal goals but proved to be flexible and pragmatic, a good listener and negotiator. It was a while before people realized it, but the five-year effort by elements of the Board to assert management authority was over.

Jack B. Hoey, former president of the People's Gas Company, ascended to the Board's chair in 1985.

Lauterbach's role was unique in the College's history. No other Board president/chairman ever had as much influence over the affairs for the College. The period from Miller's death in 1978 until Lauterbach's resignation in 1985 could appropriately be called "the Lauterbach years." He did not succeed in "taking the College back from the faculty," but he certainly demonstrated that in a tight job market, you could freeze pay or delay contracts and teachers would grumble but not leave. More significantly, he delivered a bitter dose of fiscal discipline that probably strengthened the College's financial health.

Dean of students
Jerry M. Boone
was named acting
president in 1985
after the resignation
of Allen Splete.

Boone had been dean of students at Westminster for three years when he became interim president, and he set out to rebuild a college with a decimated administrative staff, an unfinished financial retrenchment program and a mutually suspicious faculty and Board. At his first faculty meeting on June 6, 1985, he was able to announce that the Board had elected new officers. The faculty that had expressed no confidence in the executive committee just four months before now passed a resolution commending the Board for choosing new leaders and expressing a desire to work closely with them.

To fill the vacancy at academic affairs, Boone picked Clarence Harms, chairman of the biology department, as interim dean. Harms agreed to serve temporarily, with the understanding that he would return to the biology department once a permanent dean could be found. Both Boone and Harms were respected, even popular figures on campus, and their elevation brought an immediate rebound in faculty morale. The two men had plenty of other senior vacancies to fill: director of alumni affairs, director of public relations, director of annual fund/deferred giving, director of admissions, registrar, head librarian and director of the physical plant. While the upheaval took its toll on the administration, relatively few senior members of the teaching faculty left.

Hoey and the Board still expected their president to balance the budget, trim personnel and reduce the percentage of tenured faculty, but they went along when Boone argued that stability and trust needed to be re-established first. Hoey and Boone had differences of opinion but developed a good working relationship.

The key to a balanced budget and avoiding faculty job loss was maintaining enrollment. There was an essential ratio between the number of paying students who showed up and the number of teachers the College could afford to pay. In the fall of 1985 enrollment dropped from 1,321 the previous year to 1,150, a much larger decline than anticipated, but Boone's team, supported by the new Board leaders, attacked this problem and brought enrollment back up to 1,176 in the fall of 1987, then to 1,217 in the fall of 1987. The size of the faculty was reduced by seven for 1986-87 and increased by two for 1987-88. A 6 percent increase in student fees for 1986-87 helped to offset a 6 percent increase in the budget for salaries. Raises were not dispensed across-the-board, however. Boone and Harms found that some employees, especially women, were underpaid and moved to correct that discrimination. Student charges were adjusted to reflect actual costs, with the result that, for

1987-88, tuition went up 9.4 percent, room charges 6.9 percent, and board was cut by 13.3 percent. The total package ($9,420) rose 5.4 percent.

Meanwhile, the search for a permanent president moved forward. The Board restricted the actual search committee to trustees but enlisted faculty, alumni and students representatives for an advisory committee, and the two committees sometimes met together.

Boone was one of many candidates for the permanent presidency as the search expanded. Early in the process the name of Oscar E. Remick surfaced. Remick had put himself and Alma College in Michigan on the map by attracting national publicity about its academic program and organizing successful fund-raising campaigns. He rebuffed an early job feeler, saying that he still had much to accomplish at Alma. As the June 1986 deadline for finding a new president approached, Robert F. Patton, chairman of the search committee, asked for an extension. He wanted to get Remick to change his mind. Boone and Harms agreed to stay on a second year in their interim capacity, but at this point Boone withdrew as a candidate for the Westminster presidency and accepted an offer to become president of Ferrum College in Virginia.

In November 1986, Remick finally agreed to make an exploratory visit to Westminster to evaluate the situation, share his findings with the Board and determine if he might become a candidate. That visit produced results, and on Feb. 10, 1987, the Board announced that Remick would become Westminster's twelfth president on July 1. Unlike Splete, Remick would enjoy the full backing of the Board and faculty and bring back stability and collegial cooperation to the College, a happy situation that endured as the College celebrated its 150th birthday. ❖

—————— CHAPTER 21 ——————

Student Consumers:
Packaging and Selling College Education

T he period from the end of World War II until the twenty-first century saw sweeping social, cultural and economic changes in the nation that had a major impact on higher education in general and especially on private liberal arts colleges like Westminster. The revered concept of the liberal arts education – on which Westminster, like so many other small private colleges, was founded – came under pressure on several fronts. It survived at Westminster, but not without changing. Those forces of change can be grouped under three overlapping headings:

- ◆ **The democratization of higher education.** The so-called G.I. Bill that flooded college campuses with World War II veterans at mid-century profoundly reshaped colleges socially, economically and academically. No longer was college a training ground for would-be professionals from well-to-do families. Higher education was reinvented as a classless entitlement, available to all academically qualified students who applied. Financial aid became a right.

- ◆ **Increased demand for vocational training.** With great strides in science and technology, rapid population growth and the emergence of a global economy, how people earned their livings changed dramatically. Demand for focused, practical pre-employment education grew as on-the-job training became inadequate for a growing number of jobs. The line between professional and labor employment faded. No longer could a college or university focus on educating a few well-defined professional groups. A host of community colleges and vo-tech schools sprang up to help meet this need, and more traditional colleges and universities revamped their offerings and repositioned themselves in this new market. For Westminster and its peers, it meant finding a new balance between a traditional liberal arts curriculum and a responsive, vocationally oriented curriculum.

  John Forry, English professor and academic dean, was largely responsible for reviving the College's liberal arts emphasis in the 1960s.

- ◆ **Market influences.** A radical shift in supply and demand occurred as many new colleges, university branches and specialized institutions entered the market, especially in the 1950s and 1960s, followed by a flattening of the population growth curve that eventually led to a scarcity of college-age young people by the 1970s and 1980s. After more than a century in which young people competed against their peers to get into good colleges, good colleges found they had to compete aggressively against each other to attract a sufficient number of qualified students. This shift of power to the student-consumer forced colleges to embrace a marketing mentality and apply it to how they designed and sold their curricula to prospective students and their parents. The result was that popular curriculum designs, academic calendars, courses and even grading policy came to dominate higher education. More than ever before, Westminster (like so many of its peers) confronted a need to package the education it offered as a marketable commodity.

Vocational Influences

In theory, liberal arts colleges produced individuals with well-rounded educations and the ability to think and articulate. How they used that education to find their vocation was not the college's concern, although colleges jealously guarded their reputations for turning out students well prepared for post-graduate education or teaching. In practice, Westminster like many of its peers could be flexible and pragmatic, responding to changing needs and opportunities. As we have seen (Chapter 6), Westminster was founded largely to educate future teachers and clergymen and provided an English and scientific course, alongside the more traditional classical track, as a more practical way to prepare future school teachers. As early as 1903, the College offered courses in "education" that could be considered vocational.

And during the Depression, when vocational anxiety was high, Westminster attracted students with its two-year secretarial training program, as noted in Chapter 10. But until the post-war influx of new students, there was a clear philosophical line between vocational training and a liberal arts education, and Westminster could meaningfully be defined as a liberal arts college. By 1990, that line was a blur.

When author David Breneman, a former liberal arts college president, began research on a book about the future of the liberal arts college, he was surprised to discover that instead of the 600 or so he expected to find, only 212 colleges in the country met his criteria. Westminster was not on that list, published in the October 1990 *Bulletin of the American Association of Higher Education*. By Breneman's standards, a liberal arts college granted no more than 60 percent of its degrees in vocational programs. In 1990, Westminster awarded slightly over 61 percent of its degrees in vocational programs.

While there has been a general consensus over the years that Westminster should preserve its liberal arts heritage and that its forays into vocational training should be limited, opinion has varied, and there have been swings both toward and away from vocationalism. As we might expect, faculty teaching history, language, literature, religion, philosophy and the arts have tended to champion Westminster's liberal arts tradition, while those teaching vocational subjects defended the importance of such study.

Some of the vocational inroads of the 1930s and 1940s were abandoned in the late 1950s and early 1960s while John Forry was academic dean. Journalism, introduced in 1934, was phased out of the curriculum in the late 1950s. Rocky relations between President Orr and the journalism faculty and students, many of whom wrote for the *Holcad*, may have contributed to the demise of journalism. But the decision made in the early 1960s to drop the separate secretarial and business education offerings was clearly a curriculum reform; a position as coordinator of audio-visual aids was created for Robert F. Galbreath Jr., who had headed those programs. His business education department was folded into the Department of Economics and Business Administration in September 1962.

An effort also was made at that time to limit the number of students majoring in the two large vocational programs, elementary education and business administration, by restricting admissions of students planning majors in those areas, but that attempt proved ineffective because students weren't required to declare majors before being admitted and were free to change majors afterwards. Those two fields continued to attract large numbers of students.

Another step was the extension in June 1960 of the core curriculum standards to all students, including business, music and education majors. All were required to take two semesters of freshman composition, including an introduction to literary genres; an introduction to the humanities (a survey of the literatures, religions, and philosophies that had shaped western civilization); a fine arts survey; a speech course; three religion courses; two semesters of a laboratory science; one or two years of a foreign language; a history course; and at least one course in sociology or psychology and one in political science or economics. On paper at least, a broad education was guaranteed.

During the 1960s, vocational degrees were dropped, including bachelor of music education (1963), bachelor of science in education (1963), and bachelor of business administration (1967). The master of science in education degree was changed back to the master of education in 1964. These changes brought the College back to three long-standing undergraduate degrees: bachelor of arts, bachelor of science, and bachelor of music. Along with the master of education, these continued to be the only degrees offered by Westminster from 1967 through 2002.

Efforts were made to enrich the liberal arts experience. In the fall of 1960 Westminster joined the Washington Semester Program of American University in Washington, D.C., providing opportunity for students to study the national government in action by spending one semester of their junior year in Washington. But the swing toward liberal arts was moderate; some programs with vocational overtones were developed. For example, in the spring of 1963 the United Presbyterian Church officially approved Westminster's Christian education program.

And practical accommodations were made for students in a hurry. In October 1962 the Board approved, on recommendation of the faculty, an advanced graduation program that made it possible for students to finish in three years by continuing through two or three summers. The summer school program was extended to enable students to earn 12 hours if they attended two five-and-a-half-week terms.

By the late 1960s and early 1970s, the academic pendulum was swinging away from prescribed requirements like Westminster's 1960 core curriculum toward a program that gave students more freedom of choice. While student unrest across the country focused primarily on social and political problems, a more militant generation of students may have made colleges more responsive to curriculum changes they favored.

In August 1967, Earland Carlson arrived as Westminster's first president with substantial experience in higher education. He came from Millikin University in Illinois, where he had been vice president for academic affairs and where a new 4-4-1 academic calendar recently had been adopted. A year later, Phillip Lewis arrived from Hastings College in Nebraska to become Westminster's academic dean. Both men were aware of the trend in U.S. colleges toward a more open curriculum, and they wanted to open doors to change at Westminster.

As part of the comprehensive self-study program put in motion by Carlson, a committee was set up to study academic calendars. This committee recommended changing to the 4-1-4 calendar, which was growing in popularity at that time. This calendar included a January term in which students took only one course, sandwiched between two compressed semesters in each of which students normally took four classes. The 4-1-4 calendar was approved by the faculty and Board in the spring of 1969, to become effective for the 1970-71 academic year.

The move to 4-1-4 had vocational overtones. In January 1971, Westminster initiated a field experience/internship program; students could earn academic credit by serving as interns in offices, public schools, laboratories, and social service agencies. Originally limited to the January term, the program was extended in 1976 to include internships that lasted for a full semester (four months) or even the entire academic year. With the transition to 4-1-4, the freshman composition, humanities and fine arts requirements disappeared. The lone writing requirement was essentially remedial; able students could test out of the course. Students could also test out of the foreign language requirement or satisfy it with high school credits. Students had to choose four from a long list of humanities and fine arts courses and two each from lists of social and natural science offerings. Only one religion course was required. Students were not inhibited from choosing the easiest courses or the most popular professors. High enrollment was a measure of faculty success; teachers were implicitly encouraged to sell their courses to students who were shopping for an agreeable schedule.

It was inevitable that such a sweeping change from the traditional calendar and curriculum would meet with some opposition from the faculty. Some objected that the January term courses, which could not be regular catalog courses, together with the dilution of area requirements, would undermine the academic integrity of the College. There was also concern about the teaching load, which at first was supposed to be seven courses per year. When that was changed to six, faculty opposition diminished. Also many faculty members came to enjoy the prospect of designing their own courses, including travel seminars. Once 4-1-4 was approved, by a substantial majority of the faculty, it became so popular that when Oscar Remick later wanted to eliminate the January term, it took another selling job to get the faculty to give up 4-1-4.

By the late 1970s, after a couple of recessions and a much tighter job market, students and their parents were looking harder at what colleges could offer in the way of post-graduate employment prospects. And members of the faculty at this time, worried about their own job security, were looking for ways to attract students. In this atmosphere, majors that seemed to offer vocational advantage flourished.

At Westminster, at some point during the 1977-1990 period, a student could major in computer science, industrial relations, management science, international economics and business, health science, environmental science, international politics, computer information systems, telecommunications, organizational behavior, cognitive science, information arts, accounting, and public relations. Most such majors were modular constructions, built from existing course offerings, internships and independent study but packaged and rationalized as coherent fields of study.

The inevitable reaction came in 1997, when the College revised its curriculum to re-emphasize what it called "liberal studies." Distribution requirements returned. All freshmen had to take two four-hour interdisciplinary courses, Inquiry I and II, taught largely from a common syllabus by faculty from many different departments. These courses explored human society, culture and different value systems. Students also had to take a pair of two-hour courses in written and oral communication, later expanded to two separate four-hour courses, both of which were required. Liberal Studies also required all students to take at least one "cluster" of two linked courses from different disciplines. For example, a literature professor teaching children's literature and a psychology professor teaching child psychology might "cluster" their courses and offer them in consecutive time slots. Students would register for the cluster, and the teachers normally would attend each other's classes. Typically about six clusters were offered each semester.

Traditional area requirements gave way to "intellectual perspectives." To graduate a student had to take at least one course in each of seven different areas:

- ◆ Foreign languages,
- ◆ Religious and philosophical thought and tradition,
- ◆ Humanity and culture,
- ◆ Quantitative reasoning,
- ◆ Scientific discovery,
- ◆ Social thought and tradition and,
- ◆ Visual and performing arts.

Faculty were expected to make these courses somewhat interdisciplinary, integrative and intellectually stimulating. Seniors concluded with an advanced "capstone" course, sometimes lasting two semesters, in their major. The course was intended to integrate the major into the broader liberal arts education. To implement the new curriculum, Westminster received a three-year $230,000 grant from the U.S. Department of Education Fund for the Improvement of Post-Secondary Education. The impact of computers, the Internet and information technology on Westminster's curriculum is so important that it requires a chapter of its own – Chapter 23.

A Marketable Education

Westminster had long walked a fine line between sensitivity to the needs of students and maintaining the rigor and integrity of its academic program. But in the 1970s, market influences became increasingly difficult to ignore. A drop in the birth rate back in the 1950s finally hit colleges with a drop in the number of college-age young people. A decade of aggressive expansion of two-year community colleges exacerbated the problem. Suddenly, too many colleges were chasing too few students. Scarce students became customers to be wooed rather than applicants to be screened. A college education was packaged and sold, often with the aid of marketing professionals.

The influence of marketing was conspicuous in the inflation of college grades. As the quality of high school education declined, colleges like Westminster had to lower admission standards. Yet grades went up. Graduating *summa cum laude*, once a rare feat, became commonplace. The Westminster class of 1960, for example, included 16 of 144 who graduated with honors (11 percent), none with *summa*. The class of 1980 included 102 honors graduates in a class of 344 (almost 30 percent), including seven *summas*.

New groups of potential students were courted. In September 1975 Westminster initiated an experimental Lifelong Learning Program, designed to appeal to older employed or married students by granting some credit for learning outside the classroom and allowing them to earn a bachelor's degree through supervised semi-independent study.

Ancient languages, the bulwark of Westminster's first curriculum, had limited market appeal by the 1980s (and were briefly considered for extinction in the retrenchment heat of 1983-84). However, Westminster continued to offer a Latin major and a Greek minor in 2002, its sesquicentennial year.

Market influences naturally got stronger as enrollment dropped and weaker as it rose. Undergraduate enrollment, which had been subsiding from the post-war G.I. boom, hit bottom at 789 in 1953. In that year, there were 242 students enrolled in the graduate program, 17 special students and 29 student nurses enrolled in college courses designed to supplement the nurses training program at Jameson Hospital in New Castle, a Westminster program that ran from 1952 until 1983. Thus, there was a total enrollment of 1,077. After that, it began to rise until total enrollment topped 2,000 for the first time in 1966-67 with 1,427 undergraduates, 547 graduate students, 40 nurses, and 26 specials for a total of 2,040.

The "Annual Enrollment: 1950-2000" graph, which tracks undergraduate enrollment rather than total enrollment, shows a long, steady climb from 1954 to 1970. Most of those years coincided with the Orr administration (1949-67) when Orr was raising funds and erecting buildings to handle the strong growth in the size of the student body. As undergraduate enrollment approached the 1,500 mark, he decided that it would be wise to cap enrollment at 1,600 as the optimum size for Westminster – a number his expanded campus could accommodate comfortably. In fact, it peaked at 1,560 in 1970. In the late 1960s and early 1970s, so many well-qualified students were applying that the College could stay within that cap by raising admission standards. As the graph shows, enrollment reached a plateau by 1970 and remained relatively stable during the next decade.

Annual Enrollment: 1950-2000

Figures are given for the fall term undergraduate enrollment and do not include special students or graduate students.

1950	922	1967	1,476	1984	1,196
1951	816	1968	1,486	1985	1,155
1952	805	1969	1,520	1986	1,134
1953	789	1970	1,560	1987	1,193
1954	795	1971	1,550	1988	1,263
1955	847	1972	1,524	1989	1,389
1956	863	1973	1,530	1990	1,420
1957	891	1974	1,525	1991	1,380
1958	935	1975	1,474	1992	1,387
1959	1,007	1976	1,517	1993	1,409
1960	1,013	1977	1,538	1994	1,433
1961	1,076	1978	1,527	1995	1,441
1962	1,105	1979	1,505	1996	1,362
1963	1,197	1980	1,460	1997	1,353
1964	1,215	1981	1,439	1998	1,363
1965	1,367	1982	1,326	1999	1,371
1966	1,427	1983	1,305	2000	1,357

Then enrollment dropped precipitously between 1981 and 1986, when the pool of eligible high school graduates ebbed. Those were the years of Lauterbach, Splete and retrenchment, covered in Chapters 19 and 20. By the second year of Jerry Boone's interim presidency (1986-87), it had begun to rise again.

To maintain enrollment, Westminster's academic leaders have had to become pragmatic about market influences. "We need to organize ourselves in ways that our prospective clientele – the students we hope to attract – can recognize as meeting their needs," vice president and academic dean John Deegan explained in a 2000 interview. If you want to see market influences, he suggested, "go to a college fair. The colleges represented display their materials, and future students walk up and down the aisles browsing and asking questions."

Deegan shed some light on how curriculum development occurred at the close of the twentieth century. At President Tom Williamson's request, Westminster compared itself to a group of other colleges – peers, competitors and role models – to see where it was missing opportunities. It came up short in the area of health-related professions, clearly a vocational area but "one of the fastest-growing sectors of our economy," Deegan noted. So Westminster made plans to institute a physical therapy program, not by adding expensive faculty, courses and labs but by packaging courses already in the curriculum and arranging with Duquesne University in Pittsburgh for Westminster's physical therapy students to transfer there after four years to take their clinical work at Duquesne. After that, when a student at a college fair asked, "Do you offer physical therapy?" Westminster would have something to offer him, Deegan explained.

"Colleges like Westminster, with modest endowments, are heavily dependent on tuition income," he noted. "If we don't get the students, it undermines our ability to carry out our mission. What meets the needs of one generation of students doesn't necessarily work for another generation. What we teach reflects the world we live in."

The Graduate Program

The resurgence of graduate education, especially in the College's third half-century, had little or no effect on the undergraduate curriculum but broadened the College's educational mission. This may have helped to attract faculty in some departments, consistently provided a net contribution to earnings, and sometimes helped to recruit undergraduate students by cultivating good relations with their high school teachers, principals and guidance counselors. That program waxed and waned as it positioned itself to meet the needs for certification and continuing education of public school educators – and as it faced changing competition from other institutions.

As we have seen (Chapters 6 and 10), Westminster moved quickly into both pre-college and post-graduate education in its first decade but withdrew from graduate education in 1912. The College reentered the ranks of the graduate degree-grantors in 1945, just in time for the post-war boom in both undergraduate and graduate enrollment. At that time, Westminster became the first college or university between Cleveland and Pittsburgh to offer an M.S. in education (subsequently a master of education). Graduate students, generally teachers from western Pennsylvania and eastern Ohio who commuted to night and summer classes, could earn the degree by taking 36 course credits or 30 course credits and writing a master's thesis. Until 1967, an oral examination also was required, but it was dropped when enrollment grew so large that it became difficult to schedule so many individual exams. The premise of the graduate program was frankly vocational, of course, but included liberal arts courses (e.g., high school history teachers took courses taught by history professors). The number of liberal studies credits required for a M.Ed. dropped from six in 1945 to three by 2000.

Education professor Joseph Henderson headed the College's graduate program from 1960-1980.

Largely under the leadership of Lewis H. Wagonhorst (1949-60), Joseph R. Henderson (1960-80) and Samuel A. Farmerie (1980-99), the graduate program was crafted to provide to teachers, administrators and staff specialists of the public school systems the training they needed to be effective and especially the courses they needed to meet the growing requirements for certification and advanced degrees. The core program was a master of education degree that would meet the continuing education requirements of classroom teachers and qualify them for a higher spot on the salary scale. But as school administration and specialized instruction grew, Westminster opportunistically added specialized training for principals and superintendents, for guidance counselors, for reading specialists and supervisors, for administrative specialists and visiting teachers, and in the academic areas of history, English, social studies and religion. Many of the specialized programs were geared to meet certification requirements in Pennsylvania and Ohio.

Over the years, thousands of public school employees drove to New Wilmington to take a succession of summer and night classes. Between 1945 and 2000, more than 4,000 of them earned Westminster master's degrees. Most lived and worked within an hour's drive of the campus. Enrollment grew as Westminster introduced new offerings that these teachers and administrators needed and shrunk as other institutions with lower tuition or locations closer to urban centers introduced similar offerings. Most of the courses were taught by the same faculty who taught undergraduates during the day and in classrooms that otherwise would have been empty. With relatively low costs, the graduate program has made a consistent but usually modest operating profit – under $200,000 until 1997 but approaching $500,000 by 2000.

Enrollment has been volatile. The program enjoyed steady and often rapid growth between 1945 and the mid-1960s, hitting a peak of 582 students in the spring of 1966. Keeping up with demand was a perpetual scramble; the situation was repeatedly described as "unmanageable" in Board minutes. Then it fell to a low of 70 in the fall of 1984, largely due to increased competition, and the program's future was in doubt. During the financial retrenchment of the Splete administration, the graduate program, with its enrollment then regularly below 100, came under cost-cutting scrutiny, even though it was still marginally profitable. Splete recommended cuts to the Board that included terminating the counselor education program, but his sudden dismissal and the confusion that followed meant that no action was taken on these recommendations. The counselor education program subsequently rebounded (from 11 in 1984 to almost 80 in 2000) to become a bulwark of the graduate program. Had it been cut in 1984, the entire graduate program probably would have been lost, Farmerie has said.

When Westminster was unable to beat lower-cost providers, it struck cooperative deals with them for joint offerings. Plans for a doctoral program at Westminster were scrapped when Youngstown State came out with a similar offering. Instead, Westminster teamed up with the University of Pittsburgh in 1998 on a program where doctoral students would begin at Westminster and finish at Pitt. By the spring of 2000, about 20 students had completed the Westminster leg of the program and enrolled at Pitt. Over the years, cooperative programs also have been offered with Penn State, Slippery Rock and Edinboro. ❖

CHAPTER 22

Pomp and Difficult Circumstances

Westminster College wanted, needed, courted Oscar Remick. He was a minister, a scholar and a clearly successful president of a small liberal arts college, Alma College, that faced many of the same challenges that Westminster was facing. Politically shrewd, Remick had measured Westminster's divisions and determined that he would need solid Board support and its acceptance of his own unchallenged leadership. After six years of upheaval, Westminster welcomed Remick in 1987 as a savior, much as the College had welcomed Will Orr in 1949. In both cases, unrealistic expectations contributed to inevitable disappointments, but both men restored stability and provided unchallenged leadership.

Remick, 55, looked almost perfect. He was an ordained Presbyterian minister with a divinity degree from Eastern Baptist Theological Seminary. He held a master's degree from the University of Pennsylvania and a Ph.D. from Boston University. He had taught philosophy for many years on college faculties. Best of all, in seven years he had upgraded Alma academically and financially. And he had crafted a marketing and public relations plan that was giving the college a national reputation and attracting students. For the first time, Westminster had a president fully prepared for the challenges he would face. All his predecessors had to learn on the job to various degrees. Westminster was hoping Remick would do for Westminster what he already had done for Alma.

Oscar E. Remick, Westminster's 12th president (1987-1997), restored stability to the College after six years of upheaval.

Once Remick arrived on July 1, 1987, he moved quickly to reorganize the Board. A package of changes was approved at the March 1988 Board meeting. Membership was increased from 28 to 36. No trustee could serve longer than two consecutive four-year terms but could be re-elected after leaving the Board for at least a year. The chair and vice chair still were elected by the Board but could serve no more than one three-year term. Six associate, non-voting members were added – three from the faculty and three from the student body. The president became an *ex officio* member of the Board and an officer of the corporation, along with the chair and vice chair.

Robert F. Patton '50 was named chair of the Board in 1988.

In elections held at that same meeting, Robert E. Lauterbach rotated off the Board after 17 years. Jack Hoey and Richard Kennedy retired as chair and vice chair, respectively, and were replaced by Robert Patton and Donald Wiley. Thomas V. Mansell stayed on until October to complete 50 consecutive years as a trustee. Lauterbach, Kennedy and Mansell were named *emeriti* trustees.

Another change in practice broke the power of the executive committee, which for many years had met before Board meetings to screen all business and recommend action to the full Board, which usually approved what the executive committee advised. Now the Board's ten standing committees would report directly to the full Board. The president and his vice presidents would work with the Board committees and provide liaison with the faculty, but faculty representatives already served on five of those ten committees, and some of them also had student representatives. The College was swinging back to the Miller/Carlson model of participatory governance.

The College bylaws had been revised in 1979 to give the Board chair unprecedented powers to bypass the president and deal directly with the faculty and staff. The president's powers were reduced, and all references to the academic dean were removed. (See Chapter 19.) In 1988, the bylaws were revised again, this time to remove the chairman's administrative powers and vest them in the president and his vice presidents, all of whom serve at the pleasure of the president. The chairman was given specific powers – to preside at meetings, appoint committees, and lead the review of the presidents' performance by the Board. Essentially, it became the role of the Board to hire the right president, support him and replace him when necessary. Real authority was concentrated in the president.

The faculty welcomed Remick as a fellow scholar who would respect them and work to strengthen Westminster's academic reputation. He was a colleague who enjoyed discussing history, philosophy, and religion. But he had an agenda that was not always what many faculty members wanted or expected. Remick intended to bring back the two-semester calendar, drop the January term, go back to measuring academic credits in hours instead of course credits and return to the eight-course teaching load. The increased teaching load was immediately unpopular. Remick's popularity with the faculty took another blow when the Board, in October 1988, approved new tenure guidelines that provided for a non-tenure track designed to reduce the percentage of tenured faculty from 82 to 60-65. While his calendar may have

The current president's manse, enlarged and remodeled during the Remick administration.

seemed traditional, he was in step with the times. He wanted to see Westminster thrive in the competitive marketplace and tried to exploit rather than resist the trends toward market responsiveness and vocationalism discussed in Chapter 21.

Remick's leadership style was reflected in the way he reorganized the administrative staff. He intended to be Westminster's ambassador to the world, winning valuable friends, favorable publicity and generous donations. Day-to-day administration of the College would be delegated to four vice presidents. All four of his vice presidents started when he did in 1987, and only one of them, a recent graduate, had any past association with Westminster. Since all four were hired while Remick was still at Alma, he relied heavily on search committees to do the initial screening but was responsible for the final selection.

For the key post of academic affairs and dean of the College, Remick picked Grace M. Allen, who brought impressive credentials (degrees from Cambridge and New York University), but she was unable to fill the post satisfactorily. She had barely arrived when illness forced her to take a sick leave of several months. When she tried to return to work, her performance was shaky, and the College bought out the second year of her contract. Remick had to start looking for a new dean. The vice president for development and institutional relations, Kevin Garvey, a 1977 Westminster grad, stayed until 1993, when he resigned and was replaced with Arthur Rathjen, who had worked with Remick at Alma on a fund-raising campaign that brought in $29 million, $3 million more than its goal. William J. Birkhead, vice president for finance and management services, still held that post in 2002, and Robert O. Thomas Jr., vice president for student affairs, stayed until 1996, after which his position was eliminated.

William J. Birkhead,
vice president
for finance and
management
services since 1987.

Faculty disillusionment with Remick really set in when an unexpected rash of repairs forced him to postpone scheduled increases in faculty salaries. Shortly after he arrived, he got the bad news that campus buildings were badly run down and needed extensive, expensive repairs. If Orr was known as the builder who left Westminster with an impressive physical campus, it was Remick's less glamorous destiny to be the president who repaired it. Year after year, scarce money went into necessary but unrewarding projects like fixing leaky roofs.

Remick had to ask the Board in 1988 for permission to draw $1.25 million from the endowment to pay for the first round of urgent repairs. Even the ten-year-old Natatorium needed a new roof. Before Remick's administration ended, 17 buildings required new roofs – virtually every building except the older ones with tile roofs. The bill for roof repairs alone came to more than $1.28 million. As one porous roof after another sucked up funds and faculty raises were deferred because of the expenses, English professor James Perkins brought down the house when he observed during a faculty meeting that if he believed in reincarnation, he'd like to come back as a leaky roof. "Decisions to invest in facility repairs instead of the College's 'educational mission' were agony for Dr. Remick," according to Birkhead. "Had he inherited a campus in good physical repair in 1987, it might have been quite a different looking decade for the College."

It wasn't just roofs. The electrical wiring in the dormitories needed to be replaced. So did the telephone system, installed in 1982. The messy prospect of tearing up the campus and its buildings to install all new electrical wiring and telephone cables raised an important question: Since the disruption and expense were inevitable, should the College seize the opportunity to install a fiber optic network and provide Internet access in every student room? And so the most conspicuous legacy of the Remick administration was born, partly of vision, partly of dire necessity. Westminster would be among the first online colleges in the nation, a potent selling point in the marketing of the College. One consequence was that Westminster earned a high ranking (83rd out of 3,631) in the *Yahoo! Internet Life* listing of "America's Most Wired Colleges" for the year 2000. But the decision also saddled Remick with a heavy financial burden for the rest of his administration. By the time his administration ended in 1997, Westminster had spent $13.2 million on infrastructure upgrades and repairs. The consequences of that decision will be reported in detail in the next chapter.

Remick had a go-getter's temperament and an austerity agenda, not an ideal combination, and his administration had to walk a fine line between penny-pinching and confident expansion. He was an effective speaker who did a good job of selling his vision of Westminster to outside supporters. As Westminster's public persona, it was his style to do things first-class, which made for effective marketing and public relations but sometimes caused resentment among those bearing the brunt of the austerity.

While faculty and staff raises remained modest, Remick's own compensation reflected the tight market for talented college presidents, who increasingly were wooed like corporate CEOs with high salaries and perks. Thus Remick's starting salary of $110,000 was substantially more than the $60,000 salary the College paid Splete in each of his three years.

The manse, built in 1950 for $50,000, was expanded and remodeled – at a cost of almost $341,000 – to suit Remick's need to entertain in style. To be sure, he hosted the faculty generously, with charbroiled steaks, a professional orchestra and tables and chairs for several hundred on the manse lawn for a fall faculty picnic. But some of those attending observed that they would rather eat hamburgers and listen to student musicians if it would mean a larger paycheck.

Faculty salaries were above average for Westminster's peer group at the end of the Carlson administration (1980-81) but failed to keep pace in the chaotic years that followed. (See "Salary Gap.") Raises given in Boone's second year (1986-87) helped, but Remick still inherited a faculty that was underpaid by comparison to its peers. When Barbara Faires replaced Allen in 1988 as dean and vice president for academic affairs, she launched a successful campaign to raise faculty salaries, but salaries began to lag again after 1992, when heavy debt from financing the Internet venture put financial pressure on the College.

Salary Gap
(average for all ranks)

	Westminster	Allegheny	W&J	Thiel	Waynesburg
1980-81	$21,200	$19,900	$20,500	$18,300	$19,800
1985-86	$26,600	$29,800	$28,300	$24,200	$21,800
1991-92	$38,500	$40,000	$43,400	$35,300	$30,500
1997-98	$43,700	$49,000	$51,600	$41,400	$37,600
2000-01	$60,100	$65,500	$71,000	$53,500	$57,200

Source: *Academe*, the AAUP magazine

Remick's primary mission, of course, once stability was restored, was to market Westminster and persuade good students to enroll and donors to write checks. In 1991, after several years of behind-the-scenes preparation and solicitation of special gifts, Westminster kicked off the "Heritage for the Future: A Campaign for Westminster," with a goal of raising $35 million. Details of that campaign are covered in Chapter 17, but it wasn't until June 1997 that it met its goal. Still, it had amassed the largest dollar total of any Westminster campaign to date. The projected buildings did not materialize because donors chose to direct their pledges to student scholarships, faculty chairs and the endowment. The result was, according to a 2001 Middle States evaluation report, that the campaign eventually hit its target but failed to raise "the money needed for the College's capital needs in the mid-1990s."

Despite a few bumps in the road, the Remick administration was working, and Westminster was moving forward again. The Board moved to preserve that progress in Remick's third year by offering him a seven-year contract that would provide for a 10-year term and break the pattern that marked the short presidencies of Lauterbach, Splete and Boone. To assure a smooth leadership transition at the end of Remick's term, the Board approved a plan in 1995 that would elevate Remick to chancellor and have him stay on the job during the first year or two of the new president's term. That plan ran into trouble when no qualified candidate would accept the presidency under those conditions and when some economy-minded trustees questioned the wisdom of paying two large salaries instead of one. So Remick continued alone, but with the chancellor title, until June 30, 1997, when he left the College and moved to Maine. His successor, R. Thomas Williamson, stepped into the job the next day. Remick spent the 1997-1998 year as nominal chancellor but on leave, and several trustees pitched in to pay his salary for that year.

Remick brought to Westminster a sense of teamwork it desperately needed, a sophisticated administrative structure and a reputation for liberal arts excellence. His skill in marketing the College in a competitive, high-tech and ultimately prosperous era in America can be gauged by student enrollment, which increased nearly 20 percent during his presidency, and by the higher standardized test scores of those students. He may be best remembered as the president who put Westminster online, the subject of the next chapter. ❖

—————————— C H A P T E R 2 3 ——————————

The Challenge of Technology:
Westminster Goes Online

Miller Peck, mathematics professor, developed the computer program at Westminster.

A combination of foresight and misfortune – the imminent breakdown of the College's telephone and electrical wiring infrastructure – conspired to put Westminster among the early collegiate adapters of computer technology and the Internet. Faced with high bills for essential repairs in 1993 and 1994, Westminster's leaders decided to spend even more but have something new to show for it. The result: Westminster was wired, not just for telephones and electricity but as a local area computer network that brought e-mail and the Internet to the whole campus. It changed the nature of communication that tied the College together as a community and transformed the educational experience in ways the founding fathers never could have imagined.

In the new millennium, students pick up syllabi or assignments electronically, by clicking with a mouse on a course folder icon on a computer screen and downloading the material. Term papers are largely written on computers and forwarded electronically to professors, who may grade them from their own computer terminals, type in their comments and send the papers back to students' electronic mailboxes or to an electronic folder for students to pick up. Not a single sheet of paper need ever be used, and teachers' comments are always legible.

But the computer has supplemented traditional education at Westminster, not replaced it. Class attendance still is required; most students and faculty members spend as much time as ever face to face in traditional classrooms. Students can raise questions or discuss problems with their teachers by e-mail, but office hours still are observed. And unless a prof gives a take-home exam, mid-terms and finals still find many Westminster students with sharpened pencils bent over blue books scribbling answers to essay questions.

The computer network actually has strengthened the ties between faculty and students that liberal arts colleges cultivate, some veteran teachers reported. "There is more communication in between class meetings now," English professor Frederick Horn noted in a 2000 interview. "Thanks to e-mail, I hear comments from students who don't normally speak up in class. When I walk into a class, I have a better feel for what students are thinking and how we should spend class time."

Computers now permeate the campus. The trend began modestly enough, in the classroom of a young mathematics professor, Miller Peck, who joined the faculty in 1958. Peck's own interest had been piqued by a graduate course he took at the University of California at Berkeley. Students who registered for Peck's "Mathematics 364: Introduction to Applied Mathematics" course in 1963 found themselves learning about computers and programming language.

There was no computer in Peck's classroom – or anywhere else on campus or even in town. They were too large, expensive and temperamental then to be college equipment. But Peck learned from IBM that the U.S. air base in Vienna, Ohio, had a computer, and he arranged to take his students there after business hours so they could get a hands-on feeling for the subject. Computer education expanded in 1968 when Peck started teaching "Mathematics 21: Introduction to Programming." By 1965, the College had leased a bulky IBM 1130 computer with a key punch card reader and printer, kept in a third-floor Old Main math classroom and used strictly for instructional purposes. Computer Science 1 and 2 were added in 1970, solidifying Westminster's place among the first liberal arts colleges in the country to offer instruction in computer science. When the math department moved in the fall of 1966 to Patterson, the computer moved with it, then was moved again to roomier quarters under Orr Auditorium. It remained there until 1974, when the computer center was reunited with the math department in the new Hoyt Science Resources Center.

In 1971 Rick Henderson joined the College as an instructor teaching computer courses and as part-time director of what had grown to a small computer center. Helen DeWitt was hired as his assistant. By 1977, a major in computer science was offered, and the department was renamed the Department of Mathematics and Computer Science. In 1980 Bernard Bonnie joined the staff as manager of computer operations, by this time a full-time staff position.

By the early 1970s, the chemistry and physics department had joined the math department in offering instruction in computers as a scientific phenomenon. The chairman of the physics department, William Johnson, had been trained in solid state physics, the basic field of computer electronics, and was for several summers an employee-consultant at IBM. He began teaching students in the early 1970s about computer components, and in 1977 introduced "Physics 31: Computer Electronics," which became a requirement for computer science majors. Chemistry professor Robert DeSieno introduced the study of computer electronics, also in the early 1970s, and his successor in 1982, Michael Chejlava, introduced small, inexpensive computers for various operations. By 1984 personal computers were in use by some faculty.

Using the computer outside the classroom to support College operations in processing-intensive sites like the business office, registrar's office and alumni office remained on the back burner until treasurer James Sands took an interest during the 1970s. Sands, who joined the staff in 1969 as business manager, sat in on some of Peck's computer classes and began to see how the computer could streamline certain College operations. He concluded that the College could save money by spending money, so he lined up financing to buy and install computers in the registrar's office and several other offices on campus.

As the computer revolution swept through business and industry, interest was growing among students and their parents in the career opportunities presented by computers. Westminster's computer science major was growing in popularity, leading the College in 1982 to introduce a second computer major, one more rooted in practical application than scientific theory. It was called computer information systems. Paul Wallace, a 1969 graduate of Westminster who had taken courses from Peck, came back to the College in 1981 as assistant professor of computer science and in 1987 was named director of information services.

The old 1130 gave way to a General Automation computer and then to an IBM 370, both punch-card operations. Then, in the early 1980s, came the first computer with video display terminals, a PDP-11 from Digital Equipment that was used both for instruction and to support some business processing. An IBM 4341 mainframe acquired in the mid-80s was used exclusively for instruction. The first personal computers started to appear in offices and science classrooms in the early 1980s. The first computer lab, stocked with PCs, was opened in 1984.

This growing role of the computer in Westminster's curriculum and operations was a prelude to the dramatic plunge the College took in the mid-1990s into a computer infrastructure. Before it was over, practically the whole College community was linked in one computer network, and computers had gone from being an academic curiosity and a processing tool in selected offices to being the communications medium that permeated virtually all parts of the College curriculum and most areas of College operations.

That leap started with bad wiring and a growing stack of bills. By the summer of 1993 problems with the telephone system, an aging Hitachi PBX installed in 1982 at a cost of more than $800,000, no longer could be ignored. Replacing it meant digging up the campus to install new underground cables to every building on campus and installing new wiring to every office and dorm room. Since the digging and cable laying were inevitable, why not put in a second cable at the same time, one that would support a local area computer network? That was the reasoning of the telecommunications project team spearheaded by treasurer William Birkhead and Wallace as director of information services, so they proposed this strategy. In February 1994, President Remick took the proposal to the Board, which approved it, and by the summer of 1994, the campus was torn up as trenches were dug. Two spare four-inch conduit pipes were laid in each trench, providing capacity for future expansion. In one conduit, a copper cable for telephone systems was laid alongside a fiber-optic cable for the computer network. All the conduits and cables led back to the computer center in Hoyt, where the computers that would drive the network were located. Initially, in 1995, there were four Novell file servers, but that number had grown to 22 by 2000. The telephone switchboard was relocated from Old Main to the expanded computer center.

In the summer of 1995, the dormitories were wired. Any available spaces (like the abandoned pay phone booths in Russell Hall) were converted to wiring closets – hubs where the outside cables were joined to the internal wiring networks. Rooms were wired so that each student would have a telephone jack and separate jacks where they could connect their computers.

A Westminster "smart" classroom.

Rather than tear out walls in every room, visible raceway channels were installed at desktop height to carry the wires to the jacks.

Then, in 1995, while data and phone lines were being installed in the upper floors of the dormitories, another problem came to light: The electrical wiring was inadequate. Planners feared that if many students turned on their computers in their dorm rooms after dinner, the surge in usage would overload the circuits and cause the electrical systems to crash. So the project was expanded to include new electrical wiring. The work dragged on through the summer of 1996. The New Wilmington Missionary Conference, the large summer event that pressed virtually every dormitory room into service, had to relocate to the Allegheny College campus for the summers of 1995 and 1996, returning to Westminster in 1997.

The fiber-optic computer cable, linked to copper wiring inside the buildings, also was laid to every classroom, every office and, of course, to resource centers like the library. A student with a portable computer could take it to class, to a lab, to the library and back to his dorm room and find jacks in each location to plug into the network. When TitanNet went live in the fall of 1996, 75 students brought their own computers to campus and plugged them in. By 2000, that number had risen to 550, in addition to about 600 College-owned PCs, all linked to the network. In 1995, Westminster introduced its own Web site, and by 1999 prospective students could apply for admission online. By 2000, students could use the site to see their transcripts and course schedules.

The network had direct access to the Internet, so users didn't need modems and got information quicker. Ten classrooms were rebuilt as "smart" classrooms, equipped with document cameras and projection and sound systems so that teachers in those rooms could connect to the Internet or use material stored on disks for the whole class to see. In addition, the College equipped "Smart Carts" with portable electronic equipment that could be wheeled into regular classrooms to convert them temporarily into smart classrooms. The goal was to have one cart on every floor of every academic building; by 2000, the number of carts had reached ten.

Wiring Westminster did not come cheap. The financing started in 1994 with a $2.5 million, 10-year term loan from what is now National City Bank of Pennsylvania, on which the College paid a fixed rate of 7.02 percent. As expenses continued to mount, the College tapped its endowment for temporary financing – $5.2 million in May 1995, $3.4 million in January 1996, $1.3 million the following May – then arranged bank loans so that the endowment loans, which at one point reached $9.1 million, could be repaid. Replacing endowment loans with external bank loans proved to be a shrewd strategy as the endowment investments earned a return above 20 percent in fiscal years 1996-97 and 1997-98 and 12 percent in 1998-99. By the end of 1997, total indebtedness for the project topped $12.1 million, including $3.8 million still owed to the endowment.

Once the full scope of that project financing became clear, the patchwork of debt was advantageously refinanced on Feb. 18, 1998, when trustee Thomas S. Mansell, serving pro bono as legal counsel for both the College and the New Wilmington Borough Council, arranged for the New Wilmington Municipal Authority to issue $11.925 million of municipal bonds for the benefit of the College at a low tax-free rate. The Authority then lent the money to the College, to be repaid over 30 years, at an effective interest rate of 5.47 percent. The refinancing left the College with average annual debt service costs over 30 years of $759,000, but that was considerably lower than the debt service on the combined old debts.

Where did all the money go? Replacing the old telephone system cost $2.2 million. Replacing the electrical wiring came to almost $4.9 million, and building the local area computer network (servers, operating system, software) and supplying the personal computers required nearly $5.1 million, for a total outlay of $12.2 million.

This large investment helped to move Westminster to the leadership ranks of colleges using technology to support the teaching of liberal arts. However, technology is no one-time investment; it must be maintained and regularly upgraded, committing Westminster to higher annual operating costs as well as higher debt service. Wiring the College no doubt strengthened the position of the College in the marketplace and made it more appealing to many students. But it also has raised the annual operating revenue the College must attract to cover these expenses and survive financially. It was something of a gamble. However, as other colleges have had to bite the same bullet and as computerized campuses have started to become a prerequisite to operating a liberal arts college in the new millennium, Westminster's relatively early start probably reduced its overall costs and gave the College a bigger marketing boost.

John Deegan, Jr. was named vice president for academic affairs and dean of the College in 1994.

But how have computers affected the quality of education at Westminster? Its architects are understandably enthusiastic. "From the start, this network was designed primarily to enhance the teaching and learning experience," academic dean John Deegan observed in a 2000 interview. "It gives the student seamless access to the College's educational resources wherever he or she may happen to be. We explicitly designed our new curriculum in 1994 and 1995 to exploit the power of information technology and the World Wide Web. As a result, we quickly developed a regional and then a national reputation as a leader in the sophisticated use of information technology to improve teaching and learning. Dozens of other colleges have come to our campus to see what we are doing." High-tech education has contributed to Westminster's rise in published rankings of liberal arts colleges, he added.

Professors like Horn clearly liked the new resources. "With digital delivery, it's easy now to post student papers so classmates can read them and learn from each other," Horn said. "That rarely happened in the past. Now they get fresh ideas." When he teaches a film that is available on disk, he can go precisely to the scenes he wants the class to view, with no rewinding or fast-forwarding. "We can use film more effectively in our teaching now. I'm looking forward to the day when Shakespeare productions are available on DVD." Other teachers were less happy with the huge investment in technology, but the usual acceptance curve, where people come to like a new technology once they understand what it can do, seemed to be working at Westminster.

Computer literacy requirements adopted in the 1980s had become obsolete in the new millennium. "It's no longer a specific skill students address by taking a course. It something they learn in all of their courses now," Deegan said. "Every faculty member has a computer on his or her desk and uses it to some extent to be a better teacher." To bring people up to speed, the College invested almost $400,000 in faculty training, he noted, $230,000 of it from a grant from the Fund for the Improvement of Post-Secondary Education.

Westminster took pains to protect itself from the damage that computerized education could cause to a small college. "We were particularly careful not to do anything that would damage the liberal arts culture of Westminster, with its intimate, nurturing personal relationships," Deegan noted.

Without question the role of the college professor is changing from the traditional source of knowledge to a stimulator and facilitator in the student's search for knowledge. Attention seems to be centering more on the individual student with the professor giving more one-on-one time to the student who is able to advance more at his or her own pace. Who knows what's ahead for the professor? There seems to be general agreement on two points: It's going to be an exciting ride, and the college professor is not destined for early extinction. ❖

CHAPTER 24

Smiles and Surpluses:
A Growth Agenda for the New Millennium

Histories don't have happy endings, or even endings, but they must stop when they run into the present. While it would have been presumptuous to pass judgment on the Williamson administration, which was still a work in progress, it was hard, in 2002, to escape the feeling that future historians would have to consider the 1997-2002 period to be a time of unusual harmony and prosperity for Westminster College.

The arrival of R. Thomas Williamson as Westminster's thirteenth president in 1997 was not an obvious turning point for the College. It occurred as a natural succession when Oscar Remick retired. And Williamson conspicuously retained many of Remick's key people and policies. But he took over in time to catch the wave of prosperity and philanthropy that was bringing to many private colleges a generous infusion of much-needed cash. The bucolic isolation of New Wilmington, we have seen, provided Westminster with a buffer against the strong currents of the outside world but one that always was porous and that grew more so as transportation and communication evolved. Global political, social and economic forces – and the accompanying trends in higher education – were felt, often quite strongly, in this rural community. For the five years leading up to Westminster's sesquicentennial, that generally was good news.

R. Thomas Williamson was named Westminster's 13th president in 1997.

Across the nation, colleges and universities raised $23.4 billion in gifts during their 1999-2000 fiscal years, the fifth consecutive year in which giving grew more than 10 percent. Over the 1995-2000 period, gifts to higher education were up 81 percent, much of it tied to the long bull stock market, the *Chronicle of Higher Education* reported on May 4, 2001 (pp. A28-30). Like the stock market, giving to colleges began to cool down after March 2000, the report noted. But it had been nothing less than a bonanza. "The last half of the final decade of the 20th century will go down in history as one of the greatest periods of giving to American higher education," that report concluded.

Westminster's success at attracting outside contributions certainly added to its growing sense of financial security. Total giving from all sources for all purposes rose from $1.85 million in 1988-89, the first full year of the Remick administration, to $5.5 million and $5 million in 1990-91 and 1991-92, respectively, as the Heritage Campaign (Chapter 17) boosted giving temporarily. (See "Fund Raising at Westminster.") Then it receded to $2.7 million in 1995-96 before starting up again, buoyed by a strong stock market that was making Westminster's benefactors richer, by a sophisticated fund-raising organization built under Remick and then Williamson, and by the personal attention both presidents gave to fund raising. A combination of factors led to a stunning $10.56 million in 2000-2001, almost double the previous record, in the face of a declining stock market. That performance "probably won't be repeated next year," warned Gloria C. Cagigas, vice president for institutional advancement.

Fund Raising at Westminster (*all gifts for all purposes, in $ millions*)

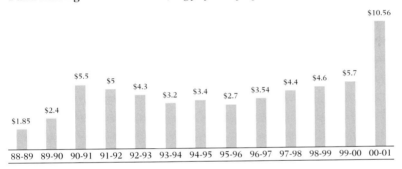

Those numbers represented a bottom line, the actual cash taken in by the College in a reporting period. Amounts may be offset by large gifts and bequests and by special fund-raising campaigns. A more stable indication of the growth of core giving was found in the Annual Fund numbers. (See "Westminster's Annual Fund.")

Westminster's Annual Fund (*in $ millions*)

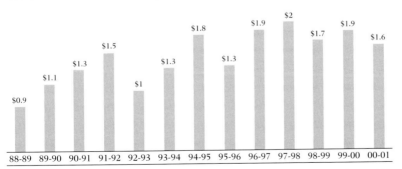

88-89 $938,874; **89-90** $1,139,826; **90-91** $1,270,588; **91-92** $1,494,821; **92-93** $1,054,540; **93-94** $1,311,768; **94-95** $1,767,313; **95-96** $1,281,552; **96-97** $1,858,367; **97-98** $2,030,9880; **98-99** $1,669,802; **99-00** $1,935,824; **00-01** $1,625,654.

Gloria C. Cagigas, vice president for institutional advancement.

Growth in giving came not just from richer donors writing larger checks; the base of participation also rose steadily from under 15 percent of all alumni making contributions in 1984 to 42 percent in 2000. When graduating seniors were asked in 2001 to make gifts to the College, 68 percent did so. The booming stock market of the late 1990s clearly helped, Cagigas explained in 2001. Even though overall giving was up, she reported that some donors were holding off on paying pledges until specific stocks they planned to sell recovered from the 2000 downturn. Stable leadership and a sense among alumni that the College was back on track after the turbulence of the 1980s also helped, she said. So did the adoption of sophisticated fund-raising strategies. "We went from a 'shotgun' approach of sending one letter to 16,000 alums to a personalized, targeted appeal emphasizing mission and explaining how their gifts support students and faculty. We used testimonials from recipients of student scholarships and faculty development grants," she reported. "In addition to Annual Fund support, having a comprehensive institutional plan with specific funding goals gave donors other opportunities to support the College." Recent success has brought Westminster, at its sesquicentennial anniversary, to a strategy of confident growth and found the College spending more liberally in pursuit of a higher level of academic performance and prestige.

It is safe to say that the choice of Williamson marked another step in the long trend toward choosing leaders for the College who were executives with proven skills in fund-raising and development and away from choosing Presbyterian ministers or academic scholars. Will Orr was the last in a long line of men to step directly from the pulpit to the presidency, but every president or acting president before Williamson had been, at some point, a minister, a college professor with academic credentials or both, except for Cleland and Lauterbach, who served briefly as agents of the Board during times of controversy. But Carlson (a lay scholar), Splete (a lay scholar) and Remick (an ordained scholar), all Ph.D.'s, already were experienced administrators in higher education when they were called to Westminster after a national search. None had historic ties to the College.

Williamson, a law school graduate, never held a position on a teaching faculty. He was a professional administrator. Born in 1946 in Detroit, Mich., he was graduated from the College of Wooster in 1968, spent two years in the Navy and then worked six years for McCormick & Co. while earning his law degree at the University of Baltimore. Then he found academia, serving as director of the Economic Development and Technical Assistance Center at the State University of New York, Plattsburg, from 1976 to 1982. He then moved on to Clarkson University, Potsdam, N.Y., to become vice president for development and external affairs (1982-87), acting president (1987-88) and executive vice president (1988-97), and was instrumental in increasing Clarkson's endowment eight-fold.

Part of the unusual harmony that marked the first five years of the Williamson administration was a matter of timing. Williamson had the good fortune to arrive at a time when fiscal crises at Westminster and many other private, liberal arts colleges were abating. Giving, as we have seen, was up dramatically. Enrollment was rising. The substantial infrastructure investments in roofs and wiring that sucked funds out of the budget during the Remick years already had been largely absorbed.

For the 1996-97 fiscal year, the final year of the Remick administration, the College operated in the black by $607,000 before discretionary fund transfers, with revenue of $23.4 million and expenses of $22.8 million. In October of 1997, following through on an earlier Remick suggestion, the College's trustees approved a funding method that drew more heavily on the College's endowment to fund annual operations. The method was put into practice beginning in 1998-99. This factor, coupled with Williamson's success at holding down expenditure increases, led to larger operating surpluses before discretionary transfers in the years following 1996-97. In fiscal year 1997-98, Williamson's first year as president, revenue totaled $24.3 million, expenses totaled $22.2 and operating surplus totaled just over $2 million. In fiscal year 1998-99, revenue rose to $25.5 million and expenses to $23.2 million leaving a $2.3 million operating surplus. For the 1999-2000 fiscal year, revenue of $26.6 million topped expenses of $24.5 million, again leaving operations in the black by slightly more than $2 million before discretionary transfers. For the 2000-2001 fiscal year, revenue of $28.3 million and expenses of $26.1 million left a surplus of $2.2 million. With such prosperity, it fell to Williamson to set a strategic course that generally was popular.

But part of the harmony came from Williamson's personality and leadership style. Faculty leaders who had clashed with his predecessors found him to be disarming – pleasant, unpretentious, a good listener, a hard worker, and someone who dispatched unpopular decisions quickly and matter-of-factly, in ways that tended to dispel rancor. Part of his technique, he acknowledged in a 2001 interview, was to "let people know that you're vulnerable and you need their help." He credited Remick's participatory reorganization that put faculty members on Board committees with reducing the tension between faculty and Board.

The polarization that had plagued the College for much of the time since the 1940s diminished during the Remick years and essentially evaporated during the first four Williamson years. Williamson's collegial leadership style and willingness to delegate responsibility placed him generally in the ranks of the participatory presidents rather than the paternalistic presidents, at the same time that his role atop a complex administrative pyramid made him more like a corporate CEO than any of his predecessors except perhaps for the actual corporate CEO, Robert Lauterbach. However, as we have seen (Chapter 22), the role of the college president as head of an academic corporation already was becoming clear in the Remick administration.

Only once in the first three-and-a-half years of his presidency did Williamson override his cardinal rule to listen and follow sound advice, he recalled in 2001. That came when a faculty-staff committee recommended tearing down the old Thompson-Clark building. By his own account, he "dug in his heels" and insisted that it be renovated instead, a decision perhaps more sentimental than economic, but hardly the kind of issue that would polarize faculty and administration. Sentiment was no small factor in this case because that was Westminster's first science building, erected when S.R. Thompson, father of science teaching at Westminster, donated his life savings ($20,000) to build a facility with laboratories and asked the College to dedicate it to his 18-year-old daughter, who died in 1886 while a Westminster student. (See Chapter 6.) Built in 1893, it is the second oldest building on campus, after Hillside (1885).

For the first time since Old Main was destroyed in 1927, crowds gathered on campus on July 31, 1998, to watch a historic College building go up in flames. West Hall, the old Conservatory of Music built by W.W. Campbell in 1907, had been Westminster's third-oldest building. English teachers, whose offices had been in West Hall, shed some tears for lost books and papers, then moved into temporary quarters (two trailers) for three years until they were installed in the even older Thompson-Clark building that Williamson had insisted on restoring.

Another potentially tough decision for Williamson involved the future of athletics at Westminster and whether the College belonged in the ranks of the NCAA's Division II or III, an issue reported in Chapter 18. "There was a time when I think it was the hope of the athletic department that we would put more money into recruiting and scholarships so that we could compete at the Division II level, but I felt that we couldn't get there from here, and that we might bring down the whole College if we tried, so that decision was fairly easy. Jim Dafler, director of athletics, did a wonderful job of managing that transition," he reflected in 2001. By giving up a limited number of designated athletic scholarships, Westminster actually could offer more academic scholarships to all students, some of whom also were athletes, and expand participation in sports, he observed. Differences of opinion between coaches and college presidents can be explosive, as Westminster had seen (Chapter 11), but this time they were not.

The West Hall fire (July 31, 1998) and the day after.

Williamson came to consider faculty cohesiveness an important strength at Westminster. "At Clarkson faculty meetings, various factions would send their gladiators forth to battle for scarce resources. I found more cooperation at Westminster," he said in a 2001 interview. "That's one of its strengths. At various times in Westminster's history, there have been gaps in the

administration, and the faculty would step in and keep the College going until the next inhabitant could be found for the front office. They have been the enduring constant. As a result, the culture here is so strong that even a president cannot mess it up."

But that cohesiveness was not altogether inherited; it also was encouraged, he admitted. "When I arrived, I encountered people who felt aggrieved about one thing or another, and I asked them to freeze their ideas about 'what should have happened' two years ago and accept things as they were now as our base line and help me move forward from there. Once they saw that I was asking the same thing of everyone, I was impressed with their reasonable approach to virtually all issues."

In some ways, gauging the performance of Westminster under Williamson was remarkably easy and clear-cut because the new president moved quickly to spell out goals in terms that were quite specific and measurable. He committed the College to a five-year strategic plan, approved by the Board in May 1998, and a series of milestones that would make Westminster's progress – or lack of progress – completely conspicuous. Thus, to a considerable degree, the record of the early years of the Williamson administration did not need to await the judgment of history but could be seen in the annual report cards the College issued on its own performance.

Thus, Westminster set out to join the ranks of the top 100 liberal arts colleges in the United States, as measured by *U.S. News & World Report*, starting from 128th place in 1997 and working its way up in steps until it reached 100 by 2003. Actual performance found Westminster at 123rd in 1998, right on schedule, 114th by 1999, and 106th by 2000, almost two years ahead of schedule. In 2001, a reorganization of college classifications increased the number of schools in Westminster's category. Even though Westminster improved in all criteria, its rank was 115. The goal is still the top 100.

Another major financial goal was to build the College endowment from $61 million in 1997 to $100 million by 2003. Progress again exceeded expectations as the endowment hit $75 million in 1998, $5 million ahead of plan; $84 million in 1999, $10 million ahead of plan; and $90 million in 2000, $11 million ahead of plan. In 2001 it stood right on schedule at $85 million.

Employee salaries were slated to rise gradually from 86 percent to 100 percent of the median for a selected peer group of 20 colleges. Westminster reached its 1998 and 1999 goals of 87 percent, and 90 percent, and topped its 2000 goal of 93 percent with a 94 percent showing.

Net revenue from undergraduate tuition and fees was targeted to grow from $10.8 million in 1997 to $15 million by 2003. The College met its target for 1998 and slightly exceeded it for 1999, then fell behind the pace by $409,000 in 2000, but in 2001 it picked up, though it came in $852,000 short of the goal. Another goal was boosting alumni participation in annual fund giving from 40.2 percent to 43.2 percent, and progress through 2000 was roughly on track at 42 percent and stayed at about the same level in 2001. Although the completion of specific projects and raising funds to meet their expected cost were part of the plan, and although targets were set for endowment growth and tuition and fee revenue, no long-range targets were set for annual giving or overall fund raising.

Harold Burry Stadium, named for Westminster's famed football coach, now includes a two-story press box, refurbished bleachers, and a new track, installed in 2001.

While the College generally was meeting or even outperforming its financial plan, goals for student enrollment were proving harder to reach. Success was defined as increasing undergraduate enrollment from 1,402 in 1997 to 1,520 by 2003. Actual enrollment hit 1,423 in 1998, right on plan, but fell to 1,408 in 1999 rather than rising to 1,425 as planned. In 2000 it bounced back to 1,433, still 32 shy of the goal for that year, then rose slightly to 1,438 in 2001. Particularly disappointing was the volume of applications for admission. The goal was to increase applications from 1,022 in 1997 to 1,400 by 2003, but the numbers declined to 1,020 in 1998, to 975 in 1999 (well below the 1,200 target), rose to 1,050 in 2000, and rose again to 1,181 in 2001 – lagging behind the aggressive goal by 119 but still registering the highest level of applications in the College's history. The projected rise in freshman SAT scores from 1079 to 1100 failed to materialize as average scores came in at 1096 for 1998 but fell to 1080 in 1999, then rose to 1091 in 2000 and dropped to 1075 in 2001. Likewise the goal of upgrading the academic caliber of the incoming freshman classes proved hard to attain. The plan was to increase the percentage of students who had graduated in the top 10 percent of their high school classes from 22 to 31. The reality was that the number rose to 26 percent in 1998, dropped to 22 percent in 1999 and bounced back to 25 percent in 2000 and 2001. It was easier to attract money than students in the early years of the twenty-first century, even with a market-oriented curriculum, a burnished physical plant, leading-edge computer technology and a rising academic reputation.

Raising academic standards for faculty was easier to control. By fall 2000, the percentage of the full-time faculty holding the highest degree available in their discipline had increased from 83 in 1994 to 91.

Improvements to the physical campus moved ahead on schedule.

◆ The 5,100-square-foot Remick House, which held the admissions and financial aid departments, was completed on schedule at a cost of $1.4 million and dedicated in May 1999. A $500,000 grant covered 36 percent of the cost.

◆ The $3 million renovation of Thompson-Clark Hall was completed on schedule by the beginning of January 2001 and housed the English and public relations; modern languages; and communication studies, theatre and art departments. A twelve-month $1.5 million challenge gift was met in eleven months with gifts from alumni, friends, corporations and foundations.

- The 6,900-square-foot Thomas V. Mansell education wing of Memorial Field House, financed partly with a $500,000 gift from the New Castle-based Hoyt Foundation, was completed in 1999 at a cost of $1.5 million.

- The 11,000-square-foot James F. Edwards wing of the Field House was completed by October 2001 at a cost of $2.1 million. Edwards '42, a former cross country star, gave $500,000 for the project.

- Construction was under way in 2002 on the $13 million Campus Center, connecting the Walton-Mayne Student Union with Charles Freeman Hall. Fund raising got a boost from a $3 million challenge gift from Andrew McKelvey '57. The complex, which will include a food court, game room, bookstore, lounge, career center, conference rooms and the campus radio and TV stations and the Center for Excellence in Teaching and Learning, was scheduled to open in 2003.

- The renovation of Old Main at an undetermined cost was scheduled to begin in 2003.

If George C. Vincent and D.H.A. McLean, the two clergymen/scholars who listened to 20 students "recite" at opposite ends of the sanctuary of the "old Seceder Church" in the spring of 1852, could have returned to Westminster College in 2002, they no doubt would have been dazzled by the size and bustle of the place with its 21 buildings, 1,450 students, 97 faculty members, full-time staff of 170 (some with titles like "administrative systems coordinator" and "telecommunication network engineer") and its $38 million annual operating budget. And the 18 country pastors, farmers and merchants who enjoyed "a hearty laugh" when the audacious suggestion first was made that they start a "college" would have enjoyed an even heartier laugh to see the fruits of their faith and labor 150 years later.

The Remick Admissions House was completed in 1999 at a cost of $1.4 million.

They would have been impressed and not entirely pleased by the worldly sophistication of the student body, rendered incredulous by the technological virtuosity of the "smart classrooms," shocked by the fleet of student automobiles in various parking lots.

They probably would have been appalled by the ignorance of Greek and Latin that existed not only in the student body but among the faculty. But they would have been impressed by the depth of knowledge represented in the proliferation of disciplines that made up a modern college. They

By 2002, work was progressing on the College's $13 million Campus Center.

might have felt ambivalent about how liberal the curriculum of a liberal arts college had become, but they would have felt a sense of satisfaction that their principles of diversity, tolerance and practical education had borne such fruit. They could easily have been inclined to strut a bit about how right they had been in endorsing coeducation and extending to women the opportunities of higher learning.

And they would have applauded the faith with which Westminster College, 150 years later, continued to move confidently into an uncertain future. If this fantasy could be realized and the people who started Westminster College in 1852 could have come face to face with the constituents of the place in 2002, it's easy to think that they would have enjoyed each other immensely, offered congratulations all around, and then thanked their Creator and joined hands for a chorus of "Blest Be the Tie that Binds." ❖

—————— A P P E N D I X   A ——————

Faculty & Staff of Westminster College
1852 – 2002

This list of full-time persons is arranged in chronological order of appointment. For those persons who served at least twenty years, the date of retirement and years of service are given. Those persons who are still serving in 2002 are identified by an asterisk (*).

– Compiled by H. Dewey DeWitt

YEAR	NAME	DISCIPLINE
1852	George C. Vincent	Greek Literature and History
1852	D. H. A. McLean	Mathematics
1853	James Patterson	President; Mental and Moral Philosophy
1853	Andrew M. Black	Hebrew Literature and Greek
1853	John W. Harshaw	Latin Literature
1853	J. A. Goodwillie	Natural Science
1853	Janet S. Lowrie	Mathematics and Natural Science
1856	James B. Cummings	Natural Science (retired 1884, 28 years)
1856	William Findley	Latin Literature, later Greek and Mental Science
1858	William Mehard	Mathematics (retired 1889, 31 years)
1866	W. H. Jeffers	Latin Literature
1866	Mrs. W. H. Wilson	French, German, Italian
1866	Ella Mehard	Instrumental Music
1866	N. Coe Stewart	Vocal Music
1867	Robert Audley Browne	President; Mental Science and Latin Literature
1867	Sarah McMichael	Principal in the Ladies Department
1869	John D. Irons	Latin and Hebrew
1869	Mary Stevenson	Instructor in the Ladies Department
1871	John D. Shafer	Latin Literature and German, later Greek
1872	Eliakim Tupper Jeffers	President; Mental and Moral Philosophy
1872	J. W. Stewart	Latin
1873	John Knox McClurkin	Latin, later Greek
1873	John Edgar	English
1873	Nathan Winegart	German
1873	Kenneth McIntosh	Constitutional Law
1874	Mary Shafer	Principal in the Ladies Department
1874	Ella Reed	Assistant in the Preparatory Department
1874	Andrew H. Harshaw	Latin
1875	R. H. Carothers	English and German
1875	Mary E. Rippey	Science
1877	Oella J. Patterson	English
1877	Duncan M. McKinley	Greek and Mathematics

YEAR	NAME	DISCIPLINE
1878	R. O. Graham	Chemistry
1879	William Coventry Lawther	Greek
1880	John McNaugher	Greek
1881	John C. Rolfe	Latin
1881	John Mitchell	Latin and Greek
1883	W. W. Wallace	Mathematics
1883	W. M. Milroy	Greek
1884	Robert Gracey Ferguson	President; Mental and Moral Science (retired 1914, 30 years)
1884	R. B. Taggert	Greek
1884	S. R. Thompson	Physics
1884	T. M. Austin	Music
1884	Perry Kuhn	Maintenance (at least 20 years)
1885	Mary A. Morrison	Art
1885	Mary Samson	Governess of Ladies Dormitory
1886	Adah M. Strock	Art
1886	Alice B. Finley	Music
1886	J. Calvin Adair	Chemistry
1886	Mrs. Thurman	Governess of Ladies Dormitory
1887	Margaret McLaughry	English
1887	W. A. Fankboner	Chemistry
1887	Linnie Hodgens	Art (retired 1908, 21 years)
1888	Anna M. Wallace	Music
1888	H. J. Hotchkiss	Mathematics
1889	Ralph W. McGranahan	Latin
1889	John N. Swan	Chemistry and Mathematics
1889	Louise Ball Robertson	Matron of Ladies Hall
1889	James M. Robertson	Physics
1889	Clara L. Whissen	Music
1890	Eva Shontz	Elocution
1890	James D. Barr	Latin
1891	E. P. Thompson	Chemistry
1891	Mary Ferguson	Music
1891	Christian Thelan	Music
1892	Hulda E. Campbell	Instructor
1892	Flora J. Irons	Instructor
1893	John J. McElree	Latin (retired 1918, 25 years)
1893	Arthur J. Hopkins	Chemistry
1893	Charles A. Douglas	Music
1893	Idella R. Merritt	Voice
1893	Edith L. Winn	Music
1894	Agnes Reed	English
1894	Ina M. Hanna	Physics
1894	Charles C. Freeman	Chemistry, Dean and Acting President (retired 1944, 50 years)
1894	P. O. Cable	Physical Education and Baseball
1895	Hannah E. Peebles	English
1895	Daniel Hahn	Music
1895	Adella Hahn	Music
1895	E. W. Guilford	Physical Education
1896	Morgan Barnes	Greek

YEAR	NAME	DISCIPLINE
1896	Mary Cotton Kimble	Music
1896	Horace Greeley Byers	Physics
1896	W. J. Holmes	Physical Education
1897	Rolla Roy Ramsey	Physics
1897	Martin Luther Peterson	Music
1897	Maude Morrow McNall	Music, Piano
1897	Grace Acheson	Elocution
1898	Mary Houston Brown	Modern Languages
1898	George Cummings	Physics
1898	Marie C. McConnell	Elocution
1899	Isaac Newton Moore	Physics
1901	James O. Campbell	History and Political Science (retired 1921, 20 years)
1901	James M. Shaffer	Mathematics (retired 1921, 20 years)
1901	Sarah Foster Brownlee	Governess of Ladies Dormitory
1901	Hugh Lambie	Physical Education, Director of Athletics
1902	John Abram Shott	Physics (retired 1933, 31 years)
1902	Ella Mary Warner	Music
1902	Olive Pyle	Art
1902	Agnes Oliver	Elocution
1903	W. T. Hewetson	English
1903	Frank C. McGill	Greek
1903	Elizabeth Rebekah Speer	Music
1904	Lois Knott	Modern Languages
1904	Murrey Kerr Martin	Latin
1905	James H. Grier	Greek
1905	Almon W. Vincent	Music
1905	Agnes Vincent	Music
1906	Robert McWatty Russell	President; Christian Evidences
1906	James D. Barr	Greek
1906	Anna Heyberger	French and German
1906	Arthur D. Howard	Biology and Geology
1906	Paulina Alexander	English
1906	William Wilson Campbell	Music
1906	Nona Yantis	Piano and Harmony
1907	Wilson T. Moog	Pipe Organ and Piano
1907	Donna Louise Riblette	Vocal Ensemble
1907	William T. Troup	Latin and Greek
1907	Owen J. Neighbors	Mathematics and Physics
1907	Elizabeth L. Randall	Oratory
1907	May Alexander	French and German
1907	Leneral P. Moorehouse	History and Calisthenics
1908	Corinne Mercer	Secretary to the President (retired 1950, 42 years)
1908	Sarah A. Pratt	Dean of Women
1908	Benjamin W. Bridgman	Physics and Mathematics
1908	Owen W. Mills	Biology and Geology
1908	Alta Aileen Robinson	English
1908	Bertha Muller	French and German
1908	Bess Stewart	Greek

YEAR	NAME	DISCIPLINE
1908	Mabel McCoy Henderson	English
1908	Lucie M. Manley	Art
1908	Mona Downs	Vocal Culture and Ensemble
1909	Edwin L. Beck	English
1909	Clara Louise Shaffer	Vocal Culture and Ensemble
1909	Luigi Von Kunits	Violin
1909	May Scott	History
1909	Margaret Earla Mitchell	English
1910	Elbert P. Moses	Public Speaking
1910	James Cooper Lawrence	English and History
1910	Marguerite Forrest	Vocal Culture and Ensemble
1910	Oscar Dewitte Hollenbeck	Mathematics and Physical Director
1911	Elizabeth C. Torrey	Dean of Women
1911	Henry Ernest Smith	English
1911	Edward F. Kurtz	Violin and Orchestra
1911	Selmar Janson	Piano and Harmony
1911	Isabella Gareissen	Vocal Culture and Ensemble
1911	Luella E. Kiekhoefer	Modern Languages
1911	Carolyn G. Nelson	Public Speaking and Calisthenics
1911	Willard H. Gildersleeve	Physical Education, director
1912	Mabel Boak	Dean of Women
1912	Robert Metcalf Smith	English
1912	Marjorie Bryant	Public Speaking
1912	William E. Duckwitz	Piano and Music History
1912	Edward Royce	Piano and Composition
1912	Mary C. Douthett	Piano
1912	Adolph Walter	Woodwind Instruments
1912	E. C. Cowden	Brass Instruments
1913	Helen J. Martin	Dean of Women
1913	Frank L. Tinkham	Physical Education, Athletic Director
1913	Esther M. Dixon	Modern Languages
1913	Agnes Clancy Smith	English
1914	Alice E. McClure	Bible and Missions
1914	Catherine MacLaggan	Modern Languages
1914	Wesley W. Howard	Singing
1914	J. H. Veasey	Registrar and Local Treasurer
1914	James Weber	Superintendent of Buildings and Grounds
1915	B.W. Bridgman	Local Cashier
1915	Sarah J. Knott	Dean of Women, Psychology
1915	Florence Hutchison	Art
1915	Marian Hover	Public Speaking
1916	W. Charles Wallace	President; Christian Evidences
1916	John J. Welsh	Buildings and Grounds
1916	George K. Pattee	English
1916	Lewis K. Oppitz	Physics
1917	Walter E. Rogers	Biology and Geology
1917	Roger F. Gephart	Latin
1917	Herbert Solon Hollopater	Public Speaking
1917	Caroline Meyer	Librarian
1917	J.A.C. McQuiston	Business Manager
1918	Emma Louise Stone	Romance Languages

YEAR	NAME	DISCIPLINE
1919	James A. Swindler	Physics (retired 1954, 35 years)
1919	Bert E. Quick	Biology and Geology (retired 1946, 27 years)
1919	William F. Luebka	English
1919	Martha Mae McKnight	Public Speaking and Physical Culture
1919	Per Nielson	Music
1919	Julian Raymond Williams	Piano and Organ
1919	Violet A. Nethersole	Piano and Harmony
1919	Evelyn Neil Fitch	Voice
1920	Naomi Williams	Public Speaking and Pageantry
1920	Cleo A. Matheny	English and History
1920	Alice Cunningham	Romance Languages
1920	Frances Turney	Romance Languages
1920	Ella R. Moyer	Piano
1920	Louise L. Grant	Voice
1921	R. J. Love	Bible
1921	Walter Peterson	Ancient Languages
1921	Minnie Belle McQuiston	Dean of Women
1921	Irving Garwood	English
1921	Hulda L. Ise	English
1921	Elmer Beecher Russell	History
1921	E. J. Eberling	Economics and Business Administration
1921	E. H. Balz	Chemistry
1921	Rachel Hibbard	Modern Languages
1921	Elizabeth Stewart	Modern Languages (retired 1950, 29 years)
1921	Sara E. Conrad	Modern Languages
1921	Gertrude McCain	Mathematics
1921	Isabel Ramsey	Stenographer-Recorder (retired 1963, 42 years)
1921	Elsie Pershel Eberling	Violin
1922	Paul J. Appell	English
1922	Jessie L. Mockel	Music
1922	Nettie H. Johnson	Music
1922	Mrs. C.B. Robertson	Dean of Women
1923	Norval Brelos	Music
1923	Dwight Dyer	Athletic Director
1923	Gilbert W. Mead	English
1923	F. Earl Ward	English
1923	Mary C. McConagha	Public Speaking
1923	Charles D. Bohannan	Economics and Business Administration
1923	Helen L. Madden	Piano
1923	Elizabeth B. Whiteman	Librarian
1923	Andrew A. McDonald	Director of Publicity, Manager of Athletics
1924	Captain William McKee	Economics and Business Administration (retired 1958, 34 years)
1924	John D. Lawther	Psychology, Basketball Coach
1924	A. D. Fraser	Ancient Languages
1924	George D. DeMille	English
1924	J. George Lutz	Chemistry
1924	Edna C. McCabe	Modern Languages
1924	Elberta Kagy	Violin
1924	Mary Louise Lloyd	Music

YEAR	NAME	DISCIPLINE
1924	Marian W. Redway	Librarian
1925	Gilbert Taylor	Latin (retired 1953, 28 years)
1925	Charles A. Dawson	English
1925	Franz Bellinger	Music
1925	Alice Nieveen	Music
1925	Paul E. Pendleton	English
1925	Robert X. Graham	English
1925	Margaret E. Robertson	English
1925	Mildred A. Ailman	Librarian
1926	Jack Hulme	Swimming Coach, Director of Physical Education
1926	John E. Caughey	Bible
1926	Royal A. Gettman	English
1926	W. S. Vance	English
1926	Hunter D. Farish	History
1926	Lois W. Doolittle	Modern Languages
1926	Juanita C. Robinson	Modern Languages
1926	James W. Coleman	Physical Education
1927	Alan B. Davis	Music (retired 1955, 28 years)
1927	Marjorie Brown	English
1927	Mrs. James A. McLaughry	Modern Languages
1927	Ruby L. Guilliams	Music
1928	Harold L. Black	Mathematics
1928	John Orr	Bible, Acting Dean, Acting President (retired 1954, 26 years)
1928	Ben Euwema	English
1928	A. T. Cordray	Public Speaking
1928	John G. Moorhead	Mathematics and Physics
1928	Florence W. White	Modern Languages
1928	Dorothy C. Kirkbride	Piano (retired 1970, 42 years)
1928	Esther M. McKray	Violin
1929	Harlow S. Osgood	Chemistry
1929	Eldon C. Murray	Violin
1929	Agnes G. Martin	Music
1929	Mrs. Ben Euwema	Mathematics
1930	Leon S. Marshall	History
1930	Harry Fox Young	Education
1930	Thomas V. Mansell	Economics and History
1930	Mae E. Haas	Music
1930	Monique Lussan Mercat	French
1930	Malcolm H. White	Business Manager
1931	Hershel V. Beasley	Chemistry
1931	G. Ross Ellis	Business Administration (retired 1975, 44 years)
1931	Bertha A.Bay	Business Administration
1931	Baldwin Sears	Purchasing Agent
1931	Gordon Bach Nevin	Organ
1931	Edward H. Freeman	Piano
1931	Florence Mae Thomas	Music
1931	Mrs. A.T. Cordray	English
1932	Robert F. Galbreath	President

YEAR	NAME	DISCIPLINE
1932	Harold J. Brennan	Art
1932	Herbert L. Davis	Chemistry
1932	Foster B. Steele	Mathematics
1932	Avery Jonah Gronfield	Hebrew
1932	Ruth E. McConnell	English
1932	Ronald E. Jones	Economics
1932	Arthur D. Kirkbride	Business Administration
1932	Margaret F. Reed	Business Administration
1932	Pearl Hoagland	Education and Psychology
1932	Donald O. Cameron	Violin (retired 1965, 33 years)
1932	Lynn McCuskey	English and History
1932	Mary E. Turner	Dean of Women
1932	Haskell R. Patton	Business Manager
1932	William A. Johns	Director of Public Relations
1932	Margaret F. Reed	Assistant Librarian
1932	Jack Hulme	Assistant Director of Physical Education
1933	Francis S. Sowersby	Business Administration
1933	Carl Ernest Rankin	Education
1933	Albert J. Tener	Speech
1933	Helen Yoder	Assistant Librarian
1933	Louise Kepple	Accountant
1933	James V. Baker	History
1933	Thomas V. Mansell	History
1933	Mona Sowash	French
1933	Walter Biberich	German (retired 1973, 40 years)
1933	Ada I. Peabody	Music (retired 1971, 38 years)
1934	Alex C. Burr	Dean of the College
1934	Edward T. Miller Jr	Business Administration
1934	Homer E. Cooper	Education
1934	Chauncy E. Goodchild	Biology
1934	Richard M. Patterson	Voice
1934	J. Ralph Neale	Bible
1935	Wallace R. Biggs	Journalism
1935	Robert J. Swenson	Business Administration
1935	Grace May Ackard	Secretarial Science
1935	Norman H. Diamond	Hebrew
1936	Mary M. Purdy	English (retired 1956, 20 years)
1936	Virginia T. Everett	English
1936	Joseph C. Dewey	Education, Director of Placement
1936	Jessie E. Ashworth	History
1936	Francis Craig	Health
1936	Donald C. Mathews	Biology
1936	Wallace R. Biggs	Director of News Bureau
1936	L. Laverne Strausbaugh	Speech
1937	Branson Beeson Holder	Economics
1937	Donald Lawrence	Secretarial Science
1937	Glenn J. Taylor	Speech
1937	Max H. Guyer	History
1937	Grover C. Washabaugh	Physical Education (retired 1961, 24 years)
1938	Emma M. Campbell	English
1938	McCrea Hazlett	English

YEAR	NAME	DISCIPLINE
1938	Reid Bingham Duncan	History
1938	Maxwell Kelso	Dean of the College
1938	Albert Koper	Chemistry
1938	William L. Reuter	Education
1938	Lola Sewall	Mathematics
1939	Albert J. George	Modern Languages
1939	Herbert C. Graebner	Economics
1939	Ruth Sewall	Music
1939	Franklin J. Shaw	Psychology
1940	D. Ralph Appleman	Music
1940	Russell N. Cansler	Secretarial Studies
1940	W. Brainerd Jamison	Bible
1940	Lowell Leland	English
1940	Wilanne Lorimer	Physical Education
1940	Edward A. Metcalf	Chemistry
1941	Dallmeyer Russell	Piano
1941	Frank M. Brettholle	Economics
1941	Margaret C. George	English
1941	Margaret Graff	Psychology
1941	Helen Hauck	Librarian
1941	David Henderson	History
1941	Carroll H. Leeds	Education
1941	Juanita R. Moorhead	Spanish
1941	G. W. H. Powell	Chemistry
1942	Michael Radock	Journalism
1942	Jose D. Arevalo	Spanish
1942	Wayne H. Christy	Bible (retired 1983, 41 years)
1942	Robert F. Galbreath Jr.	Secretarial Studies (retired 1977, 35 years)
1942	Sarah B. Hamilton	Secretarial Studies
1942	Neil A. McNall	History
1942	Clara E. McCandless	Assistant to Business Manager
1942	Susan Scurr	Dietitian
1942	Helen Y. Hauck	Librarian
1942	Carroll H. Leeds	Director of Teacher Placement
1942	Anne C. Skoog	Assistant Librarian
1942	Mabel C. Kocher	Librarian (retired 1975, 33 years)
1943	Leila McNeill	English
1943	T. R. Wiley	Spanish (retired 1967, 24 years)
1943	Donald Barbe	Speech
1943	Harold Burry	Physical Education, Football Coach, later Director of Athletics (retired 1980, 37 years)
1943	Melvin Hetzler	Physical Education
1943	Clyde English	Organ
1943	Eve Goodenough	Psychology
1943	R. Glenn Hall	Mathematics
1943	J. Levan Hill	Engineering Drawing
1943	Samuel Hopfer	Physics
1943	Paul Keenan	Chemistry
1943	J. Byers King	Mathematics
1943	Harriet Jackson Sarver	Mathematics

YEAR	NAME	DISCIPLINE
1943	Elsie Leffingwell	Secretarial Science
1943	Irvin G. Wyllie	History
1943	Miriam M. Cosel	Dietitian
1943	Leila P. Ernest	Dietitian
1943	Helen McClelland	Assistant Librarian
1943	Hugh M. Hart	College Physician
1944	Mary Jane Stevenson	Dean of Women
1944	Frank Brettholle	Business Manager
1944	Emmett Davidson	Economics
1944	Ludwig Lenel	Music
1944	Elizabeth Butz	Music
1944	Alona Elizabeth Evans	Economics
1944	Jane Hawkins	Librarian (retired 1978, 34 years)
1944	Beulah Mae Kimble	Journalism
1944	Donna Mae Pound	Physical Education
1944	Alice K. Schuster	History
1944	Katharine Shattuck	English
1944	James H. Stevenson	Physics
1944	Martha Barnhill	English
1944	Zelma Whittenberg	Education
1944	Charles E. Holley Jr.	Chemistry
1944	Gertrude Minner Rodgers	Accountant
1945	Nellie Barbe	Cashier and Accountant
1945	Horace Fowble	Bookstore Manager
1945	Robert E. Maxwell	Alumni Director
1945	John Reed Spicer	Dean of the College
1945	Charles D. Starr	Chemistry
1945	Albert James Cox	History
1945	Helen V. Cushman	Speech
1945	James W. Evans	Music
1945	Charles I. Sager	Music
1945	Benedict Hall	Biology
1945	J. Irvine Reaney	Education, Director of Graduate Study
1945	William J. Thomas	Journalism
1945	Harry Manley	Government
1945	John W. Creighton	Economics
1945	Jane C. Little	Secretarial Science
1946	H. Lloyd Cleland	President
1946	W. J. Harper McKnight	Dean of the College and Pastor
1946	R. Ross Houston	College Physician
1946	Joseph M. Hopkins	Bible (retired 1985, 39 years)
1946	C. Robert Kelly	Bible
1946	Donald E. Hoffmaster	Biology
1946	George O. Hollibaugh	Biology
1946	Peter J. Zucchero	Biology
1946	E. G. Haas	Chemistry
1946	Lowell Hicks	Chemistry
1946	Ralph F. Lengerman	Chemistry
1946	C. A. Walker	Business Administration
1946	Elster C. Short	Education
1946	Reed Groniger	Education

YEAR	NAME	DISCIPLINE
1946	Beulah Campbell	Education
1946	George Bleasby	English (retired 1975, 29 years)
1946	Amy Charles	English
1946	John Forry	English
1946	Ann Shane Jones	English
1946	Maxine Gilliland	English
1946	Myrta McGinnis	English
1946	Elizabeth Nixon	English
1946	Jane Laird Orluk	History
1946	George Conway	Mathematics
1946	Wayne McGaughey	Mathematics
1946	Blanche Carrier	Psychology
1946	Harvey Mercer	Secretarial Science
1946	Arlene Risher	Secretarial Science
1946	Melvin P. Moorhouse	Speech
1946	W. Paul Gamble	Radio and Alumni Director, later English and College Historian (retired 1977, 31 years)
1946	Alice Ligo	French (retired 1967, 21 years)
1947	E. Lucille Frey	Biology (retired 1970, 23 years)
1947	Eleanor Feigenbaum	Biology
1947	Frank M. Semans	Biology
1947	Benjamin H. Pringle	Chemistry
1947	Samuel H. Sloan	Business Administration
1947	Zita Hanford	Business Administration
1947	Malcolm J. Carr	Business Administration
1947	Harold Lundvall	Business Administration
1947	Richard Stewart	Business Administration
1947	Everett Handy	Education
1947	Paul E. Brown	Mathematics (retired 1976, 29 years)
1947	James H. Ralston	Music
1947	Robert M. Woods	Physics (retired 1973, 26 years)
1947	James C. Laurence	Physics
1947	Robert S. Carter	Psychology
1947	Claude F. Eckman	Psychology
1947	Donald E. Lathrope	Sociology
1947	David E. McArthur	Speech
1947	Helen Sittig	Dean of Women
1948	Charles L. Dietz	Art
1948	W. George Faddis	Art
1948	Myron Simpson	Biology
1948	Donald G. Hartman	Biology
1948	J. Oliver Collins	Chemistry
1948	Edwin C. Gangloff	Chemistry
1948	John G. Zimmerman	Chemistry
1948	Henry Calvert	Business Administration
1948	Milvin A. Steiner	Education
1948	Ella Mae Stagg	Languages
1948	Edwin Galbraith	Mathematics
1948	Frank H. Bohnhorst	Music
1948	Clayton L. Straw	Physics

YEAR	NAME	DISCIPLINE
1948	John W. Reid	Psychology
1949	Will W. Orr	President
1949	George C. Collins	Journalism-News Bureau
1949	Charles G. Ridl	Physical Education, Basketball Coach, later Director of Athletics (retired 1985, 37 years)
1949	Robert A. McGill	English
1950	William Vander Lugt	Dean of the College
1950	Bertha Hutchison	Manager of TUB
1950	Lewis H. Wagenhorst	Education
1950	Joseph N. Johnson	Education
1950	Ethel Cowles	Physical Education
1950	Robert E. Higgins	Psychology
1950	Bruce J. Carlton	Speech
1950	Charles G. Curtis	Sociology
1950	Wallace N. Jamison	History
1951	Frank McClanahan	Medicine-Health
1951	Allegra Ingleright	Education
1951	Martin Ridge	History
1951	Ronald Carley	Music
1951	Margaret McBride	Physical Education
1951	William G. Burbick	Speech (retired 1984, 33 years)
1951	James M. Lewis	Speech
1951	Denton Albright	Psychology
1952	Hugh Rawls	Biology
1952	Thomas F. Cummings	Chemistry
1952	John R. Edwards	Education, Director of Admissions
1952	Gildo Gene Santavicea	Education
1952	Ernest L. Saul	Education
1952	Delber L. McKee	History (retired 1988, 36 years)
1952	Donald K. McKee	History
1952	J. Hilton Turner	Ancient Languages (retired 1984, 32 years)
1952	Merrill Palmer	Mathematics
1952	Clarence J. Martin	Music (retired 1993, 41 years)
1952	Arthur Birkby	Music
1952	Mary B. Scanlon	Music
1952	Carl E. Waisenon	Sociology
1952	J. Wiley Prugh	Bible
1952	Robert G. Carey	Journalism-News Bureau
1953	Frank McClanahan	College Physician
1953	Jack Taylor	Art
1953	Paul Schwartz	Business Administration
1953	Albert G. Sweetser	Business Administration
1953	Carol J. Nicklas	Business Education
1953	Roger A. Max	Chemistry
1953	Olive R. Hewitt	Education
1953	Charles H. Cook	English (retired 1985, 32 years)
1953	Edward R. Cain	Political Science
1953	Charlotte Forsberg	Speech-Drama
1954	Thomas M. Gregory	Bible and Philosophy
1954	George Y. Bijani	Biology
1954	Elsie M. Hileman	Business Education

YEAR	NAME	DISCIPLINE
1954	Ruth B. Mikich	Business Education
1954	Mary A. Barbour	Education
1954	A. M. Schmuller	Education
1954	Henry VanHouten	Education
1954	Sherod M. Cooper	English
1954	Paul Whitney	English
1954	George Masterton	Sociology
1954	Frances V. Henry	Speech
1954	Vernon Wanty	News Bureau
1954	Isabelle K. Smith	Cashier and Accountant
1955	Norman R. Adams	Bible
1955	Margaret Gamble	Business Education
1955	Herman DeHaas	Chemistry
1955	Clyde Amon	Chemistry
1955	Arthur L. Jensen	History (retired 1989, 34 years)
1955	John L. Huyck	Music
1955	Marilyn E. Dimitroff	Physical Education
1955	John G. Albright	Physics
1955	Leone M. Westover	Speech
1955	Martha Whitehill	Dean of Women
1955	Paul M. Musser	Field Representative-Churches
1955	Dorothy Nowling	Dietitian
1956	Cleo M. Hummel	Biology
1956	Charles Carlson	Business and Economics
1956	Amos Nevin Sponseller	Business and Economics
1956	Joseph F. Schwartz	Business and Economics
1956	H. Dewey DeWitt	Chemistry (retired 1993, 37 years)
1956	Joseph R. Henderson	Education (retired 1980, 24 years)
1956	George W. Cobb	English
1956	Elizabeth Keen	English
1956	Mary Ellen Williams	English
1956	Josef H. Wiehr	German
1956	James A. Duran	History
1956	James L. Smith	Mathematics
1956	Raymond H. Ocock	Organ (retired 1993, 37 years)
1956	Jane Walker	Physical Education
1956	E. Seaton Carney	Physics
1956	Roger T. Wolcott	Sociology (retired 1993, 37 years)
1956	David L. Colton	Director of News Bureau
1956	Jay W. Newman	Manager of Bookstore
1957	Carl H. Larson	Art
1957	Teunis Vergeer	Biology
1957	Charles F. Saylor	Education
1957	Margaret Means	Education
1957	Sara K. Scent	English
1957	Dan E. Wilson	English
1957	Charlene Stewart	Mathematics
1957	Isaac E. Reid Jr.	Music (retired 1982, 25 years)
1957	Lois Carnahan	Physical Education
1957	Billy G. Garland	Physical Education
1957	Robert Dorrell	Speech

YEAR	NAME	DISCIPLINE
1957	Robert Hall	Speech
1957	Norma E. Langham	Speech
1958	James A. Clark	Economics
1958	Ruth L. Meyers	Education
1958	Virginia Fulcomer	Education and Psychology
1958	Paul W. Pillsbury	English
1958	R. Dale Tuttle	English
1958	Conrad Wiley	English
1958	Harry G. Swanhart	History (retired 1996, 38 years)
1958	J. Miller Peck	Mathematics (retired 1999, 41 years)
1958	Barbara L. Lapsley	Language
1958	Dorothy Colton	Physical Education
1958	Cleve D. Oliver	Physical Education
1958	Anthony Clark	Speech
1958	Donald H. Wood	Speech
1958	Graham M. Ireland	Dean of Men (retired 1988, 30 years)
1958	Robert M. Ashbaugh	Admissions
1958	William E. Blackburn	Superintendent of Properties (retired 1987, 29 years)
1958	Clara Thomas	Assistant Librarian
1959	Robert D. Robinson	Art
1959	William Stuart	Business Education
1959	Richard A. Hendry	Chemistry (retired 1998, 39 years)
1959	Gerald Simmons	Chemistry
1959	J. Edward Smith	Education and Psychology
1959	Edna Oswalt	Education and Psychology
1959	Julia D. Marshall	Education and Psychology
1959	Charles R. Andrews	English
1959	Hilda Radzin	Language
1959	James E. Rees	Music
1959	Janet M. McNutt	Physical Education
1959	Charles Cox	Speech
1959	Robert Clark	Speech
1959	Judson McConnell	Dean of the Chapel (retired 1985, 26 years)
1959	Donald J. Pace	Assistant Business Manager
1959	Robert Campbell	Assistant Alumni Secretary
1960	John Kowalek	Art
1960	Chin An Yang	Bible and Philosophy
1960	Edward Gese	Biology (retired 1984, 24 years)
1960	Clara Cockerille	Education
1960	C. Arthur Christopher	Education
1960	Norman McWhinney	English
1960	James Vizas	English
1960	Ilse Linneman	Language
1960	Raymond Swift	Music
1960	John L. Walker	Assistant Director of Admissions
1961	Nelson E. Oestreich	Art (retired 1988, 27 years)
1961	Bardarah McCandless	Bible
1961	Michael W. Fabian	Biology
1961	Robert S. Bailey	Business Administration
1961	Einar Bredland	Education and Psychology

YEAR	NAME	DISCIPLINE
1961	Richard V. Chambers	Education and Psychology
1961	Harry C. Pry	Education and Psychology
1961	Frank J. Donovan	English
1961	Selma Tate Ceusnez	Language
1961	Alice McFarland	Language
1961	Charles Shannon	Language
1961	Stanley E. Tagg	Music
1961	William S. McGinnis	Physical Education
1961	Edward F. Douglas	Speech
1961	Frederic Newhart	Speech
1961	William T. Bolyard	Director of Student Affairs
1961	Howard S. Stewart	Registrar
1961	Jack B. Critchfield	Director of Admissions
1961	Charles K. Henderson	Director of Public Information
1962	Robert A. Coughhenour	Bible
1962	Norlyn Bodkin	Biology
1962	Ronald P. Bergey*	Accounting
1962	Kenneth M. Long*	Chemistry
1962	A.H. Solomon	Education and Psychology
1962	Edmund M. Hayes	English
1962	Lauren R. Stevens	English
1962	Adam J. Bisanz	Language
1962	George Clemens	Language
1962	James K. Sewall	Language (retired 1987, 25 years)
1962	Karen Lee Berry	Math
1962	Carolyn J. Bessy	Physical Education
1962	Marjorie A. Walker	Physical Education (retired 1993, 31 years)
1962	Clarence N. Stone	Political Science
1962	Richard V. Stevens	Speech
1962	Katherine McClure	Dean of Women
1962	Gertrude Chapin	Assistant Librarian
1963	Jack B. Rogers	Bible and Philosophy
1963	Percy Warrick Jr.	Chemistry (retired 1992, 29 years)
1963	Richard O. Davis	Education
1963	Jeanne Braham	English
1963	Marion A. Fairman	English
1963	Marilyn J. Denton	English
1963	Arthur H. Auten	History
1963	James A. Cummins*	Language
1963	Francis M. Webster	Physical Education
1963	Richard L. Bestwick	Physical Education
1963	John D. Cowlishaw	Physics
1963	Roger C. Johnson	Physics
1963	Walter H. Slack	Political Science (retired 1996, 33 years)
1963	Mary P. Fray	Librarian (retired 1984, 21 years)
1963	James R. Meurer	Sociology
1963	Douglas R. VanderYacht	Speech
1963	William R. Haley	Speech
1963	William H. Hassler	Director of Student Affairs
1963	Philip A. Snyder	Director of Public Information.
1963	Frederic C. Stoop	Assistant Director of Development

YEAR	NAME	DISCIPLINE
1964	James A. Hopper	Art
1964	Thomas W. George	Biology
1964	Robert H. Luce	Biology
1964	Russell D. Chambers	English
1964	Wesley Craven	English
1964	Howard C. Adams	Languages
1964	Dale Z. Kilhefner	Mathematics
1964	Carol A. Schoenhard	Music (retired 1984, 20 years)
1964	William L. Greer	Sociology
1964	Raymond C. Fenn	Speech
1964	Richard A. Sinzinger	Speech
1964	Leon D. Radaker	Education
1965	William H. Harvey	Biology
1965	William E. Stanclift	Chemistry
1965	James T. Shanklin	Economics and Business Administration
1965	William L. Edwards	Education and Psychology
1965	Janet H. Eagleson	Education and Psychology
1965	David B. Gray*	Education and Psychology
1965	Daniel L. Van Dyke	Education and Psychology
1965	Christopher Brown	English
1965	Irving L. Gray	English
1965	Nancy E. James	English (retired 1990, 25 years)
1965	C. Clyde Jones	History
1965	Donald T. Moen	Languages
1965	Rudolf Herrig	Languages (retired 1986, 21 years)
1965	Paul R. Chenevey*	Music
1965	Lewis Songer	Music
1965	D. Ralph Bouch	Physical Education
1965	Thomas C. Heard	Physics
1965	Robert C. Sproul	Religion
1965	Walter E. Scheid	Speech (retired 2000, 35 years)
1965	Sara G. Hawkinson	English
1965	Gertrude M. Lewis	Education
1965	Floyd J. Zehr	Physics (retired 2000, 35 years)
1965	Jean Antes	Associate Dean of Students
1965	Philip Snyder	Public Information
1965	Galen Hover	College Physician
1966	Robert B. Hild	Art
1966	Robert V. Travis	Biology (retired 1996, 30 years)
1966	Robert L. Milam	Economics and Business Administration
1966	Arthur D. Chesler	Economics and Business Administration
1966	Lawrence M. Douglas	Education
1966	Samuel A. Farmerie	Education (retired 1996, 30 years)
1966	David V. Hessong	Education
1966	Charles E. Skinner	Education
1966	Frederick D. Horn*	English
1966	James S. Beddie	History, Political Science, Sociology
1966	Robert C. Beider	History, Political Science, Sociology
1966	Peter N. Kidman	History, Political Science, Sociology
1966	Lawson A. Pendleton	History, Political Science, Sociology
1966	E. Ernest Wood	History, Political Science, Sociology

YEAR	NAME	DISCIPLINE
1966	Thomas R. Nealeigh	Mathematics (retired 1989, 23 years)
1966	Verna Wilfert	Mathematics
1966	William J. Catherwood	Music
1966	Dorothy McFarland	Physical Education
1966	J. William Carpenter	Religion and Philosophy
1966	Alfred D. Jensen	Religion and Philosophy
1966	Frederic C. Stoop	Director of Development
1966	Mitchell G. Simon	Director of Public Information
1967	Earland I. Carlson	President
1967	George C. Gilbert	Art
1967	Verl D. Rhoton	Biology (retired 1990, 23 years)
1967	Elizabeth W. Smith	Biology
1967	Robert E. Conway	Education (retired 1990, 23 years)
1967	Earl Houts	Education
1967	Robert H. Fogg	English
1967	Earl C. Lammel	Theatre (retired 1996, 29 years)
1967	Caroline Lelear	English
1967	Terry-Howard Wallace	English
1967	M. Robert Ewing	History and Political Science
1967	William W. Burns	History and Political Science
1967	W. John Mathieson	Languages
1967	Susan Pope Webb	Languages
1967	Carol A. Godsen	Physical Education
1967	William C. Davis	Physical Education
1967	John H. Ginaven	Physics
1967	Edwin G. Tobin	Assistant Director of Admissions
1968	John Mansell – H.L Shaffer	College Physicians
1968	G. Alan Sternbergh	Director of Career Planning and Placement (retired 1990, 22 years)
1968	Robert Latta*	Assistant Director of Admissions, Director of Financial Aid
1968	George Trivoli	Business and Economics
1968	Robert P DeSieno	Chemistry
1968	L. Jerold Miller	Education (retired 1994, 26 years)
1968	Jon Lawry	English
1968	Larry Sells	English
1968	Jacob Erhardt*	German
1968	Warren D. Hickman*	Mathematics
1968	Kenneth Whipkey	Mathematics
1968	Joseph B. Fusco	Physical Education, Football Coach, Director of Athletics (retired 2000, 32 years)
1968	C. Ronald Galbreath*	Physical Education, Basketball Coach
1968	Rita Gregg	Physical Education
1968	Irene F. Walters	Physical Education (retired 1990, 22 years)
1968	George Murphy	Physics
1968	Dale Willis	Speech
1968	Phillip A. Lewis	Dean of the College
1969	John Bush	Sociology
1969	Harold Davis	Physical Education
1969	William Bothell	Art
1969	Clarence E. Harms*	Biology

YEAR	NAME	DISCIPLINE
1969	Paul Frary	Economics and Business
1969	David Dyer	Economics and Business
1969	Terry Imar	Education and Psychology
1969	James Badal	English
1969	Russell Barnes	English
1969	Franz S. Mandarich	Spanish
1969	Herman DeHoog	Music
1969	Paul Johnson	Philosophy
1969	B. Eugene Nicholson*	Physical Education, Football Coach
1969	Raymond Ondako	Physical Education, Basketball Coach
1969	Susan Stewart	Physical Education
1969	Roy Knestrick	Sociology
1969	Jerome Henderson	Speech and Drama
1969	Louis Lager	Speech and Drama
1969	Thomas R. Giddens	Assistant to President
1969	James D. Sands	Business Manager
1969	Lorraine A. Sibbet	Assistant Dean of Students
1969	Harry W. Shoup	Director of Development
1969	Larry A. Judge	Director of Public Information
1969	William N. Jackson	Dean of the Chapel
1969	Robert Seidewitz	Director of Food Service, Business Manager
1970	David K. Brautigam*	Assistant Librarian
1970	Russell Terwilliger	Director of Counseling Center
1970	John C. Vance	Director of Deferred Giving
1970	Mary Beth McLaughry	Director of Annual Giving
1970	Thomas W. Carver	Assistant Dean of Students
1970	Raymond G. Preston	Alumni Director
1970	Patrick C. McCarthy*	Biology
1970	Robert Levine	Chemistry
1970	James Bradley	Economics and Business
1970	Loren Casement	Economics and Business
1970	Pirie Sublett	History
1970	A. Dwight Castro*	Languages
1970	Nancy Genovese	Languages
1970	Eliot M. Newsome	Music (retired 1993, 23 years)
1970	S. Kipley Haas*	Physical Education
1970	George Waggoner	Physical Education
1970	G. Samuel Lightner IV*	Physics
1970	Gary Mullin	Political Science
1970	Willard Overgaard	Political Science
1970	Andrew Abell	Psychology
1970	Peter Macky	Religion (retired 1997, 27 years)
1971	John E. Jelacic	Economics and Business
1971	Marta Messier	English
1971	Betty Bernack	Language
1971	Richard Bancroft	Music
1971	Irene Sample	Music
1971	Ronald Rossi	Psychology
1971	Stephen Shry	Psychology
1971	William L. Johnson*	Physics
1971	Jon M. Patterson	Sociology

YEAR	NAME	DISCIPLINE
1971	Carolyn Combs	Speech
1971	Richard E. Henderson	Director of Computer Center
1972	Robert Godfrey	Art
1972	John Philip Fawley*	Biology
1972	Robert E. Meadows	Economics and Business
1972	Eugene G. Sharkey*	History
1972	Nancy Mandlove	Language
1972	Roger N. Campbell	Physical Education
1972	W. Thomas Nichols	Political Science (retired 2000, 28 years)
1972	David G. Guthrie	Theatre (retired 1999, 27 years)
1973	Robert L. VanDale	Religion (retired 1998, 25 years)
1973	Richard R. Carroll	Economics
1973	John A. Griffiths	Education
1973	Eloise Snavely	Education
1973	Helga W. Kraft	Language
1973	Ellen Wood Hall	Language
1973	Eva H. Cadwallader	Philosophy (retired 1996, 23 years)
1973	James L. Twerdok	Director of Food Service
1973	James A. Perkins	English
1974	T. Hinds Wilson	Economics and Business Administration
1974	Paul G. Wozniak*	Economics and Business Administration
1974	G. Eugene Hill	Education (retired 1998, 24 years)
1974	Frank Frankfort	History
1974	Carol S. Fuller	Language
1974	Sara A. Gearhart	Language
1974	David J. Rooney	Physical Education
1974	Dale E. Hess	Political Science
1974	Frederick E. Smith	Librarian
1974	Charles M. Closz	Controller
1974	Richard W. Cochrane	Director of Deferred Giving
1975	Molly P. Spinney*	Librarian
1975	Daniel E. Fischmar*	Economics
1975	Michael Malzer	Economics
1975	Arthur C. Kelley	Education
1975	William J. McTaggert	English (retired 2001, 26 years)
1975	Thomas J. Bolgar	Physics
1975	Judy M. McMichael	Psychology
1975	Mark C. Klinger	Speech and Theatre
1976	Alvis Brown	Education
1976	Allen C. Johnston	Education (retired 2001, 25 years)
1976	Marlene A. Miller	Education
1976	Richard L. Sprow*	English
1976	William R. Frey	Physical Education
1976	Barbara T. Faires*	Mathematics
1976	Alan G. Gittis*	Psychology
1976	Richard B. Perkins	Sociology
1977	Edith D. Streams	Assistant to the President
1977	Donald C. Wallace	Dean of the Chapel
1977	Gary D. Lilly*	Sociology
1977	Catherine Muder Huebert	French
1977	Darwin W. Huey*	Education, Director of Graduate Program

YEAR	NAME	DISCIPLINE
1977	Daniel C. Messerschmidt	Economics
1978	Phyllis G. Kitzerow*	Sociology
1978	Patricia F. Lamb	English
1978	R. Scott Osborne	Speech
1978	Grover A. Pitman*	Music
1978	D. Scott Renninger Jr.*	Physical Education
1978	William McKnight Wright	Dean of Students
1979	Linda Natiello Freidland	Associate Dean of Students
1979	Martha T. Garing	Assistant Dean of Students
1979	Elizabeth Ellis Hines*	Admissions, Registrar, Development
1979	James C. Holden	Director of Counseling Center
1979	Robert G. Barlett	Physical Education
1979	Katherine Blacklock	Physics
1979	George T. Brunish	Mathematics and Computer Science
1979	Mary W. Hill	Education
1979	John R. Holloway	Biology
1979	Kathy Koop*	Art
1979	Tom E. Rosengarth*	Business Administration
1979	Diana V. Veith	Psychology
1980	Paul H. Yackey	Vice President of Development
1980	James R. Christofferson	Treasurer
1980	Bernard F. Bonnie*	Manager of Computer Operations
1980	Steven V. Baumeister	Librarian
1980	Byron L. Carnahan	Physics
1980	Terry W. Fuller	English
1980	Lynn L. Foltz*	Financial Aid Statisticin
1980	Stephen V. Grillo	Art
1980	Frederick R. Neikirk Jr.	Political Science
1980	Jo-Ann S. Rasmussen	Speech
1980	Monika Rudzik	Chemistry, Biology (retired 2001, 21 years)
1981	Robert E. Lauterbach	Interim President
1981	Elizabeth B. Shear	Director of Public Relations
1981	John C. Fisler	Director of Annual Fund-Deferred Giving
1981	David L. Barner*	Broadcasting
1981	Dorita F. Bolger*	Librarian
1981	C. Paul Clark	Education
1981	Paul N. Wallace*	Computer Science
1981	E. Paige Wisotzka	French
1982	Allen P. Splete	President
1982	Jerry M. Boone	Dean of Students, Interim President
1982	Wayne R. Nickerson	Dean of the Chapel
1982	William E. Beckman	Business Manager
1982	Karla S. Bacon	Assistant Director of Admissions
1982	Michael Chejlava	Chemistry
1982	Henry R. Klimesz	Economics and Business
1983	Mary F. Dorsey	Assistant Dean of Student Affairs
1983	Judith Duda*	Director of Student Health Center
1983	David N. Frohman	Physical Education
1983	Gail L. Miller*	Business Administration
1983	Vijay K. Verna	Business Administration
1983	Sandra K. Webster*	Psychology

YEAR	NAME	DISCIPLINE
1984	Zane G. Gizzi	Assistant Director of Admissions
1984	David M. Wahl	Vice President of Development
1984	Carol M. Bove*	French
1984	James E. Hall*	Mathematics
1984	Jesse T. Mann*	French
1984	Victoria S. Tietze	French and Latin
1985	Cynthia J. Carle	Director of College Relations
1985	Martin D. Kennedy	Assistant Director of Annual Fund
1985	Kimberlee A. Killmer*	Director of Human Resources
1985	Joanne Recchione	Coordinator of Publications
1985	Sandra L. Shearer*	Manager of Bookstore
1985	Donald E. Shelenberger*	Business Manager
1985	Patricia P. Whitman	Controller
1985	Nancy C. Wright	Director of Continuing Education
1985	Collene B. Allen	Biology
1985	Leonard J. Barish	Telecommunications
1985	Peggy L. Cox*	Art
1985	Patricia M. Grayson	Psychology
1985	Robert G. Klamut Jr.	Physical Education
1985	Amy J. Luginbuhl	Mathematics and Computer Science
1985	Carl C. Peters	Economics and Business
1985	Andrew W. Smith	Mathematics and Computer Science
1986	Katherine A. Henry	Admissions Counselor
1986	Jill A. Jack	Admissions Counselor
1986	Benjamin A. Jones	Director of Physical Plant
1986	Katheleen H. Dolan	Spanish
1987	Oscar E. Remick	President; Philosophy
1987	Grace M. Allen	Vice President for Academic Affairs, German
1987	William J. Birkhead*	Vice President for Finance
1987	Kevin J. Garvey	Vice President for Development
1987	Robert O. Thomas	Vice President for Student Affairs
1987	David W. Stewart	Chief of Security
1987	Jeffrey E. Tobin	Director of Alumni and Parent Relations
1987	Shaun J. Toomey*	Athletic Trainer
1987	Kelly A. Variotta	Assistant Director of Alumni Affairs
1987	Keturah F. Laney*	Chapel
1987	Sarah K. Huey*	Director of Learning Center
1987	Drea Howenstein	Art
1987	Gabriel G. Manrique	Economics
1987	Sheryl L. Postman	Spanish
1987	Alex Starr	Theatre
1988	Charles M. Chirozzi*	Chief Engineer
1988	Guy A. Combine	Director of Audio-Visual Services
1988	James E. Dafler*	Basketball Coach, Director of Athletics
1988	Neal A. Edman*	Dean of Student Affairs
1988	Camille Hawthorne*	Associate Dean of Student Affairs
1988	T. Lynn Fox*	Manager of Computer Labs
1988	R. Dana Paul	Director of Admissions
1988	Anthony C. Peyronel	Director of Communications
1988	Jon Kinel	Physics
1988	Ellen L. Ruckert	Computer Science

YEAR	NAME	DISCIPLINE
1988	Charles G. Yarbrough	Speech
1989	Gloria C. Cagigas*	Director of Development and Planned Giving, later Vice President for Institutional Advancement
1989	David J. Grober	Director of Annual Giving
1989	L. Eugene DeCaprio*	Director of Celebrity Series
1989	Daniel P. Irvin	Associate Director of Communications
1989	Jeffrey C. McCabe	Director Physical Plant
1989	Joy Cable	Mathematics and Computer Science
1989	Blase B. Cindric	Computer Science
1989	Carolyn K. Cuff*	Mathematics
1989	Elizabeth A. Ford*	English
1989	Lewis K. Grell	Education
1989	Peter A. Groothuis*	Economics
1989	William J. Johnson	Theatre
1989	Abul K. Khan	Chemistry
1989	Nora M. Lane	French
1989	Cynthia A. Laurie	Psychology
1989	Kevin L. Ross	Economics
1989	Corinne L. Ruby	Mathematics and Computer Science
1989	Linda J. Smaltz	Economics and Business
1989	Robert J. Stokem	Speech
1989	Valeria A. Whitecap	Speech
1990	Melissa K. Barnes	Director of Career Planning and Placement
1990	Bruce A. Bartoo	Director of Annual Giving
1990	Nathaniel P. Boyle	Budget Reporting Officer
1990	Mary C. James*	Assistant, later Director of Alumni Affairs
1990	Thomas K. McMahon*	Coordinator of Business Systems
1990	Gary L. Swanson*	Director of Audio-Visual Services
1990	Diana M. Reed*	Preschool Teacher
1990	Verena Botzenhart-Viehe*	History
1990	Marilyn S. Corrado	Business Administration
1990	Daniel Hrozencik	Mathematics
1990	Joanne M. Leight	Physical Education
1990	Richard McCallster	Spanish
1990	Richard J. Stemple	Telecommunications
1990	David G. Swerdlow*	English
1990	Ann E. Throckmorton*	Biology
1990	David C. Twining*	History
1990	Ross A. Wastvedt*	English
1990	Michael R. Zianni	Biology
1991	Sean M. Kelly*	Physical Education
1991	Paul R. Darlington	Director of Safety and Security
1991	David G. Steele	Development Officer
1991	Kent D. Carter*	Business Administration
1991	Mary Donald Mbosowo	French
1991	Karen K. Sracic	Library
1991	Betty Richardson	Counselor
1992	Jeffrey F. Machi	Coordinator of Telemarketing
1992	Jeffrey P. Salamon	Director of Marketing Communications
1992	Kathleen Scholl	Education

YEAR	NAME	DISCIPLINE
1992	Deborah C. Shale*	English
1992	Claudia Nadine	French
1992	Mandy B. Medvin*	Psychology
1992	David Krus Jr.	Physics
1992	James C. Rhoads Jr.*	Political Science
1992	Colleen Beckovich	Associate Director of Communications
1992	Jennifer L. Thompson*	Director of Westminster Fund
1992	Amy Rose Wissinger	Director of Publications
1992	Philip King	Minority Student Adviser
1992	Carol L. Yova*	Director of Lifelong Learning Program
1993	Arthur H. Rathjen	Vice President for Development
1993	Gary K. Cameron	Budget and Reporting Officer
1993	Bradley P. Tokar*	Associate Director of Admissions
1993	M. Keen Compher*	Biology
1993	Charlene K. Endrizzi*	Education
1993	Tat P. Fong	Economics
1993	Glenn Grishkoff	Art
1993	Martha R. Joseph*	Chemistry
1993	Thomas P. Kelliher	Computer Science
1993	Jeffrey J. Kripal*	Religion
1993	Nancy A. Macky*	English
1993	Kristin Park*	Sociology
1993	Jesse (Jizhong) Song	Librarian
1993	Tammy L. Swearingen*	Physical Education, Assistant Athletic Director
1993	Timothy T. Wooster*	Chemistry
1993	Angela Broeker	Music
1994	Ina Martin Rexford	Director of Planned Giving
1994	Ron Treacy	Director of Communication Services
1994	John Deegan Jr.*	Vice President for Academic Affairs and Dean of the College; Political Science
1994	David Feuerman	Communication Arts
1994	Mark T. Taylor*	Grant Writer/Researcher
1994	Linda M. Meade'	Assistant, then Director of Career Center
1994	Kelly A. Hartner*	Enterprise Network Manager
1994	Joyce E. Hoellein*	Education
1994	Bryan S. Rennie*	Philosophy
1994	Zachary D. Zuwiyya	Spanish
1995	Amanda A. DeShong	Chemical Hygiene Officer
1995	Joseph M. Onderko*	Sports Information Director
1995	Craig W. Mosurinjohn	Director of Career Center
1995	Debi S. Behr*	Preschool Teacher
1995	R. Tad Greig*	Music
1995	Ann L. Murphy*	French
1995	Douglas P. Starr	Music
1996	Mark A. Meighen*	Senior Director, Marketing Communications
1996	Susann E. Rudloff*	Coordinator of Advancement Programs
1996	Edward S. Cohen*	Political Science
1996	Linda P. Domanski*	Education
1996	Kathleen A. Hric	Education
1996	Jan M. Reddinger*	Coach, Softball and Basketball

YEAR	NAME	DISCIPLINE
1996	Cary W. Horvath*	Communication Studies
1996	Russell E. Martin*	History
1996	Sheila A. McBride	Communication Studies
1996	Mark A. Sciutto	Psychology
1996	Virginia M. Tomlinson*	Sociology
1997	R. Thomas Williamson*	President
1997	Sharna C. Moore	Development Officer
1997	Linda M. Volpe*	Assistant to the Dean
1997	Joseph M. Balczon*	Biology
1997	Camila Bari de Lopez*	Spanish
1997	Roman Garrison	Religion
1997	Milagros Z. Swerdlow*	English
1997	Suzanne G. Prestien*	Public Relations
1997	Leslie D. Thomas	Theatre
1997	Michael P. Muth*	Philosophy
1998	Douglas L. Swartz*	Dean of Admissions
1998	Barbara I. Quincy*	Counselor
1998	Owen Wagner*	Director of Physical Plant
1998	Girish Thakar*	Soccer Coach
1998	Larry R. Ondako*	Physical Education
1998	Jason B. Nevinger*	Assistant Director of Admissions
1998	Deborah L. Parady*	Graphic Designer
1998	John Ackley	Computer Science
1998	Christine A. Martin*	Controller
1998	John P. Bonomo*	Computer Science
1998	John R. Garell	Computer Science
1998	Margaret J. Morris Lowe	Chemistry
1998	Kang-Yup Na*	Religion
1999	Lori A. Micsky*	Chemical Hygiene Officer
1999	Patrick S. Broadwater*	Publications Coordinator
1999	William J. Maloney*	Director of Church Relations
1999	John N. Lechner*	Public Safety, Assistant Dean of Student Affairs
1999	Deanna L. Drisko*	Web Master
1999	Don E. Goodlin Jr.*	Software Specialist
1999	Jeffrey Knapton*	Desktop Systems Manager
1999	Cheryl Gerber*	Assistant Director of Financial Aid
1999	Connie L. McGinnis*	Assistant Director of Celebrity Series
1999	Kathleen J. Edmiston*	Assistant to the Director, Career Center
1999	Ann L. Coble*	Religion
1999	Margaret A. Gingerich	Music
1999	Eileen E. Hendrickson*	Theatre
1999	Terri L. Lenox*	Computer Science
1999	Leigh C. Monhardt	Education
1999	Raymond A. Niekamp	Communication Studies
1999	Timothy A. Sherwood*	Chemistry
1999	John M. Klein*	Coach, Football and Baseball
1999	Molly A. Burnett*	Assistant Dean of Students
1999	Regina M. Sharbaugh*	Admissions Counselor
2000	Jerome M. Schmitt*	Football Coach
2000	E. June Garner*	Registrar

YEAR	NAME	DISCIPLINE
2000	Jennifer A. Hough*	Admissions Counselor
2000	James H. Herschel*	Assistant Controller
2000	Barry S. Bonnell	Biology
2000	James L. Cherney*	Speech
2000	Timothy Cuff*	Humanities
2000	Nancy Zipay DeSalvo*	Music
2000	Andrea K. Grove*	Political Science
2000	Elizabeth A. Harrison*	Music, Organ
2000	Robin Anna-Karin Lind*	Music, Choral
2000	Benita H. Muth*	Humanities
2000	John C. Robertson*	Biology
2000	C. David Shaffer*	Computer Science
2000	Betty P. Talbert*	Business Administration
2000	Bradley L. Weaver*	Broadcast Communications
2001	Steven M. Allen*	Chaplain
2001	Branislav Cikel*	Assistant Enterprise Network Manager
2001	Jeannette Hooks*	Diversity Coordinator
2001	Anne H. Bentz*	Music
2001	Carla A. Bluhm*	Psychology
2001	Helen M. Boylan*	Chemistry
2001	Amy H. Camardese*	Education
2001	Craig L. Caylor*	Physics
2001	Joshua C. Corrette-Bennett*	Biology
2001	Jennifer M. DiLalla*	English
2001	William J. Evans*	Education
2001	Alane S. Ferland*	Mathematics
2001	Bethany F. Hicok*	English
2001	Scott A. Mackenzie*	Theatre
2001	Delores A. Natale*	Public Relations

Intercollegiate Athletics
Summary of Team Records, 1884 – 2001

1884-85
Baseball 0-2.

1885-86
Baseball 1-2.

1886-87
Baseball 3-0.

1887-88
Baseball 0-1.

1888-89
Baseball 2-1.

1889-90
Baseball 2-1.

1890-91
Baseball 3-4.

1891-92
Football 0-1; Baseball 4-2.

1892-93
Football 3-1; Baseball (n/a).

1893-94
Football 2-2; Baseball 1-1.

1894-95
Football 1-3-1. Baseball 2-0-1.

1895-96
Football 4-1; Baseball 12-8, Conference
Champions; Track & Field (no record).

1896-97
Football 3-3-1; Baseball 5-3; Track & Field
(no record).

1897-98
Football 1-6-2; Basketball 4-2; Baseball 7-3;
Track & Field (no record).

1898-99
Football 2-8-1; Basketball 2-4; Baseball 5-3;
Track & Field (no record).

1899-1900
Football 6-2, Northwest Pennsylvania
Champions; Basketball 3-6; Baseball 11-6,
Conference Champions; Track & Field (n/a).

1900-01
Football 2-5; Basketball 2-5; Baseball 9-0;
Track & Field 1-0.

1901-02
Football 2-4-2; Basketball 3-5; Baseball 1-6;
Track & Field 1-0, National Champion Relay
Team.

1902-03
Football 3-4-4; Basketball 6-5; Baseball 7-10;
Track & Field 1-0.

1903-04
Football 3-5-1; Basketball 2-4; Baseball 3-3;
Track & Field (no record), National
Champion Relay Team.

1904-05
Football 4-3-2; Basketball 6-5; Baseball 2-1;
Track & Field (no record).

1905-06
Football 9-2; Basketball 12-2, Western
Pennsylvania Champions; Baseball 2-8;
Track & Field (no record).

1906-07
Football 6-2; Basketball 7-1; Baseball 7-7;
Track & Field (no record); Tennis
(no record), District Champions.

1907-08
Football 7-2-1, Conference Champions;
Basketball 6-9; Baseball 5-7; Track & Field
(no record); Tennis (no record), District
Champions.

1908-09
Football 8-2; Basketball 4-6; Baseball 3-8;
Track & Field 0-1.

1909-10
Football 4-6; Baseball 11-7, Western
Pennsylvania Champions; Track & Field 2-0,
Western Pennsylvania Champions; Tennis
(no record).

1910-11
Football 6-2; Women's Basketball 2-0;
Baseball 7-8; Track & Field 0-1; Tennis (no
record).

1911-12
Football 2-4-1; Women's Basketball 1-1;
Baseball 6-6; Track & Field 3-1; Tennis
(no record).

1912-13
Football 3-6; Women's Basketball 1-0;
Baseball 6-8; Track & Field (no record).

1913-14
Football 6-1-1; Women's Basketball 1-0;
Baseball 6-8; Track & Field 0-1.

1914-15
Football 5-3; Women's Basketball n/a;
Baseball 5-10; Track & Field 0-3;
Tennis 0-1-2.

1915-16
Football 2-5; Cross Country n/a; Men's
Basketball 0-4; Women's Basketball 1-2;
Baseball n/a; Track & Field 0-4; Tennis 1-2.

1916-17
Football 2-5-1; Cross Country n/a; Men's
Basketball 2-2; Women's Basketball 1-2;
Baseball 0-1; Track & Field (n/a); Tennis 0-1-1.

1917-18
Football 2-7; Men's Basketball 8-6; Women's
Basketball 3-1; Track & Field 0-1; Tennis 2-0.

1918-19
Football 3-2; Men's Basketball 6-4; Women's
Basketball n/a; Baseball 4-2; Track & Field 0-
1; Tennis 2-1.

1919-20
Football 2-3-2; Men's Basketball 6-7;
Women's Basketball 2-1; Baseball 1-7; Tennis
1-3.

1920-21
Football 0-6-2; Men's Basketball 2-14;
Women's Basketball 1-0; Baseball 8-4; Track
& Field (no record).

1921-22
Football 1-6-2; Men's Basketball 3-7;
Women's Basketball 6-1; Baseball 4-16; Track
& Field (no record).

1922-23
Football 0-8-1; Men's Basketball 10-8;
Women's Basketball 6-3-1; Baseball n/a;
Track & Field 1-1; Tennis 1-0.

1923-24
Football 1-7; Men's Basketball 9-8; Women's
Basketball 1-2-2; Baseball n/a; Track & Field
0-1; Tennis 8-1.

1924-25
Football 4-4; Men's Basketball 7-10;
Women's Basketball 1-7; Track & Field 2-0;
Tennis 12-0-1, Conference & District
Champions.

1925-26
Football 2-6; Cross Country 5-0, Conference
Champions; Men's Basketball 2-11; Women's
Basketball 0-6; Track & Field 1-1; Tennis 5-3,
Conference Champions.

1926-27
Football 1-4-1; Cross Country 1-2; Basketball
10-5; Swimming 2-0; Track & Field 0-2;
Tennis 5-1, Conference Champions.

1927-28
Football 2-3-2; Cross Country 3-2,
Conference Champions; Basketball 17-3,
Conference Champions; Swimming 0-2;
Track & Field 1-3; Tennis 4-5.

1928-29
Football 4-5; Cross Country 3-2, Conference
Champions; Basketball 15-2, Conference &
District Champions; Track & Field 2-1;
Tennis 5-0, Conference Champions.

1929-30
Football 3-4; Cross Country 0-4; Basketball
14-2, Conference Champions; Track & Field
2-1; Tennis 3-3.

1930-31
Football 4-5; Cross Country 1-3; Basketball
13-1, Conference & District Champions;
Track & Field 3-0; Tennis 2-4.

1931-32
Football 3-6; Cross Country 2-1, Conference
Champions; Basketball 16-2, Conference &
District Champions; Track & Field 1-1.

1932-33
Football 4-6; Cross Country 0-4; Basketball
19-6; Track & Field 1-1; Tennis 2-4.

1933-34
Football 2-6; Cross Country 2-1; Basketball
22-4, Conference Champions; Tennis 5-2.

1934-35
Football 3-6-1; Cross Country 0-2; Basketball
19-3; Tennis 3-4; Golf 0-1.

1935-36
Football 2-5; Basketball 20-6; Tennis 8-4;
Golf 0-5.

1936-37
Football 2-4-1; Basketball 14-7; Tennis 6-4;
Golf 0-3.

1937-38
Football 1-4-2; Basketball 15-5, District
Champions; Tennis 1-2-1; Golf 1-3.

1938-39
Football 1-4-3; Cross Country 1-6; Basketball 15-6; Swimming 1-5; Tennis 2-10; Golf 0-4.

1939-40
Football 3-5; Cross Country 4-3; Basketball 11-7; Swimming 2-6; Tennis 6-4; Golf 0-8.

1940-41
Football 2-6; Cross Country 5-0, District Champions; Basketball 20-2, Pennsylvania State Champions, NIT Tournament; Swimming 3-7; Track & Field 3-1; Tennis 8-2; Golf 1-4.

1941-42
Football 5-3; Cross Country 8-0, Tri-State Champions; Basketball 16-5; Swimming 9-0; Track & Field 0-2; Tennis 5-2.

1942-43
Football 4-4-1; Cross Country 4-1; Basketball 12-7; Swimming 3-1.

1943-44
Basketball 11-8.

1944-45
Basketball 14-5, Tri-State Conference & District Champions.

1945-46
Basketball 16-5.

1946-47
Football 3-1-4; Soccer 1-6; Basketball 20-4; Swimming 6-5; Track & Field 2-2; Golf 12-2.

1947-48
Football 1-7; Soccer 6-1; Cross Country 8-1; Basketball 15-9; Swimming 11-1; Track & Field 4-3; Golf 12-2.

1948-49
Football 3-4-1; Soccer 4-2-1; Cross Country 2-7; Basketball 15-8; Swimming 6-5; Track & Field 6-0; Golf 9-1-1.

1949-50
Football 2-5-2; Soccer 4-2-2; Cross Country 3-5; Basketball 25-4, NAIA National Tournament; Swimming 7-4; Baseball 7-2; Track & Field 2-4; Tennis 1-7, Golf 9-3-2.

1950-51
Football 2-6-1; Soccer 5-2; Cross Country 3-3, Tri-State Champions; Basketball 22-6, NAIA National Tournament; Swimming 8-3; Baseball 3-5; Track & Field 4-1; Tennis 2-6; Golf 9-2-2.

1951-52
Football 5-4; Soccer 1-4-1; Cross Country 3-3; Basketball 15-7; Swimming 7-2; Baseball 4-4-2; Track & Field 2-3; Tennis 3-7; Golf 3-5.

1952-53
Football 6-2; Cross Country 4-3, Tri-State Champions; Basketball 10-13; Swimming 5-5; Baseball 7-5; Track & Field 1-4; Tennis 3-5; Golf 3-6-1.

1953-54
Football 8-0, Tri-State Conference Champions; Cross Country 2-2; Basketball 17-6; Swimming 3-4; Baseball 8-4-1; Track & Field 4-1; Tennis 4-3; Golf 7-3.

1954-55
Football 6-1; Cross Country 1-2; Basketball 14-11; Swimming 3-4; Baseball 10-3; Track & Field 6-1, Tennis 9-2, Tri-State Conference Champions; Golf 2-9.

1955-56
Football 6-0-1, Tri-State Conference Champions; Cross Country 2-4; Basketball 13-11; Swimming 1-5; Baseball 8-4; Track & Field 8-0, Tri-State Conference Champions; Tennis 2-6; Golf 2-7.

1956-57
Football 8-0, Tri-State Conference Champions; Cross Country 2-6; Basketball 11-11; Swimming 3-6; Baseball 5-8; Track & Field 7-1, Tri-State Conference Champions; Tennis 5-5; Golf 6-4.

1957-58
Football 4-4; Cross Country 2-6; Basketball 13-12; Swimming 4-5; Baseball 14-1; Track & Field 8-2, Tri-State Conference Champions; Tennis 7-4; Golf 1-10.

1958-59
Football 6-1-1, West Penn Conference Champions; Cross Country 7-3, West Penn Conference Champions; Volleyball 4-1; Women's Tennis 1-0; Men's Basketball 19-8, NAIA National Tournament; Women's Basketball (n/a); Swimming 1-6; Baseball 10-5-1; Track & Field 7-1, West Penn Conference Champions; Men's Tennis 11-4, West Penn Conference co-Champions; Golf 11-1-2.

1959-60

Football 6-2, West Penn Conference
Champions; Cross Country 6-3, West Penn
Conference Champions; Volleyball (no
record); Men's Basketball 24-3, NAIA
National Tournament; Women's Basketball
(n/a); Swimming 4-4; Baseball 7-7; Track
& Field 6-2, West Penn Conference
Champions; Tennis 10-1, West Penn
Conference Champions; Golf 6-5-1.

1960-61

Football 5-3, West Penn Conference
Champions; Cross Country 5-3; Volleyball
3-2; Men's Basketball 23-5, NAIA National
Tournament; Women's Basketball 2-1;
Swimming 0-7; Baseball 11-2; Track & Field
3-4; Tennis 8-1, West Penn Conference co-
Champions; Golf 5-5.

1961-62

Football 6-2, West Penn Conference
Champions; Cross Country 5-2; Field
Hockey (n/a); Volleyball 1-0; Men's Basketball
26-3, NAIA National Tournament; Women's
Basketball (n/a); Swimming 4-5; Baseball
13-4; Track & Field 4-3; Tennis 6-2; Golf
7-3, West Penn Conference Champions.

1962-63

Football 6-2, West Penn Conference
Champions; Cross Country 4-3, West Penn
Conference Champions; Field Hockey (n/a);
Volleyball (n/a); Women's Tennis (n/a); Men's
Basketball 15-7, West Penn Conference
co-Champions; Women's Basketball 0-2;
Swimming 2-8; Baseball 9-6; Track & Field
6-1; Men's Tennis 9-0, West Penn
Conference Champions; Golf 10-0, West
Penn Conference Champions.

1963-64

Football 5-2-1, West Penn Conference co-
Champions; Cross Country 9-2, West Penn
Conference Champions; Field Hockey (n/a);
Volleyball (n/a); Women's Tennis (n/a); Men's
Basketball 17-7, West Penn Conference
Champions; Women's Basketball 1-4;
Swimming 2-5; Baseball 8-4; Track & Field
5-2; Men's Tennis 4-4; Golf 10-1, West Penn
Conference Champions.

1964-65

Football 8-0, West Penn Conference
Champions; Cross Country 9-4-1; Field
Hockey (n/a); Volleyball 5-1; Women's Tennis
(n/a); Men's Basketball 14-9, West Penn

Conference Champions; Women's Basketball
2-2; Swimming 0-7; Baseball 12-4, West
Penn Conference Champions; Track & Field
7-1; Men's Tennis 4-4; Golf 11-0, West Penn
Conference Champions.

1965-66

Football 5-3; Cross Country 9-2, West Penn
Conference co-Champions; Field Hockey
(n/a); Volleyball 1-1; Women's Tennis (n/a);
Men's Basketball 10-12; Women's Basketball
(n/a); Swimming 1-7; Baseball 11-5; Track &
Field 5-1; Men's Tennis 6-2; Golf 8-0-1, West
Penn Conference Champions.

1966-67

Football 6-2-1; Cross Country 6-5; Field
Hockey 2-1-1; Volleyball 3-2; Women's
Tennis 1-3; Men's Basketball 22-6, NAIA
National Tournament; Women's Basketball
4-2; Swimming 0-7; Baseball 12-6; Track
& Field 4-2; Men's Tennis 6-2, West Penn
Conference Champions; Golf 7-1, West Penn
Conference Champions.

1967-68

Football 6-2, West Penn Conference co-
Champions; Cross Country 7-3; Field
Hockey 1-1-1; Volleyball 3-5; Women's
Tennis 1-2-1; Men's Basketball 22-8, NAIA
National Tournament; Women's Basketball 6-
1; Swimming 0-6; Wrestling 0-6; Baseball 6-
7; Track & Field 7-1; Men's Tennis 4-3, West
Penn Conference Champions; Golf 10-0,
West Penn Conference Champions.

1968-69

Football 6-2; Cross Country 6-4; Field
Hockey 1-2-2; Volleyball 5-3; Women's
Tennis 1-3; Men's Basketball 20-6; Women's
Basketball 5-2; Swimming 1-6; Wrestling 4-3;
Baseball 10-5; Track & Field 7-0, West Penn
Conference Champions; Men's Tennis 7-1;
Golf 9-1, West Penn Conference Champions.

1969-70

Football 6-2; Cross Country 5-4-1; Field
Hockey 1-3; Volleyball 3-7; Women's Tennis
4-0; Men's Basketball 14-10; Women's
Basketball 2-4; Swimming 2-7; Wrestling 2-6;
Baseball 5-6; Track & Field 4-2; Men's
Tennis 6-2; Golf 7-1.

1970-71

Football 10-0, NAIA Division II National
Champions; Cross Country 7-4; Field
Hockey 3-1; Volleyball 2-8; Women's Tennis

3-3; Men's Basketball 13-10; Women's Basketball 1-5; Swimming 0-7; Wrestling 5-3; Baseball 7-11; Track & Field 5-2; Men's Tennis 5-0; Golf 5-2.

1971-72

Football 8-1-1; Cross Country 10-0; Field Hockey (no record); Volleyball 7-6; Women's Tennis 1-4; Men's Basketball 12-10; Women's Basketball 2-4; Swimming 1-6; Wrestling 1-6; Baseball 11-9; Track & Field 6-1; Men's Tennis 4-3; Golf 8-1-1.

1972-73

Football 7-1; Cross Country 9-3; Field Hockey 4-0; Volleyball 5-7; Women's Tennis 4-3; Men's Basketball 13-8; Women's Basketball 2-4; Swimming 0-6; Wrestling 4-4; Baseball 10-4; Track & Field 4-1-1; Men's Tennis 6-2; Golf 10-0.

1973-74

Football 7-1; Cross Country 7-1; Field Hockey 1-2; Volleyball 9-10; Women's Tennis 5-3; Men's Basketball 7-14; Women's Basketball 7-1; Swimming 0-7; Wrestling 2-10-1; Baseball 10-11; Track & Field 3-2; Men's Tennis 7-3; Golf 11-2.

1974-75

Football 7-2; Cross Country 5-2-1; Field Hockey 2-2; Volleyball 4-7; Women's Tennis 2-5; Men's Basketball 8-14; Women's Basketball 3-4; Swimming 5-4; Wrestling 4-7; Baseball 17-10; Track & Field 5-3; Men's Tennis 7-3; Golf 9-3.

1975-76

Football 6-1-1; Cross Country 3-5; Field Hockey 0-3; Volleyball 7-10; Women's Tennis 7-3-1; Men's Basketball 11-11; Women's Basketball 2-9; Swimming 6-4; Wrestling 3-8-1; Baseball 13-9; Track & Field 1-4-1; Men's Tennis 5-4; Golf 11-1.

1976-77

Football 10-1, NAIA Division II National Champions; Cross Country 3-5; Field Hockey 1-2; Volleyball 11-7; Women's Tennis 7-3-1; Men's Basketball 15-6; Women's Basketball 3-8; Swimming 9-2; Baseball 15-6; Track & Field 6-1; Men's Tennis 7-3; Golf 11-3.

1977-78

Football 11-0, NAIA Division II National Champions; Cross Country 6-2; Field Hockey 1-4; Volleyball 13-4; Women's Tennis

7-3-1, Keystone Conference Champions; Men's Basketball 20-4; Women's Basketball 1-11; Swimming 9-1; Baseball 9-6; Track & Field 6-2; Men's Tennis 5-4; Golf 10-2-1.

1978-79

Football 6-2-1; Cross Country 5-3; Field Hockey 1-5; Volleyball 5-7; Women's Tennis 5-5; Men's Basketball 22-4; Women's Basketball 1-10; Swimming 7-3; Baseball 10-9; Track & Field 7-1; Men's Tennis 4-6; Golf 8-4.

1979-80

Football 4-5; Cross Country 4-6; Field Hockey 1-6; Volleyball 10-8; Women's Tennis 8-4; Men's Basketball 13-11; Women's Basketball 4-11; Swimming 9-3; Baseball 11-15; Track & Field 3-3; Men's Tennis 3-9; Golf 6-5; Softball 15-4.

1980-81

Football 5-3; Cross Country 5-4; Field Hockey 1-7; Volleyball 10-7; Women's Tennis 6-7; Men's Basketball 12-12; Women's Basketball 7-10; Swimming 9-1; Baseball 15-9; Track & Field 2-2; Men's Tennis 1-12; Golf 9-3; Softball 5-6.

1981-82

Football 5-3; Cross Country 5-4; Field Hockey 1-8; Volleyball 17-8; Women's Tennis 7-5; Men's Basketball 21-7, NAIA District 18 Champions; Women's Basketball 13-9; Swimming 7-4; Baseball 27-8; Track & Field 2-2; Men's Tennis 4-8; Golf 10-1; Softball 7-6.

1982-83

Football 9-2; Cross Country 3-6; Field Hockey 1-7; Volleyball 15-15; Women' Tennis 6-5; Men's Basketball 16-10; Women's Basketball 13-11; Swimming 8-3; Baseball 16-8; Track & Field 3-3; Men's Tennis 9-3-1, NAIA District 18 Champions; Golf 6-2; Softball 15-6, NAIA District 18 Champions.

1983-84

Football 9-2; Cross Country 6-6; Field Hockey 0-8; Volleyball 8-17; Women's Tennis 6-4, NAIA District 18 Champions; Men's Basketball 17-11; Women's Basketball 4-17; Swimming 6-7; Baseball 13-10; Track & Field 2-1-1; Men's Tennis 11-2; Golf 7-1; Softball 10-5, NAIA District 18 Champions.

1984-85

Football 5-2-1; Cross Country 3-7; Volleyball 17-13; Women's Tennis 5-4-1, NAIA District 18 Champions; Men's Basketball 15-12;

Women's Basketball 11-11; Swimming 6-5; Baseball 17-20; Track & Field 3-3; Men's Tennis 11-4, NAIA District 18 Champions; Golf 7-2, NAIA District 18 Champions; Softball 21-7, NAIA District 18 Champions.

1985-86
Football 5-4; Cross Country 6-2, NAIA District 18 Champions; Volleyball 17-19; Women's Tennis 6-4, NAIA District 18 Champions; Men's Basketball 19-9; Women's Basketball 8-12; Swimming 6-5; Baseball 16-11; Track & Field 3-1, NAIA District 18 Champions; Men's Tennis 6-3, NAIA District 18 Champions; Golf 33-20-2; Softball 19-7, NAIA District 18 Champions.

1986-87
Football 6-3; Soccer 1-9; Cross Country 7-6, NAIA District 18 Champions; Volleyball 14-20; Women's Tennis 7-2; Men's Basketball 21-4; Women's Basketball 18-8; Swimming 7-4; Baseball 3-16; Track & Field 2-0, NAIA District 18 Champions; Men's Tennis 5-4, NAIA District 18 Champions; Golf 20-8; Softball 15-11, NAIA District 18 Champions.

1987-88
Football 9-2; Soccer 1-13; Cross Country 7-1, NAIA District 18 Champions; Volleyball 18-20; Women's Tennis 7-4; Men's Basketball 21-5; Women's Basketball 19-4; Men's Swimming 7-6; Women's Swimming 7-4; Baseball 11-13; Track & Field 5-0, NAIA District 18 Champions; Men's Tennis 6-3, NAIA District 18 Champions; Golf 53-18; Softball 21-6, NAIA District 18 Champions.

1988-89
Football 14-0, NAIA Division II National Champions; Soccer 3-10-1; Men's Cross Country 4-1; Women's Cross Country 5-0; Volleyball 22-11; Women's Tennis 9-3, NAIA District 18 Champions; Men's Basketball 20-6; Women's Basketball 10-13; Men's Swimming 6-6; Women's Swimming 9-3; Baseball 7-10; Track & Field 2-2, NAIA District 18 Champions; Men's Tennis 6-6, NAIA District 18 Champions; Golf 60-24-1; Softball 22-4, NAIA District 18 Champions.

1989-90
Football 13-0, NAIA Division II National Champions; Soccer 7-8-2; Men's Cross Country 6-2, NAIA District 18 Champions; Women's Cross Country 4-2, NAIA District 18 Champions; Volleyball 27-13; Women's

Tennis 9-3, NAIA District 18 Champions; Men's Basketball 21-7; Women's Basketball 13-10; Men's Swimming 8-2; Women's Swimming 9-1; Baseball 14-11; Track & Field 0-2, NAIA District 18 Champions; Men's Tennis 5-7, NAIA District 18 Champions; Golf 43-19; Softball 23-11, NAIA District 18 Champions.

1990-91
Football 11-2; Soccer 8-8-1; Men's Cross Country 4-4; Women's Cross Country 6-2, NAIA District 18 Champions; Volleyball 29-13; Women's Tennis 6-5, NAIA District 18 Champions; Men's Basketball 16-9; Women's Basketball 2-20; Men's Swimming 9-2; Women's Swimming 10-1, freshman Kristen Zukowski NAIA National Champion in 100-yard butterfly; Baseball 8-22; Track & Field 1-1, NAIA District 18 Champions; Men's Tennis 4-6; Golf 40-13; Softball 13-9.

1991-92
Football 7-3; Soccer 7-8; Men's Cross Country 3-2; Women's Cross Country 3-7; Volleyball 22-15; Women's Tennis 7-3; Men's Basketball 21-7; Women's Basketball 2-20; Men's Swimming 9-2; Women's Swimming 10-0, Penn-Ohio Conference Champions; Baseball 11-18-1; Track & Field 1-2, NAIA District 18 Champions; Men's Tennis 4-6; Golf 29-18, NAIA District 18 Champions; Softball 15-10, NAIA District 18 Champions.

1992-93
Football 10-1; Soccer 4-11; Men's Cross Country 5-13; Women's Cross Country 7-13; Volleyball 29-12; Women's Tennis 7-1-1; Men's Basketball 17-12; Women's Basketball 6-19; Men's Swimming 10-1, Penn-Ohio Conference Champions; Women's Swimming 9-2; Baseball 13-9; Track & Field 13-7, NAIA District 18 Champions; Men's Tennis 5-9, NAIA District 18 Champions; Golf 84-17; Softball 16-7.

1993-94
Football 10-3, NAIA Division II National Runner-Up; Soccer 6-9-2; Men's Cross Country 7-21; Women's Cross Country 15-15; Volleyball 28-7; Women's Tennis 3-5, KECC Champions; Men's Basketball 25-3, KECC Champions, NAIA National Tournament; Women's Basketball 9-15; Men's Swimming 6-4, Penn-Ohio Conference Champs; Women's Swimming 3-

7; Baseball 13-20; Track & Field 14-7, KECC Champions; Men's Tennis 5-8, KECC Champions; Golf 26-26; Softball 17-15, KECC Champions.

1994-95

Football 12-2, NAIA Division II National Champions; Soccer 8-7-1; Men's Cross Country 19-12; Women's Cross Country 20-15; Volleyball 36-7, KECC Champions; Women's Tennis 8-4, KECC & NAIA Northeast Regional Champions; Men's Basketball 19-9, KECC Regular Season Champions; Women's Basketball 9-15; Men's Swimming 5-5; Women's Swimming 6-5; Baseball 20-8; Track & Field 3-4, KECC Champions; Men's Tennis 8-5, KECC Champions; Golf 62-29, NAIA Northeast Regional Champions; Softball 26-10, KECC & NAIA Northeast Regional Champions, NAIA National Tournament.

1995-96

Football 4-3-2; Soccer 8-6; Men's Cross Country 11-16; Women's Cross Country 31-16; Volleyball 28-13; Women's Tennis 5-6, KECC & NAIA Northeast Regional Champions; Men's Basketball 21-7, KECC Champions, NAIA National Tournament; Women's Basketball 17-10; Men's Swimming 7-1; Women's Swimming 3-5; Baseball 9-9; Track & Field 9-14; Men's Tennis 7-5, KECC Champions; Golf 41-32, NAIA Northeast Regional Champions; Softball 22-6, KECC Champions.

1996-97

Football 9-3; Soccer 7-6-2; Men's Cross Country 7-41; Women's Cross Country 32-16; Volleyball 28-14; Women's Tennis 7-2, KECC Champions; Men's Basketball 20-8, KECC Regular Season Champions; Women's Basketball 9-19; Men's Swimming 7-1; Women's Swimming 3-5; Baseball 12-14; Track & Field 2-3; Men's Tennis 7-5, KECCChampions; Golf 46-20, NAIA Northeast Regional Champions; Softball 22-21, KECC Champions.

1997-98

Football 9-2; Soccer 9-10; Men's Cross Country 18-15; Women's Cross Country 27-7; Volleyball 31-8, KECC & NAIA Northeast Regional Champions, NAIA National Tournament; Women's Tennis 3-7; Men's Basketball 17-10, KECC Regular

Season Champions; Women's Basketball 6-20; Men's Swimming 5-5, sophomore David Gesacion NAIA National Champion in 200-yard butterfly; Women's Swimming 6-4; Baseball 3-11; Track & Field 2-1; Men's Tennis 5-5, KECC Champions; Golf 25-52, NAIA Northeast Regional Champions; Softball 24-18, KECC Champions.

1998-99 (*)

Football 3-8; Men's Soccer 7-11; Women's Soccer 15-3; Men's Cross Country 24-13; Women's Cross Country 23-20; Volleyball 11-15; Women's Tennis 0-14; Men's Basketball 11-15; Women's Basketball 3-23; Men's Swimming 6-3, GLIAC Champions; Women's Swimming 7-2; Baseball 4-33; Track & Field (no record); Men's Tennis 5-10; Golf 26-48; Softball 20-24.

1999-2000 (*)

Football 3-8; Men's Soccer 5-11-2; Women's Soccer 6-10-1; Men's Cross Country 18-4; Women's Cross Country 16-20; Volleyball 15-20; Women's Tennis 1-13; Men's Basketball 11-15; Women's Basketball 5-21; Men's Swimming 9-1; Women's Swimming 9-1; Baseball 10-25; Track & Field (no record); Men's Tennis 3-15; Golf 43-62-2; Softball 29-15.

2000-01 (#)

Football 8-2; Men's Soccer 14-4-1; Women's Soccer 12-8; Men's Cross Country 41-12; Women's Cross Country 37-19-2; Volleyball 27-7; Women's Tennis 6-5; Men's Basketball 19-6; Women's Basketball 16-9; Men's Swimming 8-2; Women's Swimming 10-0; Baseball 18-14-1; Track & Field (no record); Men's Tennis 6-10; Golf 58-37; Softball 32-13.

* - Member of NCAA Division II Great Lakes Intercollegiate Athletic Conference (GLIAC)

- Member of NCAA Division III Presidents' Athletic Conference (PAC) – Westminster ineligible for PAC Championships due to reclassification from NCAA Division II to NCAA Division III

—————————— A P P E N D I X   C ——————————

College Financial Operations
1976 – 1989

The Late Carlson Administration

	1976-77	1977-78	1978-79	1979-80	1980-81
Tuition & fees	$4,121,163	$4,551,195	$4,910,786	$5,292,338	$ 5,910,953
Private gifts	$1,113,838	$ 916,526	$ 890,781	$ 648,816	$ 904,684
Total Revenue	$8,101,942	$8,502,327	$9,243,237	$9,715,972	$11,203,765
Instruction/research	$2,459,312	$2,678,301	$2,778,129	$2,896,823	$ 3,168,806
Financial aid	$ 569,803	$ 629,955	$ 660,725	$ 742,314	$ 938,625
Total Expenditures	$7,449,626	$8,157,178	$8,985,553	$9,664,788	$11,094,330
Net surplus/deficit	$ 652,316	$ 345,149	$ 257,684	$ 51,184	$ 109,435
Transfer to endowment	$ 546,543	$ 339,669	$ 255,644	$ 45,447	$ 97,605

The Lauterbach Administration

	1981-82 (restated)
Tuition & fees	$ 6,816,714
Private gifts	$ 1,038,122
Total revenue	$12,941,318
Instruction/research	$ 4,184,639
Financial aid	$ 1,318,088
Total expenditures	$12,727,247
Net surplus/deficit	$ 214,072
Transfer to endowment	$ 202,831

The Splete Administration

	1982-83	1983-84	1984-85
Tuition & fees	$ 6,901,929	$ 7,428,503	$ 7,123,315
Private gifts	$ 993,928	$ 1,574,202	$ 1,087,940
Total revenue	$12,837,698	$14,494,421	$13,929,730
Instruction/research	$ 4,372,206	$ 4,313,011	$ 4,169,271
Financial aid	$ 1,602,793	$ 1,978,405	$ 1,966,253
Total expenditures	$12,801,977	$14,417,595	$13,656,538
Net surplus/deficit	$ 35,721	$ 76,826	$ 273,192
Transfer to endowment	$ 25,568	$ 71,323	$ 262,542

The Boone and Early Remick Administrations

	1985-86	1986-87	1987-88	1988-89
Tuition & fees	$ 7,419,600	$ 7,832,614	$ 8,892,003	$10,580,874
Private giving	$ 923,145	$ 984,248	$ 1,034,433	$ 957,265
Total revenue	$14,139,260	$14,713,027	$16,171,374	$18,734,495
Instruction/research	$ 4,400,737	$ 4,458,086	$ 4,783,190	$ 5,103,351
Financial aid	$ 2,027,367	$ 2,020,377	$ 2,429,802	$ 3,170,832
Total expenditures	$14,077,237	$14,336,102	$15,629,398	$17,334,816
Net surplus/deficit	$ 62,023	$ 376,925	$ 541,976	$ 1,399,679
Transfer to endowment	$ 48,584	$ 50,044	$ 30,195	$ -340,654*

* Money taken from endowment

—————— A P P E N D I X   D ——————

Specific Goals for Westminster College
October 1, 1997 – October 1, 2003
(Goals Measured Each October 1st – Updated as of October 1, 2001)

#	Specific Goals	Measurement Point/Interval	10/1/97 Baseline	10/1/98	10/1/99	10/1/00	10/1/01	10/1/02	10/1/03
1.	Top 100 Liberal Arts I (LA-I) Colleges Rank	On Prior 6/30	128	123	120	115	110	105	100
	Actual Result			123	114	106	115**		
2.	Employer Connection (# of student internships)	During Prior FY	191	197	210	222	260	280	300
	Actual Result			261	271	250	289		
3.	Community Service Connections (# of Students)	During Prior FY	335	350	380	385	390	400	405
	Actual Result			350	380	257	563		
4.	New Multidisciplinary Educational Centers	On 10/1				Center #1 Established	Drinko Cntr. for Excellence in Teaching & Learning	Center #2 Established	
	Actual Result								
5.	Health Articulation Agreements	On 10/1				#1 Health Management Systems	#2 Case Western Dental School	#3	
	Actual Result					Systems	School		
6.	Employee Compensation to Median of LA-I Colleges	On 2nd prior 6/30	86%	87%	90%	93%	96%	98%	100%
	Actual Result *Does not include support staff (Hourly) data.			87%	90%	94%	***		
7.	Remick Admissions House	On 10/1		Construction Starts	Construction Completed				
	Actual Result			Jul-98	May-99				
8.	Field House Expansion	On 10/1		Construction Areas A&B Starts	Construction Areas A&B Completed	Fundraising & Construction for Areas C/D	Construction Areas C/D Completed		
	Actual Result			Oct-98	Oct-99	Oct-00	Oct-01		
9.	Thompson Clark Renovation	On 10/1		Fundraising	Construction Starts	Construction	Construction Completed		
	Actual Result			Oct-98	Oct-99	Oct-00	Jan-01		
10.	Campus Center	On 10/1		Design Phase	Begin Fundraising	Fundraising	Begin Construction	Construction Continues	Construction Completed
	Actual Result			Aug-98	Sep-99	Oct-00	Jun-01		
11.	Old Main Renovation Campaign	On 10/1					Fundraising	Fundraising	Begin Construction
	Actual Result						Jul-01		

Note: Bold Numbers are Actuals;

**Goal 1. This year's rankings are much different from last year. Westminster is now in a group of 218 colleges, instead of the 162 schools (159 ranked) we had been grouped with from 1998-2001.

***Goal 6. Purposely left blank. Complete data is not available at this time.

#	Specific Goals	Measurement Point/Interval	10/1/97 Baseline	10/1/98	10/1/99	10/1/00	10/1/01	10/1/02	10/1/03
12.	Endowment of $100,000,000	On Prior 6/30	$61 mil.	$70 mil.	$74 mil.	$79 mil.	$85 mil.	$93 mil.	$100 mil.
	Actual Result			$ 75 mil.	$ 84 mil.	$ 90 mil.	$ 85 mil.		
13.	Endowed Scholarships for Top 10% Students	On Prior 6/30		$1,000,000	$200,000	$400,000	$600,000	$800,000	$1,000,000
	Actual Result			$1,000,000	$1,000,000	$1,000,000	$1,000,000		
14.	Top 10% Students (% of First-Year Class)	Fall, Same Year	22%	26%	27%	28%	29%	30%	31%
	Actual Result			26%	22%	25%	25%		
15.	Endowed Faculty Development Program	On 10/1				NEH $500,000	$1,000,000	$1,500,000	$2,000,000
	Actual Result						$379,549		
16.	Staff Training Programs (# per year, including CE)	During Prior FY	37	36	37	38	39	40	40
	Actual Result			36	37	37	42		
17.	Minority Students (# enrolled)	Fall, Same Year	26	27	30	35	40	45	50
	Actual Result			27	26	26	35		
18.	Teaching Capacity Index (FTE Student to FTTE Faculty)	During Prior FYr	15.7	16.0	15.7	15.5	15.3	15.1	15.1
	Actual Result			16.0	15.92	15.78	14.78		
19.	Number of Applications for Admission	Fall, Same Year	1,022	1,020	1,200	1,250	1,300	1,350	1,400
	Actual Result			1,020	975	1,050	1,181		
20.	Undergrad FTE Enrollment Total (including LLP)	Fall, Same Year	1,402	1,423	1,425	1,465	1,485	1,505	1,520
	Actual Result			1,423	1,408	1,433	1,438		
21.	Graduate School Enrollment (FTE)	Fall, Same Year	48	63	68	74	80	85	90
	Actual Result			63	81	80	95		
22.	LLP Enrollment (FTE)	Fall, Same Year	64	60	64	68	70	80	90
	Actual Result			56.5	66.69	63.38	68.83		
23.	SAT Average for Entering Class	Fall, Same Year	1,079	1,095	1,096	1,098	1,100	1,100	1,100
	Actual Result			1,096	1,080	1,091	1,075		

#	Specific Goals	Measurement Point/Interval	10/1/97 Baseline	10/1/98	10/1/99	10/1/00	10/1/01	10/1/02	10/1/03
24.	Annual Fund % Participation	On Prior 6/30	40.2%	40.7%	41.2%	41.7%	42.2%	42.7%	43.2%
	Actual Result			**40.7%**	**41.1%**	**42.0%**	**41.8%**		
25.	Net Undergraduate Tuition and Fees ($ Thousands)	During Prior FY	$10,774	$11,154	$11,770	$12,400	$13,600	$14,300	$15,000
	Actual Result			**$11,154**	**$11,832**	**$11,991**	**$12,748**		

Index